The
Christian Pastor

The
Christian Pastor

THIRD EDITION, REVISED

by
WAYNE E. OATES

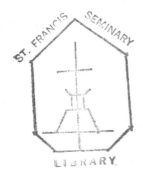

THE WESTMINSTER PRESS
Philadelphia

Book Design by Dorothy Alden Smith

Published by The Westminster Press®
Philadelphia, Pennsylvania

PRINTED IN THE UNITED STATES OF AMERICA
9 8 7 6 5 4 3 2 1

Library of Congress Cataloging in Publication Data

Oates, Wayne Edward, 1917–
    The Christian pastor.

    Bibliography: p.
    Includes index.
    1. Pastoral theology.   2. Pastoral psychology.
I. Title.
BV4011.02 1982   253   82-4933
ISBN 0-664-24372-X   AACR2

To All My Family

Contents

Preface 9

Part One
THE PASTORAL TASK

    I. The Crisis Ministry of the Pastor 17
    II. The Symbolic Power of the Pastor 65
    III. The Personal Qualifications
        of the Pastor 96
    IV. The Identity and Integrity
        of the Pastor 128

Part Two
PASTORAL METHODS

    V. The Pastor's Understanding
        and Assessment 167
    VI. The Levels of Pastoral Care 190
    VII. The Deeper Levels of Pastoral Care 219
    VIII. The Pastor as a Minister
        of Introduction 261

Bibliography 285

Index 293

Preface

You as a Christian pastor think of yourself at your best as being a shepherd of the flock of God and a minister of reconciliation whose task is the care of souls in face-to-face relationships with individuals, families, and small groups. This book is intended to be a practical guide for the average pastor in a specific church as the pastor exercises this ministry of pastoral care.

Shepherding is both a science and an art, nourished by clinical and historical tributaries of empirical and classical wisdom. This book's bid for your reading time rests on the following emphases. First, attention is given to the historical and classical perspectives of the nature and function of the pastor as a person of God amid the crucial human situations that are common ventures for persons both within and without the church. Secondly, the theological context for Christian pastoral work and pastoral counseling, which in other places is either assumed or treated philosophically, is presented here as the functional responsibility of the pastor as a symbolic representative of God the Father, God the Son, and God the Holy Spirit—of God at work in the world through the church. Thirdly, the Biblical witness to the purpose of the pastor's calling is brought into responsible and critical dialogue with later interpreters in Christian history—Chrysostom, Augustine, Luther, Calvin, and John Bunyan, to name a few. Also, findings from the behavioral sciences of education, psychology, and medicine will be presented in dialogue with Biblical and historical wisdom. One point of vivid focus will be the discussion of personal qualifications of the Christian pastor.

Furthermore, Chapter IV, "The Identity and Integrity of the Pastor," through a method of correlation, is devoted to the dilemmas that pastors undergo in the formation of the particular uniqueness that the pastor's identity brings to the Christian ministry. The struggles of the spirit occasioned by being a real person in the face of the expectations and demands of a congregation genuinely shake the foundations of all preconceptions. The perceptive results of the study by The Association of Theological Schools in the book *Ministry in America* will illume this search for identity and integrity.

This book proposes to be something of a handbook for stress management in "the Christian combat." As Augustine wrote, in a treatise by that title, "The crown of victory is promised only to those who engage in the struggle." (Augustine, *The Christian Combat*, in *The Fathers of the Church: Writings of Saint Augustine*, Vol. 4, p. 315.) The sustenance for the Christian pastor in the struggle to focus and maintain a credible identity and integrity certainly comes from the rich discoveries of recent research in the behavioral sciences. However, the field of psychotherapy today is severely fragmented by competing "therapies." The pastor who draws on the agreed-upon certainties of these will be, nevertheless, a "cut flower" if that is *all* the pastor has for sustenance. In addition to this, the pastor must have roots in the Christian heritage for stability in ever-changing enthusiasms in the behavioral sciences. The Christian pastor can bring forth things both old and new from a good treasure of the Christian witness.

In the fourth place, this edition of this book explores further the conditioning influences on the work of the pastor in the context of the church. This material has been updated to include the function of the Christian pastor as a specialist in pastoral counseling and/or psychotherapy. Since 1964, when the second edition was published, The American Association of Pastoral Counselors and The American Association for Marriage and Family Therapy have emerged with an active alternative to the parish ministry. Pastoral counseling centers and centers for Christian family therapy have taken root and shape all over North America. Intensive training and additional certification are offered and are required for this kind of ministry. Persons who are doubly qualified as ordained ministers and as clinical psychologists, social workers, or physicians have formed their identity as ministers around the subspecialty of our calling. The influences that condition the pastoral work of these specialists will be added to the chapter "The Pastor's Understanding and Assessment" in this third edition.

In the fifth place, I have raised questions with both colleagues and students about the need for a revision of the previous editions of this book. With a common voice they say that the chapter "The Levels of Pastoral Care" should be left intact and unchanged. I have done so, but have enriched it with wisdom from classical theologians and pastors. Whereas the point of view of the previous two editions was heavily reliant on a depth psychology of the individual and the group, these same insights will be reshaped and enriched by the wisdom of such intrepid pastoral teachers as Richard Baxter and Martin Luther.

In the sixth place, the second edition of this book sought to introduce the reader to the rich array of other books and journals in the rapidly expanding literature of pastoral care. This edition will differ from the previous ones in two respects. First, these references will be updated and presented in the bibliography at the end of the book. Secondly, the main body of each chapter has been written with an eye to removing as much as possible the time-binding references. Material will be used that has already

stood the test of time and therefore is far less likely to be
rendered anachronistic.

Finally, since the 1964 edition, the world has undergone
the assassination of political leaders such as the Kennedy
brothers and Martin Luther King. The great minorities of
blacks and Hispanics have become a vital force within
both the ministry and the society as a whole. The institution of the family is being revolutionized by a sexual revo-
lution, the assertion of the dignity and rights of women,
and an increase in the number of two-career marriages.

Whereas no separate treatment of these changes will be
included in this book, the work of the Christian pastor will
be discussed in this edition with these changes in mind.
However, an attempt will be made to interpret the Christian pastor as a person called to minister in the name of
Jesus Christ, the great Shepherd, who knew his sheep and
called them by name, and in whom "there is neither Jew
nor Greek, there is neither slave nor free, there is neither
male nor female" (Gal. 3:28).

The title of this book, "The Christian Pastor," was used
in the late 1890's by Washington Gladden. The warm rays
of the influence of this great pastor have given light and
inspiration to me. I am indebted to him for his title, but
I have sought to interpret this subject entirely afresh in
the light of this generation's resources and needs.

I have been dependent upon others in writing these
pages and my appreciation goes to many persons. My students have been fellow explorers with me, and this book
is an attempt to express my gratitude to them. Their difficult questions and unfailing loyalty have made this work
possible.

I express my gratitude to the Faculty of the School of
Medicine of the University of Louisville for their abundant
affirmation of me as a Christian pastor in the instruction of
our students. I experience from their commitment and
comradeship "incursions of the Kingdom of Heaven" here
and now. I am especially grateful to Mrs. Jenni Khaliel, my

research assistant, whose professional competence and colleagueship appear throughout this book. I give thanks, also, to my wife, Pauline, our two sons, William Oates and Charles Oates, M.D., and their families, and the unique fellowship I have with them, especially in their care of hurting people.

Further, I cannot name but can only express my devoted reverence for the many people who have sought my help as a counseling pastor. They have been my instructors in the ways of the human heart.

W.E.O.

School of Medicine
University of Louisville
Louisville, Kentucky

PART ONE

THE PASTORAL TASK

Chapter I

The Crisis Ministry
of the Pastor

You as a pastor move from one crisis to another with those whom you shepherd. In a single day, you may visit the mother of a newborn baby, give guidance to a person who is becoming a Christian, talk with high school or college graduates about their lifework, unite a couple in marriage, comfort a person who is bereaved, call upon someone who is confronting a serious operation, and listen to the last words of a patient who is dying. Two thousand years of Christian ministry have conditioned Christians to expect their pastors to be with them at these times of crisis. Therefore you as a Christian pastor come to the task in the strength of a great heritage. Gripped by awe in the presence of the mysterious and tremendous crises of life, you can be secure in the fact that people both want and expect you to be present at their times of testing.

In a survey of 47 denominations, which included 12,000 persons, both of the laity and the clergy, *the most expected characteristic* of a Christian pastor was stated as being that of an "open, affirming style." By this was meant, in the first place, that the pastor is capable of "handling stressful situations by remaining calm under pressure while continuing to affirm persons." (Daniel O. Aleshire, "Eleven Major Areas of Ministry," in *Ministry in America,* ed. by David S. Schuller, Merton P. Strommen, and Milo L. Brekke, p. 31.)

The crises of everyday living—birth, redemption, work, marriage, illness, bereavement, and death—are the shared experiences of all people in one way or another. They are the common ventures of life in which "the whole creation has been groaning in travail together until now" (Rom. 8:22). The straitening anxieties of these times of crisis call for a reorganization of the total personality of individuals and their families. The result may easily be disorganization. These crises either strengthen or weaken; they are either-or situations which call for ethical choices, an increase in emotional maturity, and additional spiritual resources. Therefore in these crises the careful and considerate attention of a skilled minister under the tutelage of the Holy Spirit often makes the difference between a spiritually mature and mentally healthy person and a spiritually diminished and mentally sick person.

CRISIS, CONTINUITY, AND THE FAITHFUL PASTOR

A Theological Perspective of the Crisis Ministry

As a pastor contemplates the meaning of crises in the life of the local church, its individuals, and its families, the meaning of the theology of crisis for the life of the church of Jesus Christ emerges. Primitive religions tend to spring from the periodicity of the life cycle from birth to death. The Jewish and Christian faiths lose their intimacy with human life as it is lived when their adherents ignore these common ventures of life or look upon them as "secular" concerns apart from the struggles of human crisis experiences. Paul Radin points to the religious interpretations and customs associated with marriage, birth, puberty, achievement of a professional status, death, etc., as the way in which religious inspiration must "gain its hold upon man's workaday life." Arnold van Gennep describes these religious practices, customs, and meanings as *"rites de pas-*

sage." Different "rites" help persons and groups as they are separated from one era of human life, given support and challenge in the intervening time, and then brought into full status in a new era of life. He classifies these rites as "separation" rites, "marginal or intermediate" rites, and "reunion" rites. (Paul Radin, *Primitive Religion,* p. 79; also Arnold van Gennep, *The Rites of Passage.*) Thus the spiritual community enables individuals to move from one stage of life to another without breaking the continuity of personhood. We are kept from being isolated and from being left completely alone. With the inspiration of a new relationship we are born out of an old life and ushered into a new one. For example, the church and the school, particularly the college, as typified in the student religious organization, provide for the graduate of high school a commencement ritual, some sort of "going away to college" recognition, and a new "fellowship of believers" on the college campus. But one reason that student religious organizations suffer on the campus is that they too often simply perpetuate the same way of life, identity, patterns of behavior, and dependencies of the home church. Yet young persons see themselves as having "left" or "been separated from home." They see college as a new identity, as indeed it should be, different from home and high school. But they need some sort of intermediate relationship as support while reuniting with the larger human family as represented in the college. Sometimes the dormitory group becomes this, or it may be the fraternity or the sorority. It may be the religious group which spontaneously forms of its own accord on a college campus. In every instance where a conventional religious organization really takes effect, one might safely hypothesize that the organization did *not* function as a smooth, unbroken reproduction of the kinship system of the college student's high school home and home church. Persons who do not go to college find similar transition to and reunions with their work groups, church subgroups, athletic teams, or hobby groups. College is not an indispensable way of learning, growing up, or progressing.

Anthropologists like Radin and Van Gennep are helpful in interpreting the cultural function of religion in the individual's maintenance of identity in the crises of the life cycle. Daniel Day Williams interprets the interrelatedness of the separate events of life in the context of the total destiny of the individual's salvation in God through Christ. A person does so through what Williams calls "the principle of linkage in human existence." He says: "Man, God's creature, is the being who finds every part of his experience linked with every other part. . . . That man is a whole . . . is true, but too simply true. The real situation is that man is both whole and parts, mind and body, a flow of experiences, and is a responsible, searching self. What has to be recognized is the significance of the fact that every part of his being and experience is linked actually or potentially with every other part. A trivial incident may open the way for the first time to the discovery of oneself and of God." (Daniel Day Williams, *The Minister and the Care of Souls,* pp. 26–27.)

Two observations about Williams' statement need underscoring. First, he says that a *trivial* incident may be directly and causally or symbolically linked with the person's total destiny and salvation. Thus, the wise pastor avoids the fate of paying attention to people *only* on an emergency, crisis basis. For example, it will be necessary to visit persons when they are in a great crisis. This cannot be left undone by a faithful pastor. On the other hand, a regular program of visitation of the members of the congregation as well as a carefully thought out appreciation of the very informal "marketplace" friendship with people nourishes them when all is well. For example, a pastor learned three weeks after the crisis that an inactive member of the church had broken her arm. The pastor nevertheless visited her. She considered her broken arm as "trivial," a thing that should not attract notice or "take up the pastor's time." But she was gratefully surprised by the visit. It became the occasion for unburdening her spirit of feeling rejected by the church and of expressing her need to heal this broken relationship.

You as a minister cannot become so identified with the great crises that people look upon you as a stranger except in times of great emergency. Jesus, the Good Shepherd, had time to notice children at play, acting out a funeral and playing their pipes and dancing. He had time for a "break" when he went for a meal to the home of a little man, Zacchaeus, whom he noticed in a tree. In a time of great calamity, such as an earthquake, a pastor has little time for anything but ministry to the suffering. But when a pastoral visit is made in a time of affluence, the pastor may find the total redemption of the person and the family to be linked with a harvest festival, the acquisition of a new home, a new car, or a television set. The simplicities of going to market, paying the electric bill, or playing with a child provide moments of involvement with eternity. The Christian pastor weeps with those who weep, but does not do so at the expense of rejoicing with those who rejoice.

A second observation about Williams' statement needs underscoring. He says that every part of a person's total spiritual destiny is linked *"actually or potentially"* with every other part. The trivial and the tremendous crises of life are not *necessarily* religiously meaningful to a given individual. Karl Barth says that "it simply is not so that certain situations especially weighted in the negative have, as such, a way of being the bearers of the mystery of transcendence and so of human existence. . . . The majority of men react to crises with notorious indifference." (Karl Barth, *Church Dogmatics,* Vol. III, Pt. 2, pp. 115, 118.) One would challenge Barth's easy use of the word "majority"; the whole human race has never been consulted on this matter. Nevertheless, his point is well

taken. Human crises are not *necessarily* but only potentially bearers of the mystery of the eternal God. The meaningful personal participation of the individual and the
group in a decisive and responsible commitment to God
through faith turns a potentially religious crisis into an
actual one. The "shaping environment" of the community
of faith and its ministers—official or not—makes the difference.

As such, the religious meaning of the crisis ministry of
the pastor becomes clear. You as a pastor faithfully exercise concern for persons in the name of Christ whether
their situation is critical or not. You teach people in their
search for the meaning of their past histories, the nature
of their calling in life, and the quality of hope that endows
their ultimate concerns. As crises or trivial events of the
day bring this meaning, calling, and hope to focus in the
decisions of the person or persons, they are born out of the
death of meaninglessness, purposelessness, despair, and
sin, into the life of fellowship with God through the forgiveness of sin and the acceptance of this forgiveness
through faith in Christ.

A Developmental Perspective

The common crises of human life as people live in relation to one another provide a basis for understanding the
total development of an individual amid the family and
community. You as a pastor are not *just* an "emergency
exit" for people when life becomes critical and unmanage-
able. You are a fellow participant with them as they move
from one great era of life to another. You are faithful to
them in times of crisis, and *between* crises as well. For
these crises are not just isolated events in a person's life.
A person is not bereaved of a child without at the same
time calling to mind the child's birth, the days of happy
play with the child, and the way in which the child responded to parental love. Nor do these experiences stand

apart from earlier choices of a mate and the couple's commitment to each other. Each crisis lies upon the foundation of an earlier crisis, layer lies upon layer, precept upon precept, faith upon faith, distrust upon distrust, success upon success, failure upon failure.

In the survey by Schuller and others in their book *Ministry in America,* a second way of stating the expectation of an "open, affirming style" summarizes what I have said above in these words: The pastor shows "fidelity to tasks and persons, showing competence and responsibility by completing tasks, relating warmly to persons, handling differences of opinion, and growing in skills." (Aleshire, "Eleven Major Areas of Ministry," in *Ministry in America,* p. 31.)

The developmental psychologists have much to offer pastors in their understanding of the crisis ministry as being not just an emergency "holding operation" but a participation in the spiritual becoming of those to whom the pastor ministers. For example, Erik Erikson illuminates the *continuity of experience* which he calls a person's identity. At "any given stage of development" the individuality of the person is continued as a distinct identity, is added to, focused, and clarified, or is hindered, diffused, and confused, as the case may be. As Erikson says, "Through a series of crises the individual comes to feel most himself where he means most to others—to those others who have come to mean most to him." (Erik Erikson, *New Perspectives for Research on Juvenile Delinquency,* ed. by Helen L. Witmer and Ruth Kotinsky, p. 4.) This is obviously an intricate and lifelong process.

For example, the identity formation or diffusion of adolescence is only one of a series of crises that Erikson discusses at length in his monograph *Identity and the Life Cycle.* In turn, Erikson sets forth another principle, which he calls the "epigenetic principle." By this he means that "wherever something grows" the "growing is a differentiation of preplanned parts during a given sequence of

critical periods." (Ibid., p. 7.) From his point of view, both
the task of the individual and his decisions and the task of
the shaping fellowship of other human beings in relation
to him is "together to maintain that continuity which
bridges the inescapable discontinuity between each one of
these stages. There is, for instance, discontinuity between
the trustful dependence of infancy and the stubborn autonomy of early childhood, and the second depends upon
the first." (Ibid.)

Robert Havighurst calls these critical moments "developmental tasks." The tasks arise *"at or about a certain
period in the life of the individual, successful achievement of which leads to his happiness and to success in
later tasks, while failure leads to unhappiness to the individual, disapproval by society, and difficulty with later
tasks."* (Robert J. Havighurst, *Human Development and
Education,* p. 2.) Each one of these tasks has biological
dimensions in the physical maturation of the individual,
cultural dimensions in the needs of the individual to talk,
read, write, count, and accomplish many other expected
skills "at or about a given time," and ethical dimensions
arising from the personal values and aspirations of the
individual. This concept of developmental tasks includes
the layer-upon-layer principle, or the epigenetic principle, as Erikson calls it. These tasks embrace what Havighurst calls the "teachable moment," or the concept of
timing in education and spiritual guidance. "When the
body is ripe, and society requires, and the self is ready to
achieve a certain task, the teachable moment has come,"
says Havighurst. (Ibid., p. 5.)

Thus a sense of timing within the continuity of one's
pilgrimage of selfhood becomes an *epigenetic principle of
pastoral care.* By this I mean that the *cardinal criterion of
pastoral relationships is faithfulness in establishing and
maintaining a durable relationship to individuals, small
groups, and churches.* As a pastor, you establish a covenant of concern with them. You keep these covenants. You

measure your effectiveness and choose techniques of care on the basis of both your own and their willingness to initiate, maintain, and faithfully carry through a mutually responsible covenant of acceptance of the grace of God and respect for the laws of life. You are measured not by standards of success but by standards of faithfulness, which in turn determine whatever success you have. You as the pastor and those who minister alongside you—parents, teachers, deacons, elders, stewards, vestry persons, physicians, social workers, lawyers, teachers, nurses, and status-less folk such as gardeners, lathe operators, weavers, spinners, fishermen, and miners—are to be measured by their faithfulness. You are on hand at the teachable moment, standing by in the presence of success and failure. You become a bridge of continuity that arches over the discontinuities of the crises of life in which a person is thrust into the death of one era of life and born into the life of a new era. In the agonizing test of a crucial hour, you are called to have a sense of the hope for tomorrow and to evaluate the strengths of yesterday. Thus you participate with the individuals as they come to grips with their history of past sin and failure, their sense of peril in the death of an old life, and their need for hope as they stand at the gate of a new era of their spiritual pilgrimage.

Consequently, the minister is called upon, not necessarily to do "some new thing," but rather to do more scientifically and accurately the work traditionally expected of pastors commissioned by the living Christ since the beginning of the Christian era. In order to do this adequately in modern society, you as a pastor need to take three practical steps: (1) You need to include these crises in a total plan of visitation. Visitation cannot safely or wisely be restricted to these times of crisis. To do so would be to neglect people in their times of relative peace and serenity when their decision-making capacities may well be functioning more effectively than during a crisis. Also, equipping the caring fellowship, the church, to take initiative and pay attention to those of their fellowship who are in crises must not be neglected. You cannot carry all the burdens of all the people all the time. As the pastor, you are a teacher, called to equip the saints for the work of the ministry. This is your "equipping responsibility." (2) In order to equip others, you yourself must be equipped with the devotional literature of the Bible and Christian history concerning these crises. (3) You need to know the psychological significance of these crises in the developmental history of a person. Since the publication of the first edition of this book, the following authors' works on the psychological and religious development of the human person have exercised the most influence on the conceptions in this third edition: Harry Stack Sullivan, Lewis J. Sherrill, Robert J. Havighurst, Erik Erikson, and Søren Kierkegaard. Each author in his own way approaches the interpretation of the developmental pilgrimage of the human person uniquely. The Christian pastor will find a careful study of the works of these authors worthy of consecutive attention. They and others are presented in synopsis form in my book *The Psychology of Religion.*

If you as a pastor visit people when they need you, you save lost motion in aimless and meaningless visitation. Visiting them in times of crisis lends purpose and warmth, meaning and value, to your call. Such calls establish a sense of rapport between you and the parishioners that serves as a foundation for all future pastoral care and personal counseling. The time that you would otherwise spend in getting acquainted with people who ask for counseling help can be used for more meaningful purposes. Also, your informal ministry during relatively quiescent times is enriched by your having been a faithful pastor to persons when times were not so good. These encounters become nonverbal bonds of satisfaction to you when on a happy social occasion you see laughter, joy, and fulfillment in the faces of those for whom you have cared in more difficult times. On the other hand, simple friendship and warmth with no purpose other than itself, and at times prior to any felt difficulty, has value for its own sake in the pastoral relationship, quite apart from the crisis ministry being spoken of here.

The equipment of Biblical and historical wisdom helps you to deal with crises in your own life; with the patience and comfort of the Scriptures you have hope. You can inspire hope in those to whom you minister. The literature of the Bible and that of Christian history become pastoral aids, freeing you from hackneyed phrases and trite aphorisms that are reminders of Job's comforters. Likewise, the simplicity of The Psalms and other hymnbooks of the ages purifies your speech of technical theological and psychological jargon which has a minimum of emotional strength for the average person.

However, you cannot afford to be untutored in the science of human nature and behavior. You need also to recognize the psychological significance of these everyday crises in the developmental history of a person and a community. You can best learn this by studying the results of research on each of these crisis situations: birth, conversion, vocational choice, marriage, illness, bereavement, and death. Supervised clinical pastoral education in the care of persons most in need of help at such times is also a necessity. In these crises, you can do much to promote mental health and to prevent mental disease if the time is taken to learn the difference between mental health and mental disease.

Therefore, both a thorough knowledge of the Bible and of Christian history and an empirical knowledge of the psychology of these crises are essential. But a "focused perspective" of the two is even more important. The art of living amid the everyday crises of normal growth is the province of common concern for both the pastor and the medical psychologist. In the reactions of people to these crises, the interests of religion and medical psychology intersect, both to meet and to part, in the mutually necessary emphases which they sponsor. In deed and in fact, when the religious and psychological points of view are focused upon each of these crises, one gets a true-to-life perspective that has both the breadth of empirical research and the depth of religious experience and values. Such a perspective of the crises of birth, conversion, the choice of a vocation, marriage, illness, bereavement, alcoholism, marriage conflict, divorce, retirement, and death may be discussed suggestively here.

SOME COMMON CRISES AND PASTORAL WISDOM

Theologians (such as Paul Tournier in his book *A Place for You;* Lewis J. Sherrill in his book *The Struggle of the Soul;* and Kenneth Leech in his helpful Catholic book *Soul Friend: The Practice of Christian Spirituality*) and developmental psychologists (such as Robert J. Havighurst in his book *Human Development and Education;* Howard Clinebell in his book *Contemporary Growth Therapies;* and Erik Erikson in his book *Identity and the Life Cycle*) tend to develop slightly different classifications of the psychosocial crises in the life cycle. However, these different approaches tend to operate from a common presupposition about life which Arnold van Gennep expresses: "The universe itself is governed by a periodicity which has repercussions on human life, with stages and transitions, movements forward, and periods of relative inactivity." (Van Gennep, *The Rites of Passage.*) One might add that human life is also marked by periods of retrogression, retreat, and involution. The course of human life is not an inevitable evolution. You as pastor are not only a *faithful* person, providing in yourself and the church the bridge of grace for the inevitable chasms of separation in human life. You are also an informed, disciplined, and wise person who has, through prayer and study, discerned the mind of God. You continue to learn how fearfully and wonderfully we are made and are being made by God in the crises of the process of becoming. As Luther says: "This life, therefore, is a road to heaven and to hell. None is so good that he cannot become better, and none is so bad that he cannot become worse, until at last we become what we are to be." (Martin Luther, *Luther: Lectures on Romans,* ed. by Wilhelm Pauck, p. 323.)

Therefore, the following discussion of some of the most common crises of life is open-ended. You as a pastor will, through study and reflection, want to add to it, change it about here and there, and possibly recast the whole understanding. In any event the objective of this writing will be achieved if you take this discussion as a starter for thought and develop a heart of wisdom as you begin to number the days of human life.

The Birth of a Child

The home where a new baby has arrived undergoes a crisis experience in which the pastors of all communions are expected to take an interest. This may be an occasion of great happiness and good fortune, or it can be one of tragedy and grief. At the very best, the birth of a child necessitates a total reorganization of routine in the home. Subtle changes occur in relationships between the members of the family. If the child was planned for and intensely wanted, the event of its birth brings a whole-hearted joy. If this child was not planned for and wanted, then halfheartedness has to be overcome. If the child is malformed at birth, the shock, the grief, and the search for ways to enable the child to reach its best quality of life begins.

Furthermore, the birth of a child demands a new maturity in the husband-wife relationship. If the husband has been mothered by the wife, he now is displaced by one who really needs mothering. If the wife has been accustomed to going anywhere she pleases without regard to the needs of her husband, she now is tied down to the needs of the child. If there is another child in the home, the coming of this child means that the attention of the parents must be shared with the two children. From an economic point of view, the child increases the responsibility of the parents considerably and calls for a shift in their personal values. The parents' concepts of themselves change perceptibly. They may find it difficult to imagine what they were like before they had children. Therefore, parenthood may be either a cohesive or a disjunctive crisis in the life of an individual and a family.

The first response of a Christian pastor to the advent of a child is one of worship and especially thanksgiving to God. Let the Biblical birth narratives saturate your memory, becoming the warp and woof with which to express the worship. For example, in Judges 13, Manoah's wife, though barren, was surprised by joy when a messenger of the Lord told her that she would conceive and bear a son. Manoah came to the messenger and asked him: "Now when your words come true, what is to be the boy's manner of life and what is he to do?" (Judg. 13:12).

The Book of Ruth depicts the yearning of a frustrated mother-in-law, Naomi, for a grandchild in the face of the untimely deaths of her sons. Ruth, one of the widowed daughters-in-law, meets and marries Boaz. A son is born to them. Then Naomi, the grandmotherly one, hears her neighbor's prophecy: "Blessed be the LORD, who has not left you this day without next of kin; and may his name be renowned in Israel! He shall be to you a restorer of life and a nourisher of your old age; for your daughter-in-law who loves you, who is more to you than seven sons, has borne him" (Ruth 4:14–15).

Also, Hannah was barren and upon the blessing and prayer of the priest, Eli, and her own prayers, "in due time Hannah conceived and bore a son, and she called his name Samuel, for she said, 'I have asked him of the LORD' " (I Sam. 1:20). She also said in the Temple: "For this child I prayed; and the LORD has granted me my petition which

I made to him. Therefore, I have lent him to the Lord; as long as he lives, he is lent to the LORD" (I Sam. 1:27–28).

Few events have been endowed as richly with Christian ritual as has the advent of a child. Christian baptism is conferred upon infants in much of Christendom. The formation of a household covenant knits parents, godparents, and the congregation as a whole together in a fellowship of nurturing the child. Quite independently of the sacrament of Baptism, prayers of thanksgiving for the birth or the adoption of a child are a celebration in the order of worship, for example, of the *Book of Common Prayer* of the Episcopal Church.

Churches that do not baptize children have realized in considerable numbers that this does not justify allowing the birth of a child to go uncelebrated. Therefore, services of dedication, litanies of thanksgiving for the child and the parents, and special pastoral visitation ceremonies are just a few of the ways these churches confer spiritual meaning upon a newborn child and the family.

These rituals are spiritually alive events in their own right. They need not be seen as an ecclesiastical chore or as tools for opening up conversation with families about the less public, more intensely personal, and therefore painful aspects of the birth of a child. However, such realities are often present. To the contrary, the rituals of baptism, thanksgiving, and dedication of a child can and should provide an atmosphere of love, acceptance, and trust. Thus the pastor can deal more intimately, privately, and personally with the parents' needs.

When you have patiently created an atmosphere of trust and affection, you as a pastor soon learn that not all pregnancies and childbirths are the occasion for celebration. To say the least, many have a heavy admixture of fear, embarrassment, and/or angry injustice and frustration.

The unwanted pregnancy takes many forms. A married couple have a child earlier in time than they had planned. Other ambitions for economic security, completion of education, etc., are frustrated and changed. A child may also be later in time, in that a couple may have assumed that they already had as many children as they wanted. The mother's hopes of being free at last of the care of small children are frustrated. Plans to go to work, to complete schooling, to participate with her husband in his work, etc., are again denied at worst or delayed at best. Furthermore, mothers past the age of thirty-five begin to be more and more at risk for bearing a handicapped child. In these cases, intensive prenatal evaluation to determine the child's condition can be done at most university medical schools in the department of obstetrics and gynecology or the department of pediatrics. In the event that a handicapped child is born, the staff of those departments can assess the child's real future and plan with the parents how to educate the child to develop its abilities to the highest level possible.

In a sense, every child that is born is a very incomplete creation. It is as if God gets the child to a certain completeness and now calls the parents as co-laborers in the furthering of the child's completeness. Augustine, in the fifth century, was sensitive to the incompleteness of the child: "If a child has some excess or some defect or because of some conspicuous deformity . . . [the child] will be brought again at the resurrection to the true form of human nature, so that . . . each, apart, for himself, will have as his own those members whose sum makes the complete human body." (Augustine, *Faith, Hope, and Charity,* in *The Fathers of the Church: Writings of Saint Augustine,* Vol. 4, p. 443.) The unique pastoral task in caring for these families is to see to it that they do not bear these responsibilities alone. You as pastor can mobilize the organism of the specialized professionals, of the parents of other handicapped children, and of the periodic neighborly sharing of the care of the child by other members of the church.

One of the ethical problems you as pastor meet in relation to fathers and mothers is the need for a consecrated and intelligent planning of childbirth. The only perfect means of birth control is total abstinence from all hetero-sexual intercourse. The contraceptive pill, the intrauter-ine device, the diaphragm, the male sheath or condom, and the so-called "safe period" or rhythm method of birth control are effective in a descending order of preventive-ness. However, the easing of the legal prohibition of abor-tion has revealed the extensiveness of the use of abortion as a desperate and extreme method of birth control. The technology of abortion has made it such a sufficiently safe procedure that a mood of casualness about abortion per-vades the country. Highly polarized propaganda on both sides of the pros and cons of the abortion issue obscures balanced wisdom. The procedure, it seems to me, is one most certainly indicated in conditions where the mother's life is in danger, where she has been impregnated in inces-tuous or rape attacks, or where medical diagnosis indicates that the unborn fetus is massively defective. Often a natu-ral abortion or miscarriage removes the need for a medi-cally induced miscarriage. In a preponderant majority of natural aborts of a fetus, the fetus was not chromosomally adequate to sustain life.

However, intelligent and consecrated planning of the births of children assures the child of its right to be wanted, welcome, and loved by a mother and a father both. The use of abortion as a desperate birth control method represents the lack of providence and wisdom in the sacred task of parenthood. It misses the mark of na-ture, God's care, and Christian character.

Regardless of this ideal of parenthood, many children are born to single mothers. These children begin their life's journey as partial orphans. The purpose of the church and its ministry is fulfilled and our religion is purified as we make room for these single-parent families. In a sense, the extended family "flows into" the empty places in the fam-ily broken by death, divorce, mental illness, imprison-ment, or abandonment by one or the other parent.

Religious Conversion

   In the crisis of conversion the pastor serves as a minister of reconciliation, not between a child and its parents, but between an adult and the God and Father of our Lord Jesus Christ. Not all conversion experiences meet this definition; therefore not all of them cause constructive changes in personality. Rather, many of them result in no changes at all, but merely perpetuate in different garb the same infantile character. In these cases, the conversion or pseudo conversion is an abortive, disintegrative miscarriage of creativity. It becomes a thorn in the flesh that is not assimilated into the rest of the personality, continuing as if it were entirely apart from the rest of the self. Nevertheless, conversion at its best projects religious concepts into the mind, religious practices into the habits, religious values into the conscience, and religious feelings into the affective depths of the personality. This may increase the unhappiness and conflict in the person. As one person has said, "My misery began when I was baptized." These disturbances are not *necessarily* unhealthy. Your pastoral care can make the difference. For many persons, however, the conversion experience is the beginning of their true selfhood. They achieve spiritual autonomy by "getting their own religion" apart from that of their parents, which has been breathed for them in their mothers' lullabies. Their conversion points them into the direction of a happy vocational and marital choice and becomes that portion of their personality which arises at the very core of life. In a homely metaphor, this type of conversion experience becomes the stack pole around which the rest of the personality is organized. Gordon Allport has well described it by saying that such religious experience is a man's "audacious bid . . . to bind himself to creation and to the Creator, . . . his ultimate attempt to enlarge and to complete his own personality by finding the supreme context in which he rightly belongs." (Gordon W. Allport, *The Individual and His Religion,* p. 142.)

Probably the main determinant between these two kinds of conversion in any given case is the kind of spiritual relationship that existed between the person who is converted and the family of origin, i.e., grandparents, parents, and siblings. The psychosocial functions of a normal religious experience are: (1) To lower the importance of this family. These people are fallible, human, and limited; they are not God. (2) To build in an adult a sense of ethical responsibility for the aggressive and sexual identity of the self as a person. (3) Finally, to create a larger community for an individual and give the person access to the whole human family.

Historically and psychologically the parents have always been the first pastors and priests of the individual. But next to the parents' determinative influence is the kind of pastoral care the individual receives from the pastor of the church. The chaplains of state hospitals can tell you a good deal about the part that pastoral neglect and malpractice can play in aggravating rather than healing mental disease at the crisis of conversion. No single factor is more determinative in quickening and strengthening personality growth and health than is the conversion experience that goes to the depths of the emotional life of a person. Wise pastoral care often makes the difference between an abortive and a creative conversion experience.

For example, both theologically and psychologically, there are two different kinds of conversion: (1) The progressive or maturational type of religious experience which "issues in the positive fulfillment of one's powers with self-awareness, concern for others, and oneness with the world." By "world" Leon Salzman means the realistic, everyday existence of human life. He does not mean "worldliness" in any moralistic use of the word. (2) The regressive, pathological conversion, which is "a pseudo solution . . . brought about by increasing anxieties, and has a disjunctive effect on personality." Or, because of its defensive nature and the card of entry it gives to a similarly defensive religious group, such a conversion may ward off a mental disorder. Without access to such a group, the person may decompensate into the isolation of a mental disorder. (Leon Salzman, "The Psychology of Religious Ideological Conversion," *Psychiatry*, May 1953.)

Harry M. Tiebout, in his psychiatric treatment of alcoholics, stresses the "conversion feature" in the recovery of persons in Alcoholics Anonymous. The positive function of religion is, he says, to "release the positive potential which resides in the unconscious." He says that an almost tangible wall, shell, or barrier "vanishes in [such] a conversion experience." Such an experience calls for the kind of "act of surrender" described in the Twelve Steps of Alcoholics Anonymous. (Harry M. Tiebout, "Conversion as a Psychological Phenomenon," in *The Treatment of the Alcoholic, Pastoral Psychology*, Vol. 2, No. 13 [1951], pp. 28–34.)

Classical accounts of conversion verify the progressive, process nature of the experience. A person may begin the pilgrimage of faith in either a dramatic or quietly decisive way. In either instance, nevertheless, the initial conversion is followed by a long, sometimes turbulent and sometimes ecstatic journey.

Let me cite some classical examples of persons whose conversion stories have shaped the conversion of many others. The apostle Paul, after a long struggle with his conscience for persecuting "any belonging to the Way," underwent a cataclysmic change of heart when the living Christ accosted him on his way to Damascus saying, "I am Jesus, whom you are persecuting; but rise and enter the city, and you will be told what to do" (Acts 9:5–6). He was under the orders of Jesus from then on for the rest of his life. Yet the story of his conversion is followed by the story of the struggle for the kind of *agape* commitment that put

away childish things, struggled between the law that be-
guiled his mind and the grace that empowered him to do
what he at his best wanted to do (Rom. 7:4–25).

Or, another example is Augustine. In the late summer
of 386, Augustine, feeling deeply his own self-contempt,
felt the final breakthrough of his resistance. He heard the
sound of a child's voice calling *"Tolle lege, tolle lege"*
("Take up and read"). He read the New Testament at
Rom. 13:14: "Put on the Lord Jesus Christ, and make no
provision for the flesh, to gratify its desires." Ambrose
baptized him in 387. Yet this only began his long struggle
to grapple with distinguishing the Christian faith from
philosophies he had previously espoused. He saw the life
that follows conversion as "Christian combat," a struggle
from which the person of faith does not shrink.

Martin Luther, in discovering Christian freedom from
the commercialized works theology of the sacraments
characteristic of the medieval Catholicism of his day,
speaks also of the same struggle to maturity of which
Augustine speaks. In his commentary on Rom. 12:2, he
says: "The apostle speaks of progress, for he addresses
people who have already begun to be Christians, whose
life is not static but in movement from good to better, just
as a sick man moves from sickness into health, as our Lord
shows in the half-dead man whom the good Samaritan
took care of (Luke 10:34). . . . It is of no use for a tree to
grow green and to blossom if the blossoms do not turn into
fruit. Hence, many perish when they are in blossom.
. . . If, therefore, we are always repenting, we are always
sinners, and precisely thereby we are righteous and being
made righteous; we are partly sinners and partly righteous, . . . nothing but penitents. . . . This life, therefore,
is a road to heaven and to hell. None is so good that he
cannot become better, and none is so bad that he cannot
become worse, until at last we become what we are to be."
(Pauck, ed., *Luther: Lectures on Romans,* pp. 321–323.)

Richard Baxter, born in 1615, exemplifies the impact of

suffering, such as conscience conflicts, grief, and near-death encounters. Suffering catalyzed conversions and experiences of calling in Baxter. He was converted at the age of fifteen, as a result of becoming conscience-stricken for having robbed "an orchard or two with rude boys." But his first illness, his mother's illness and death in 1634 when he was nineteen, and the long struggle with his own illness into his twenty-third year prompted in him the beginning of a long search for the source of rest and serenity in God. He thought of his care of his people, especially in preaching, "as a dying man to dying men." He said: "O brethren, surely if you had all conversed with death as often as I have done, and as often received the sentence in yourselves, you would have an unquiet conscience, if not a reformed life in your ministerial diligence and fidelity." (Richard Baxter, *Gildas Salvianus: The Reformed Pastor,* 1656, 2d ed., rev., ed. by John T. Wilkinson, p. 110.)

Furthermore, John Wesley was already a committed Christian in 1728 when he began reading William Law's *A Serious Call to a Devout and Holy Life.* He responded to a call to be a Christian missionary in America. On board ship to America, he met a group of Moravians. He saw that they had a sense of serenity amid a storm at sea. This intrigued him with his own need for an assurance of faith. Later, at a Moravian meeting on Aldersgate Street in London, Wesley heard the reading of Luther's Preface to Paul's Epistle to the Romans. Then he experienced his conversion, which he describes thus: "About a quarter before nine, while he was describing the change which God works in the heart through faith in Christ, I felt my heart strangely warmed. I felt I did trust in Christ, Christ alone for my salvation; and an assurance was given me that he had taken away *my* sins, even *mine,* and saved *me* from the law of sin and death. I began to pray with all my might for those who had in a more especial manner despitefully used me and persecuted me. I then testified openly to all there what I now first felt in my heart." (John Wesley, in

John Wesley (writings), ed. by Albert C. Outler, p. 66; Library of Protestant Thought.)

As can well be seen, none of these witnesses to conversion and the Christian life commend it as the "quick fix" offered by either the sacramental systems of liturgical churches or the forms of commercial evangelism of today. Neither is the tedious process of psychotherapy a panacea. Pastoral care consists of a durable relationship, inasmuch as in us is possible, to the persons to whom we have the unspeakable joy of faithfully and affectionately introducing Jesus Christ as their Deliverer and Redeemer.

Vocational Crises

Shifts in identity as working persons represent marked crises of vocation in the lives of persons of all ages. These crises are common to all persons who participate in life to the fullest. Here again the person who feels a sense of responsibility to God naturally turns to the minister for vocational guidance. This becomes the door into the confidence of young people which you as pastor can most easily enter. High school and college students may be defensive about their religious loyalties and resistive about their love lives, but they are eager to talk with a genuinely interested person about what they are going to do with their lives. Here the pastor confronts the strains and pressures of a competitive society upon growing personalities. When people have completed their education, they are on their own. They are expected to prove themselves, to make something out of themselves, to get up in the world, to do as well as the rest of their peers, and to be above those of their own age. This is closely geared with marital hopes. Quite often they become stalemated when marital hopes and vocational objectives conflict with each other.

Here again people fall into an either-or situation: They may be comfortable with a vocational objective that is in keeping with given abilities, or they may have such impossible goals that they think of themselves as nothing in comparison with their self-expectations. They may fear a reasonable amount of competition and prefer to get drunk rather than to take a chance on failing in work. They may have the ability to accept failure, or be so afraid of failure that they cannot act at all. Having a creative imagination and an active foresight, they may prefer dreaming *about* goals to walking *toward* them. At any rate, the completion of education and the choice of a full-time job presents a major crisis.

You as pastor can do much toward preparing the youth of your church for this crisis through group education in vocational opportunities and responsibilities. Personal interest and firm confidence in people quite frequently serve to cushion the crisis and to guide them through discouragement and anxiety. You can offer practical help to high school and college graduates in your church in finding happy places of work. This will be a pleasurable work to do. You become their mentor; they become your protégés. Some pastors find the whole months of May and June dominated by the needs of their young people in this sphere. You can plan with the whole church on ways and means of helping the young people through this crisis; the problems in religious skepticism, juvenile delinquency, and other forms of destructive adolescent rebellion can be reduced considerably.

But it is not only persons graduating from school who experience vocational crises. The working mother of today undergoes much "choice anxiety" as to whether or not she should work. She feels especially ambivalent about this if she has professional training and identity of her own. She may feel this pressure more keenly after her youngest child is in school. Some studies indicate that she can then work part-time, have others do the heavier housework for her, and be happier herself without neglecting her children.

Another group of persons in a "crisis of calling and voca-

tion" consists of those women, usually above the age of
fifty, who have always found all of their purpose in life in
being a mother and a wife. A woman in this category has
rarely, if ever, worked outside the home. Her children are
grown and have left the home. Then, usually quite suddenly, her husband dies of a heart attack or an accident,
or he might even be a suicide. In any event, the death is
sudden and she has had no preparation for life without her
husband. She fails to recover from the grief, but *the grief
itself becomes her vocation!* She refuses to take up life
again with a new purpose, or to reconsecrate her life to a
living purpose. This set of circumstances is so common in
church groups that it can be called the "wailing widow
syndrome." These persons usually come to your attention
through a daughter whose whole life routine is dominated
by a complaining mother. The daughter herself, oddly
enough, is *also* solely absorbed in being a wife and mother.
The present situation calls for great pastoral patience and
therapy of pathological grief. Also, quite apart from individual cases, the calling and destiny of women in terms of
an existence independent of marriage and motherhood
must be preached, taught, and counseled.

Such preaching, teaching, and counseling urge both
husband and wife to undergo a shift of identity as individuals and as a married couple after their children are grown
and the family has contracted to just the two of them
again. Demographic studies released in 1977 indicate that
the average longevity of the white man is 70 years and the
black man is 64.6 years and that of the white woman is
77.7 and the black woman is 73.1 years. This means that
most couples today have a probability of as much as or
more than two decades of life together *after their children
are grown.* Moving out of the identity of a protecting,
supporting, and tied-down set of parents into the vocation
of adult parents with adult children calls for a deep
reevaluation of the meaning of life. This crucial time
seems to be one in which many marriages tend to break

up or the individuals within them become sick, depressed, or alcoholic. On the other hand, it is a time of joy, celebration, and heartfelt achievement for those who have effectively faced the previous developmental tasks of life. The area of pastoral concern needs, for example, studies of conversion in the age group of the forties and fifties similar to those studies made by Starbuck with groups of college students. The "late decider" for the Christian faith and the "late decider" for the Christian ministry offer fascinating areas of study for a deeper understanding of the Christian faith. After all, the apostle Paul, Augustine, Bunyan, George Fox, and many other creative religious geniuses were in the fullness of their years when they entered the depths of the Christian faith.

In addition to the working mother and the couple whose children are grown, the person facing retirement undergoes a major crisis of separation, transition, and reunion in a new identity. Prior to World War II, retirement was a prerogative of the privileged. The population was more distinctly rural. On the farm, work in diminishing degrees is naturally possible. There were fewer people who reached the age of sixty-five. Increasing numbers of persons from the upper-lower, the lower-middle, the upper-middle, and the lower-upper classes are retiring. Furthermore, by the year 2000 it is estimated that more than 31,822,000 Americans will have passed the sixty-five mark. For those for whom work has been the center of meaning in life over and above the money that they earned, the removal of work is the removal of meaning. Thus, retirement is for many today, especially in this affluent society where there is a surplus rather than a wartime scarcity of working people, a collapse of meaning and an encounter with nothingness. But for those who have made adequate provision and preparation for retirement, both spiritually and economically, retirement can be a time of release, creative enjoyment, and productive entrée into the fruits of their labors. Effective pastoral care by the fellowship of the church and disciplined understanding of its ministers can make this difference.

The vocational heart of pastoral care addresses your most sensitive and perceptive emotions in your quest for a lasting and growing meaning in the lives of your people. You as pastor are concerned with what they are going to do with their lives at each point of arrival and departure in their developmental histories. You are concerned with the story of their manner of life in times past and you ask them: *"Quo vadis?"*—"Where are you going?" The main direction of their lives as a whole is an ultimate concern, both to them and to you.

Marriage

For people who take marriage seriously enough to consult a minister, it is a crisis. Traditionally marriage has been the concern of the churches. Even in the secular culture of today those who marry turn to a pastor for religious sanction of the step they are taking. Marriage is a crisis, not only for the persons who are marrying but also for their parents and siblings. For this cause, both the man and the woman leave their fathers and mothers, precipitating a radical reorganization of life both in their own lives and in the lives of the families from which they come. It seems almost ironical, but the family by its very nature was established with the ultimate biological and spiritual objectives of being dissolved in order that new families might be formed.

Therefore, all the early family relationships and parental training in religion are brought into focus at the time of marriage. The concept of the self of an individual undergoes marked changes. The routines of living of marital partners are transformed as they shift the centers of their attention from themselves to each other. Marriage brings religious values into bolder relief, and shows up the presence or absence of emotional stability.

You may or may not function as a marriage and family counselor when young persons confer with you about wedding ceremonies. This depends upon your willingness to take the time to do so and to discipline yourself in the careful study of the principles and techniques of marriage and family counseling. When you do this faithfully, you often make the difference between a successful marriage and a failure. In other instances you can encourage effective as well as happy marriages. When you do not attempt to give family life education on a group level and marriage and family counseling on an individual level, you are not equipped to preach against divorce. Personal neglect contributes to the "hardness of heart" that makes the writ of divorcement possible and even necessary.

The decision to marry is a culmination of a series of meaningful and often joyful crises. These crises are surrounded by many rites of separation, transition, and reunion. The process from friendship, through courtship, engagement, the wedding, and to the honeymoon represents the formation of a "covenant within a covenant." Here the individual moves into the crisis of what Erikson calls the tension between intimacy and isolation. The ministry to persons prior to the public announcement of engagement and/or the wedding itself lays the foundation for effective pastoral ministry to couples in the more formal ministry of performing the wedding. The covenant of marriage is set within the covenant of the Christian faith itself when you as pastor perform the wedding as a ministry of the church and as a representative of the church. Inasmuch as the church often has in its fellowship the families of either the bride or the groom, and sometimes both families, you have unique access to the whole fabric of the social relationships in which the marriage takes place.

Premarital pastoral care and counseling have moved through several stages since the early thirties. The depression years made us exceptionally aware of the economic factors in marital happiness. The war years presented the strains of separation and impulsive decisions of young couples. The postwar years of inflation have presented the problems of the early marriage, the increase of premarital and extramarital sexual relationships, the social-status strivings of couples, and the conflict of marital aims with educational goals. We as ministers have moved away from the "bibliographical" approach to premarital counseling in which we asked for books on sex to hand to a couple. The doubtful value of this has become apparent to more and more ministers. Pastors have also tended in great numbers to reject the "statistical actuarial" approach to premarital pastoral care and counseling. By this I mean the use of sociological statistics that predict marital happiness on the basis of factors—such as differences of education, family background, social class structures, religious preference, and race—which have been demonstrated to be operative in much marital unhappiness. Increasing numbers of pastors, however, are beginning to probe the importance of less obvious factors that have the power to overcome even such differences as have been mentioned. Education for marriage prior to marriage itself, submission to the disciplines of communication, clarification of an open covenant based upon an open-eyed awareness of each partner's weaknesses as well as strengths, and a commitment to each other in the context of commitment to Jesus Christ and the fellowship of believers are a few of these factors.

As of this third edition of this book, the area of premarital counseling is being reshaped by several social changes in the institution of marriage. A considerable number of people are extremely critical of what they consider the *oppressive* injustice of marriage itself. Others actualize a deep suspicion of the demands of a marriage covenant by simply living together without being married at all. In an even more culturally assumed way, many couples who come to the decision to be married do so after already having had sexual relations. Pregnancy more often than previously may be the signal for marriage. These shifts in mores are not restricted to one age group but extend to persons in several age groups. For example, one of the earlier presuppositions of premarital counseling was the announcement of an engagement. Today all social classes have absorbed much of the practice of earlier lower classes in simply dispensing with this time of testing of the vows to marry prior to the marriage itself. The rediscovery of the importance of the engagement is a goal for pastoral care of the future.

Without a time for counseling, pastors are forced either to be severely legalistic and dogmatic on the one hand or to adopt a casual laissez-faire attitude on the other hand. Neither seems to appeal to the compassionate but wise pastor. Consequently, a third, more difficult but rewarding approach is, it seems to me, best: Take the couple wherever you find them and challenge them to think and pray their way to a wholehearted commitment to and acceptance of their responsibility for each other. Instead of pushing the issue of true love and purity as a *summum bonum,* raise issues of the quality of trust, respect for each other's judgment, wholeheartedness of commitment, and durable hope for caring for each other in sickness and health all of their lives. The classical wedding ceremony provides a diagnostic and therapeutic pattern for such interviewing and counseling. This approach is described in detail in the book *Before You Marry Them,* by Wayne E. Oates and Wade Rowatt. For postmarital counseling, Charles Stewart's *The Minister as Family Counselor* is a useful guide. A way of maintaining a continuous update of the pastoral function in family care is for you to seek certification and membership in The American Association for Marriage and Family Therapy. 924 W. Ninth Street, Upland, California 91786.

Likewise, the theological focus of the marriage relationship as the objective basis for a lasting covenant of marriage has become the predominant theme in pastoral approaches to the care of couples at the time of marriage. The work of D. S. Bailey, *The Mystery of Love and Marriage*, still sets the tone for this approach. Also, Bailey's book *Sexual Relation in Christian Thought* gives background.

The ethical and social dilemmas posed by the pastoral responsibility for the care of divorced persons, especially at the time of remarriage, have become an increasing concern of pastors. With the easing of legal prohibitions and public attitudes toward divorce, it has too often become the first option rather than the last for the solution of marriage difficulties. A high degree of tentativeness pervades the thought of people as they enter the covenant of marriage. The simple determination to make this marriage work is still a major factor in marital success.

The pastoral responsibilities for the divorced person become specific. First, the church and its ministry are all the more responsible today for deepening a person's commitment, determination, and capability of establishing and maintaining durable, lasting human relationships of every kind, especially in the intimate covenant of marriage. Secondly, the church and its ministry are responsible for providing intensive preparation for marriage through carefully thought out plans of education, individual counseling, and forms of celebration of announcements of engagement, ceremonies of marriage, returns to the community after the honeymoon, the establishment of housekeeping either through renting or buying an apartment or house, and group fellowship during the critical first three years of marriage. Thirdly, the church and its ministry are responsible for developing a more private but nevertheless warm and accepting fellowship for persons who are divorced and prefer to remain this way rather than remarry. Fourthly, the church and its ministry are responsible for the rehabilitation of divorced and remarried couples in ways that neither compromise the integrity of the Christian ideal of marriage as a permanent covenant between two Christians nor consider the remarried persons as being sinners in a way that is either unpardonable or unique as contrasted with the other sinners in the fellowship of the forgiven. Fifthly, the church and its ministry are responsible for developing means of communication by which to discover marital discord before it has reached the point of no return, and for confronting persons who turn a second time to divorce as a solution for marital trouble with their need for both personal repentance and professional therapy for the problems that beset them. In these latter incidences, the possibilities are high that marital discord is symptomatic of deeper personality disorders that are only further complicated by divorce. And, finally, the church and its ministry should be at work in relation to civil government and lawmakers in the development of civil laws. A favorable legal climate must be developed that will contribute to the responsible solution of marriage difficulties by means other than easy divorce, such as requiring periods of waiting between procuring the license and the marriage itself, and requiring a presentation of evidence of the absence of chronic mental disorder, chronic recidivism in the divorce courts, and such diseases as alcoholism, as well as other laws that would be devised on the basis of empirical studies of the human suffering involved in marital discord and dissolution.

Physical Illness

Sooner or later the crisis of illness enters the life of most people unless they die a sudden or violent death. The physically ill person loses independence and must lean on others in a relative state of helplessness. The ill person is shocked by the abruptness of pain, panicked by the thought of sustained helplessness or death, and confused by the opinions and procedures of the medical experts in whose hands rests life. Illness may isolate a person to a life of self-concern, and the mind searches in its loneliness for some explanation of the mystery of the suffering. A patient confronts the alternative of dealing constructively with these problems, or of adopting illness as a chronic way of life. Here again is an either-or situation in which the individual and the family need the help of a skilled minister as they pass through the different stages of an illness.

Physicians have established that emotional tension and deeply rooted anxieties may cause, aggravate, or prolong an illness. Likewise, physical illness, even the sort requiring surgery, is often the prelude to psychotic disturbances. You as a pastor can positively affect these emotional tensions. Similarly, physicians have identified stress events that accumulate a "load of stress." These loads of stress are precursors of illness. You can intervene at "stress points" and help distribute and relieve these weighty times of tribulation. Remarkably enough, the stress times located in medical research correspond with the crises discussed in this chapter.

You as a minister are expected to visit the sick. The Reformation marked the recovery of the preaching ministry from sacramentalism. The translation of the Bible into the vernacular recovered the teaching ministry from the monastery. Now the intensive pastoral education in clinics and the closer cooperation of medicine and the ministry promise to recover the healing ministry from the magic and superstition of relic worship and primitive faith-healing cults, as well as from a purely secularized practice of medicine.

Many ministers look upon the visitation of the sick as a chore, dreading the discomfort of being around people who are helpless and in pain. But when you as a pastor take seriously the importance of physical and mental illness as spiritual crises of major proportions, you will find an effectual door of service and instruction set before you. You become an original explorer into the laws of character that work themselves out before your eyes. You will be doing genuine laboratory work in the patient study of the facts of human nature.

1. *The separating power of illness.* The responsibility of the church and its ministry is vivid in the care of the sick person in the decisive days prior to hospitalization in a society in which going to the hospital has become a predominant pattern in the care of the sick. The patient-to-be is diagnosed by the pastor, with a spiritual diagnosis, just as the physician diagnoses the physical/psychic disease entities. Paul Pruyser's book *The Minister as Diagnostician* will serve as a faithful guide in this process for generations to come. Furthermore, you participate with the patient and the members of the patient's family in evaluating whether or not the person has need of the physician as well as the Divine. This evaluation should be careful and specific. Determining whether a person is well or sick enough for a physician to be called precedes medical diagnosis. The pastor makes this evaluation on the basis of careful observation of the basic functions of the person, i.e., working, eating, sleeping, accustomed daily routine, and effective communication with the significant persons in the realm of relationships. When a person ceases to work, eat, sleep, meet scheduled appointments, and when that person becomes isolated and uncommunicative with the significant persons of life—such as father, mother, brother, sister, husband, wife, children, employers—one can safely assume that the person is sick and needs a physician.

2. *The inner world of the patient.* A person is enabled to accept identity as a sick person through all the rites of separation that society uses to identify a person as sick. The individual then has to come to grips with a personal inner world as a sick person.

When you care for physically ill persons, quite often you are a "stranger" to the inner world of the patient for whom you care. You may not ever have had any severe illnesses yourself, and may feel alien to the existing realities the patient is confronting. From my own experience as a surgical patient in something more than "routine" illnesses, and from my communication as a pastor and chaplain with many who have been sick, let me construct something of a descriptive psychology of the inner world of the patient who is suffering from real, organic physical pain.

The first thing to observe about any physically ill patient is the disturbed normal life routine. Financially, the routine of earning and producing has been upset. Even if the patient is a salaried or professional worker whose "base pay" is not touched, in many instances those "extra sources" of income have been cut off. If the patient is a skilled laborer, working by the day, the financial threat is more seriously felt. The patient may be quite concerned about the family, and even more agitated by the medical bills. On the other hand, if the basic desire is to avoid financial responsibility, the patient may cling to the illness as long as possible.

Furthermore, the life routine of a patient is disturbed in that the individual is separated from family and friends in an effectual and difficult way. The mother or father who has never been away from the children will be at a loss without them. Homesickness, pure and simple, is one of the problems within the inner world of the patient.

The sexual routine of married patients is also interrupted. In short-term illnesses, this is not too serious, but it becomes acute in the life of a long-term patient. The patient is thrown backward in sexual adjustment. Patients in physical rehabilitation centers find themselves exceptionally concerned, for instance, as to what their spouse will do, now that the sexual bond of their marriage has been seriously changed by their handicap. Victims of fatal diseases that cause them to linger on, such as cancer and leukemia, realize with an inner sense of quiet desperation that the sexual part of their marriage may be over. The

advent of marital distancing, infidelity, and even divorce
in the midst of the illness of one member of the partner-
ship is not an unusual thing as a result of this aspect of
illness.

The untoward interruption of the routine of the individual reduces the physically ill patient to a state of helpless
dependence. Patients may have been persons of great independence who carried unlimited responsibilities. They
may not even have been aware of their bodies, nor "have
been sick a day in their lives." They may have thought
there was "no limit to the things they could do," and that
they "could burn the candle at both ends" without pen-
alty. But now "this thing" has "hit" them. They are rendered helpless and can only capitulate to the growing
demands of a diseased body. They are now back where
they started as a baby—in a bed, made by a motherly and
antiseptic nurse, unable even to feed themselves or control their own bodily functions. They resent this dependence at first and may become quite uncooperative and
even obstreperous.

But as the heavy hand of pain clamps down, they become grateful for the right to this dependence. In the
convalescent period, they may even hang on to their status as a sick person, reluctant to become the same independent person as always. In a real sense, the physically
ill patients undergo some rather violent changes in their
self-concept. They may be shaken in self-confidence. They
may, even after having returned to their normal routine,
have an unsure hand in making decisions and accepting
work assignments. A woman may become quite inadequate in her job and the care of her children, and in her
estimate of herself as a wife. A child may have disturbances in relating afresh to the play group and to the school
situation.

The return to infantile dependence raises another con-
stellation of inner difficulties in the life of the physically ill
patient. States of unconsciousness, the effect of drugs, and

the threats to life all add together to cause old repressed and unsolved emotional conflicts to return. *Old* bereavements, *old* interpersonal alienations, *old* emotional deprivations come welling up for review. Like the ghost of Hamlet's father, these problems "walk again." As one patient told me, "All those people who have long been dead are now alive again in my dreams." The pastor's listening ministry is of great value to the patient who feels the need to talk with an understanding person as these remnants of the old self emerge for integration into the conscious selfhood of the patient.

The core of all the inner struggles of the patient, however, is the hard fact of physical pain itself. At this point, we are talking about primary pain caused by real irritation of nerve endings, such as the pinching of central nerves by shattered vertebrae. The cycle of pain needs careful attention from the point of view of the patient's reaction.

The cycle of pain begins with the stimulation or irritation of the nerve endings themselves. This is followed by shock: pain hits the patient. It carries with it a stunning, blunting, shocking effect. Theodor Reik says that shock is a primary emotion, preceding others. Shock is followed by fear. The response of the patient is a fear reaction amounting to panic. Muscles tense up, increasing the pain. This reaction differs according to immediacy, amount of control, and the degree of pain tolerance.

The fear or panic reaction calls for a muscular tonicity of bracing against additional thrusts of pain. This tension predisposes the organism to more pain, finishing or closing the cycle: pain—fear—muscle spasm—tension—more pain. The need for relaxation as a means of slowing down and eventually breaking the vicious circle is evident. The importance, therefore, of the pastor's being a calm and steady presence for the patient stands out in bold relief at this juncture of the patient's experience. All the means of relaxation at the patient's disposal are of help.

Withal, the fact of pain brings to the patient's mind the

possibility of death. The contemplation of death itself tends to populate the inner consciousness of the physically ill. They need not be seriously or critically ill; the illness itself is a reminder of their finitude, the shortness of life, the certainty of its end, and the necessity of its mortality. With many, this contemplation takes on the character of an apprehensiveness, vague and undefined. With others it intensifies into a sense of dread and horror, and may even deepen into a panic that seriously militates against recovery. With fatalistic persons, bludgeoned by circumstances or inner conflicts into a hopeless kind of despair, the thought of death may take on a definite intention *not to recover* at all. As many people have said: "There is a line in most serious illnesses in which the simple will to live becomes a significant determinant of the prognosis of the patient."

You, representing confidence and hope that transcends even death itself, by incarnating that confidence and hope in your own way of life, can do much to alleviate the fear of death. As a representative of truth and reality, by being an incarnate spirit of honesty, you can give hope without glossing over the reality of death with superficial and banal reassurances.

The patient, who knows intuitively that you are aware —if but tacitly aware—of the inner life that the patient must of necessity live, *feels* understood. This understanding is the kind of redemptive presence that becomes in itself an aid to recovery. The understanding *is* the therapy.

The hospital is a specialized community for giving patients a moratorium from the demands of society, for controlling the outside forces that affect them, and for bringing them into the close supervision of physicians and nurses who have the tools of diagnosis and therapy immediately at hand. A physician writing this would reverse this order of things. You as a minister, however, are concerned with the meaning of the spiritual moratorium of rest, protection, and freedom from demands which the hospital provides. As a wise pastor, you have a high regard for the work of the physicians and nurses when you minister to one of their patients. Nor do you wisely consider your responsibility less integral to the welfare of the patient than that of the physician.

3. *The neglect of the convalescent patient.* Much pastoral education has emphasized the role of the pastor during the acute crises of the hospitalized patient's life. Not nearly enough attention has been paid to the more subtle situation of the patients who have reunited at home, have begun to make decisions on their own about how much they will do, whether to follow the physician's advice, and just how serious the illness was and is. This would be the time, also, when they would be free of the grogginess caused by anesthetics and pain-killing drugs, and the sense of helplessness that comes to people who are nauseated, running high temperatures, and unable to perform the simplest human functions of eating, excretion, etc., without the help of others. The convalescent period, for example, is a time of partial but limited functioning; many people do not assume, for example, that a psychiatric patient will need a time of convalescence just as surely as does a surgical patient. People will assume, and so will their families, that psychiatric patients will be able to take up right where they left off before hospitalization. You might not have seen these patients on a posthospitalization basis, and therefore might be likely to fall into this way of thinking. Yet you are uniquely situated and responsible for developing rites of passage for the sick as they move back into the active community. You cannot, it seems, afford easily to neglect patients when they are at home. Modern hospitalization procedures, for financial and other reasons, work to get the patient up sooner, and out more quickly. This means a longer time at home, when members of the family take over the nursing, the caring, and the guiding of the patient.

Therefore, you and your church would do well to orga-
nize a close-knit study group of which you would be the
teacher and leader. Carefully you can gather basic information as to the situation and needs of the patient. You can
cooperate with the physicians of the patient; you can
wisely plan as to the responsibility of the church and its
ministry. More intimate consultation with the family as to
their wishes and needs would be the work of this "task
force" in the ministry to the sick. Other trained and spe-
cially skilled persons in the church—such as teachers,
physicians, social workers, nurses, and people who themselves have successfully dealt with major illnesses—should
be a part of this healing force. The patient at all stages of
the illness could be undergirded by a known fellowship,
guided by the more objective wisdom of another person,
and reunited with the responsible community upon recovery. The amount and kind of visitation during hospitalization could be governed more effectively for the patient's
good and to the relief of physicians and nurses. Rites of
reunion can be developed by the caring community to
bridge the gap between the person's identity first as a sick
person and later as a recovered person. These would include the preparation of meals by various families when
the mother of a family happens to be the sick person, the
bringing of tape recordings of the church's worship services to the home to be played on a portable tape re-
corder, the holding of more formal pastoral counseling
with the individual.

Some would ask whether the psychiatric patient is not
an exception to all that has been said here. The answer to
this is no. All these things apply more especially to those
persons and in greater degree. The basic principles of the
caring community and the counseling pastor at work are
the same. The rehabilitation of the mentally ill person is
all the more significant. State departments of mental
health are developing cultural "halfway" houses for bridg-
ing the gap between hospitalization and function in an

open society. In my own city there is such an agency
where patients can work during the day and be cared for
by physicians and nurses at night. Other facilities are available for caring for patients during the day and letting
them spend the evening with their families. The church
at work healing could do much more in the compassionate
realization of the healing strength of a caring community
in the transitional crisis of convalescent mentally ill persons. But the point here is that the basic issues are the
same with people with all manner of function-interfering
diseases. No clean line can be drawn between mental and
physical illness. However, I have given specific attention
to the pastoral care of the mentally ill in my book *The
Religious Care of the Psychiatric Patient*. Of course, the
classical work on the care of the mentally sick is that of
Anton T. Boisen, *The Exploration of the Inner World*.
Both these books were based on research done within the
confines of the hospital. What the church most urgently
needs to do is to give attention to the care of the mentally
ill person who either never goes to a hospital, is under
private psychiatric care on an ambulatory, outpatient
basis, or has been to a hospital and has returned to the
community. Here is the point at which you as a Christian
pastor see the patient more often and therefore have more
responsibility for pastoral care of the person.

Bereavement

A crisis that may come into the life of those who take the
risk of loving another person is that of bereavement. The
course of normal grief at the loss of a loved one extends
over a more lengthy period of time than is ordinarily assumed. Grief moves through stages of shock: numbness of
feeling, which seems to have organic involvements as well
as psychic ones; a refusal to accept the reality of the death
of the loved one; a period of semiconscious fantasy along
with a selective memory of events that happened in rela-

tion to the loved one; a gradual return of feeling and a flood of grief; and a transference of feelings to a new object of affection.

The Christian community has intuitively provided ways and means of ministering to bereaved persons, and you as pastor of your congregation can depend upon their help in the care of bereaved persons. Unusually powerful guilt feelings are quite often at work in bereavement, and a subtle deification of the dead loved one can cause the bereaved person to become mentally ill.

The pastor is the most thoroughly trained person into whose hands the care of the bereaved is committed at the time of the crisis. Other professions are beginning their knowledge of grief therapy. The message of the resurrection over the temporal is the lasting "renewal" of the minds of the grief-stricken that can transform them. You become a traveler between life and death with the parishioner at these times, guiding each through the valley of the shadow of death. You cannot leave this ministry to professional mourners and morticians. You have been appointed "to comfort all who mourn; . . . to give them a garland instead of ashes, the oil of gladness instead of mourning, the mantle of praise instead of a faint spirit; that they may be called oaks of righteousness, the planting of the LORD, that he may be glorified" (Isa. 61:2, 3).

The facts about bereavement have been studied extensively and appear as follow:

First, grief is a process that must be lived through. The definable stages are shock, numbness, the struggle of fantasy with reality, depression and deep mourning, a process of selective memory, and a resolution of or recovery from grief. No fixed time limit holds well for all people. Different kinds of grief require different lengths of time. However, Luther's advice in 1532 to his friend Ambrose Brendt still holds: "I would [not] account you a man, to say nothing of a good husband, if you could at once throw off your grief. Nevertheless, my dear Ambrose, I allow your mourning only in so far as it is not contrary to the will of God. For it is necessary to put a limit to one's sorrow and grief." (Martin Luther, *Letters of Spiritual Counsel,* ed. and tr. by Theodore Tappert, p. 62.)

Secondly, grief must be diagnosed and treated according to the diagnosis, because there are many kinds of grief: anticipatory grief, where the death was a lingering one and the death and dying were slow; grief that attends a person who has narrowly escaped death after having faced it for a certainty; perpetual or "no end" grief, as in cases of severe handicap because of any of a number of tragic events; and pathological grief, in which the person is psychologically disabled by the grief for a long time after a normal recovery was expected. I have dealt with these in detail in my book *Your Particular Grief.* This is a book that both you the pastor and the bereaved can read.

Thirdly, grief's slow wisdom has taught us that its great temptation is the idolatry of the dead and/or the adoption of grief as a way of life. Thus grief exercises demonic control over the life of the mourner, who, in turn, tyrannizes those who are around the person with a grief that defies their best efforts at comfort.

Fourthly, the funeral is an important ritual that enables the Christian community to provide comfort to the mourner. However, the fellowship of Christians has a variety of other rituals that can be exercised—visitation, anniversary occasions, memorial services and memorial occasions such as lectureships, educational funds, etc., all of which are calculated to pay honor to and sustain the contributions of the deceased.

The basic premise of many studies of pastoral care in times of bereavement is that damage is done to persons when these rites and patterns of interpretation become stereotyped and standardized to such an extent that they produce a stalemate of ambivalence in the mourner rather than a spontaneous, growing experience of maturity through the freedom from idolatry of the dead. Ambivalence of feeling—i.e., contradictory emotions about the same person—is the key to understanding grief. If persons deny their negative feelings, as well as extol their positive feelings toward the dead, they will develop stereotyped patterns of behavior that prevent their functioning in relation to both God and man. Therefore, the acceptance and encouragement of insight into these conflictual feelings by you is a basic principle for the pastoral care of the bereaved.

Death

No one is exempt from the crisis of dying. The ministry to the dying, as they are surrounded by their family, is inseparable from the ministry to the bereaved. It is, however, one of the most intensely personal and individualized services that you as pastor render. The dying person's request for your time and attention takes precedence over all other requests. The caring pastor feels deep gratitude for the honor of being sent for at this final crisis of a person's life.

You as a minister need to recognize the fact that many persons may be said to die mentally before they die physically. The presence of heart action and respiration are not indications of the presence of mind. The weight of sedation, the weariness of the struggle with pain, and the presence of infection in the organism militate against rationality in a dying person.

Furthermore, persons who are aware of impending death are quite often more concerned about their loved ones than about themselves. Barriers that exist between them and those whose approval they consider most worthwhile are problems. The dying persons are anxious about what will happen to their loved ones, especially to small children.

Quite regularly you as a pastor are called upon to listen to the confessions of the secret sins of dying persons, because they are concerned with middle walls of partition that separate them from God. The need for confessional ministry, although not formalized, remains an abiding reality in the spiritual hunger of the dying. Here, also, you share in the radiant pilgrimage that triumphant Christians make from mortality into immortality. You are granted glimpses into eternity, in spite of the dying person's childlike blunders in the use of God's instruments of redemption.

In the ministry to the dying, you drive a hard course between being evasive, dishonest, and falsely reassuring, on the one hand, and leaving the patient to carry the possible awareness of the imminence of death all alone, on the other hand. As a pastor you walk an equally narrow ridge between being candid, honest, and open with patients about the seriousness of their condition, and speaking with authority and assurance on an issue of which they are not certain. In doing the latter, you may remove every vestige of hope a patient has for continuing to live. Thus your ministry calls for some basic principles that take into consideration the ambiguities that have just been mentioned. These principles have been developed in careful studies by pastors and teachers with much patience in the face of death.

The first principle is close cooperation and dialogue with members of the family. The family members can also learn to listen carefully to what the patient says and to follow the lead of what they themselves say and surmise about the patient's condition. The family members can admit with the patient that the situation is critical and serious without simply throwing away every semblance of hope.

The second principle is an even closer dialogue with the physicians who are caring for the patient. The physicians can provide you with a clinical understanding of the particular patient's personal and medical history, the capacity of the patient to accept the realities of life and of death, and the basic patterns of emotional reaction. The particular patient may be depressed, hostile, withdrawn, apathetic, suspicious, dependent, ambition-driven, etc. The effects of these emotional reactions to the knowledge of the nature of the patient's disorder and the shortness of the remaining life must be assayed clinically in consultation with the physicians and the family. No static, inflexible rule of thumb should be applied in caring for a dying person. This is one time when a person has a right to the dignity of individuality and to the integrity of selfhood.

A third principle of the pastoral care of the dying involves your *private* relationship as a representative of the people of God to the dying person. Groups can do much for the person: a Sunday school class can write notes; the care of the children of a young mother can be scheduled; protection can be provided from the disorder of many well-intentioned but undisciplined visitors who insist on being morbid, etc. The family can be pulled together or apart by such a crisis, particularly if they are anxious for the goodwill of the dying person toward them concerning the dying person's "last will and testament." People at the person's place of employment can provide security in terms of attention to the ongoing care of the family, etc.; or they can be in deadly competition with one another for the dying person's position at work. But you, a sensitive and wise pastor, can copy the approach of the Lord Jesus Christ, who often even sent people out of the room when he cared for a critically ill person (Mark 5:40). This can be arranged ahead of time, in order that people will know that you want to talk with the person alone. In this atmosphere of privacy, apart from the ears of those whom the dying person loves, fears, or feels totally responsible for, you are more apt to hear the person's feelings and what intimations of life and death have been thought of.

In these quiet moments of self-confrontation I have discovered that persons facing death drop many of the cultural subterfuges of life and communicate with you as pastor concerning their deepest thoughts, their past history of fulfillment and failure, and their personal attitudes toward God. Therefore, your creation of a permissive privacy is a basic principle. Arnold Hutschneker quotes a surgeon, Dr. Frank Adair, with whom I would also agree: "The dying patient usually knows his condition and at the end is glad to go. This seems to be especially true of those patients who have deep religious convictions." (Arnold A. Hutschnecker, "Personality Factors in Dying Patients," in *The Meaning of Death,* ed. by Herman Feifel, p. 238.)

Finally, the epigenetic principle of pastoral care is never more vivid than in the care of the dying. You cannot make up to a dying patient for your absence of relationship in previous years by becoming compulsively concerned about the person's salvation all of a sudden.

From birth to death and at every significant point in between, you as a Christian pastor are commissioned by Christ and expected by the community to bring the mind of Christ and the reality of the Holy Spirit to bear upon the crises that people face. Several crises have been described here. Others, less universally confronted, but nevertheless acutely meaningful to those who do experience them, could be named. Social crises of war, famine, flood, and fire assail people en masse. Divorce and mental illness are crises of family and personal disorganization that are increasing in prevalence.

You as a pastor, along with all other persons engaged in humanitarian tasks, are a person of crisis for such times as these. Having inherited such a ministry, you can conserve your birthright and add to it your own personal spiritual fortune by assimilating all that modern research has to offer in discipline and technique and by understanding Biblical truth in terms of human needs.

Daniel Aleshire says: "Perhaps no other contemporary phenomenon has invaded the practice of ministry with the impact that pastoral care has acquired during the past three decades. Its contemporary significance is attested to by the high rating of importance given the 'Caring for Persons Under Stress' factor." (Aleshire, "Eleven Major Areas of Ministry," in *Ministry in America,* p. 32.)

Note the high levels of significance on the scale from 0–3, given this crisis ministry:

CARING FOR PERSONS UNDER STRESS

CORE CLUSTER NO.	NAME AND DESCRIPTION	AVERAGE RATING
21	*Perceptive Counseling.* Reaching out to persons under stress with a perception, sensitivity, and warmth that is freeing and supportive	2.26*
26	*Co-ministry to the Alienated.* With skill and understanding, reaching out through the congregation to the estranged, beleaguered, or isolated	1.50
23	*Caring Availability.* Responding with deep care and sensitivity to hurting people in crisis situations	2.20
22	*Enabling Counseling.* Using high levels of understanding and skill in aiding persons to work through serious problems	2.23
25	*Involvement in Caring.* Becoming personally involved in the mutual exchange among persons who seek to learn through suffering	1.73
	Factor average	1.98

NOTE: This factor structure results from the analysis of responses from clergy only. No similar structures emerge from responses of laity alone.
*Although the factor structure is determined by clergy, the average ratings are based on the responses of both laity and clergy. (Ibid., p. 33.)

Chapter II

The Symbolic Power
of the Pastor

The Christian pastor enters the responsibilities of ministry in the strength of one of the oldest callings of human beings. The function of a minister has, through centuries of Christian culture, been bred into the deeper levels of the consciousness of those whom you, the minister, serve. Therefore, you have a symbolic weight of being as well as personal influence. The symbolic strength of your role gives a weight far beyond that of your own personal appeal to people. Paul described it well when he said, "We are ambassadors for Christ, God making his appeal through us" (II Cor. 5:20). You represent and symbolize far more than yourself. You represent God the Father; you serve as a reminder of Jesus Christ; you follow the leading of the Holy Spirit; you are an emissary of a specific church; and you activate the caricatures of the Christian faith to those who are hostile, suspicious, and/or detached from the Christian faith. Nevertheless you are a shepherd to non-Christians as well as to those who are in the church.

This symbolic power elevates the importance of the unique structure and function of a pastor's interpersonal relationships with people. It places in proper perspective specific techniques of pastoral care and personal counseling. It reveals the inadequacy of stereotyped advice in given situations. The careful, intelligent, and devoted management of the unique interpersonal relationship of a pastor to an individual or a group becomes the normative definition of pastoral care and personal counseling. As such, the pastoral task is the participation in the "divine-human encounter."

All this implies a Christian context of basic theological axioms for pastoral care and personal counseling. The sovereignty of God, the principle of incarnation whereby the Word was made flesh, the activity of the Holy Spirit in contemporary living, and the function of the church as the body of Christ—these are the realities that empower the pastor. In pastoral care and personal counseling they become functional realities rather than theoretical topics of discussion. The analysis, therefore, of the symbolic power of the pastor provides an interpretation of your relationship to people in terms of your relationship to God. Such an approach gives a *theological framework for pastoral care and personal counseling.* Such a framework is needed lest the strength of secular concepts of counseling and psychotherapy force you as the pastor into a role and a relationship that are foreign to your unique place in society and in history.

Much attention has been directed toward the theological foundations of the function of the pastor. The church has been described by H. Richard Niebuhr as a community of memory and hope sharing in the memory of Jesus Christ and of the God of Israel, "united by its direction toward one God, who is Father, Son, and Holy Spirit." (H. Richard Niebuhr, *The Purpose of the Church and Its Ministry,* p. 23.) The purpose of the church and its ministry is "the increase of love of God and neighbor," and the pastor both embodies and communicates that love. This love is a rejoicing and a celebrating of the presence of both God and neighbor. It is gratitude for God and neighbor. It is reverence that "keeps its distance even as it draws near, neither seeking to absorb the loved one nor being willing to be absorbed by the loved one." This love is loyalty, i.e., the "commitment of the self by a decision of self-binding will to make the other great."

As Luther says, "It is the duty of the prudent minister to hold his ministry in honor and to see to it that he is respected by those in his charge." (Pauck, ed., *Luther: Lectures on Romans,* p. 6.) But the pastor does not command this respect apart from the grace of God which bestows God's own unmerited love upon the pastor. The reality that holds the pastor together as a person and engenders respect is the generative love of God. As Niebuhr says, "Love to this God is the conviction that there is faithfulness at the heart of all things: unity, reason, form, and meaning in the plurality of being." (H. Richard Niebuhr, *The Purpose of the Church and Its Ministry,* p. 37.)

In the most recent study, in *Ministry in America,* note what David Schuller says: "What are the most significant characteristics that people across denominational lines are looking for in their young priests or ministers? Ranking at the top is a construct or dimension whose items point to the label 'service without regard for acclaim.' This cluster of items describes an individual who is able to accept his or her personal limitations, and who, believing the gospel, is able to serve without concern for public recognition. This is reinforced by the second highest factor, namely, that of personal integrity; this describes one who is able to honor his or her commitments by carrying out promises despite all pressures to compromise. Ranking third is a factor that has to do with Christian example. The cluster describes one whose personal belief in the gospel manifests itself in generosity, and in general, a Christian example that people in the community can respect. The total group of clergy and laity allot fourth place to the characteristic of acknowledging limitations and mistakes, and recognizing the need for continued growth and learning. Ranking fifth is a cluster that has to do with the minister as a leader in community building. The items in this cluster focus on actions that will build a strong sense of community within a congregation. It includes taking time to know parishioners well and developing a sense of trust and confidence between him- or herself and the members of the parish. If you reflect on these top five criteria, you will notice that four lie within the area of the clergy's personal commitment and faith and center in the minister or priest as a person. The last of the group describes a particular leadership skill." (David S. Schuller, "Identifying the Criteria for Ministry," in *Ministry in America,* ed. by David S. Schuller, Merton P. Strommen, and Milo L. Brekke, pp. 18–19.)

It is said that the pastor is a "person of God" and an "ambassador for Christ." What kind of authority does this give the pastor and how should it be exercised? How can you as pastor exercise this "authority" without either losing your sense of urgency and commitment or becoming an authoritarian "pusher" of the ecclesiastical trappings of your social position? Your authority as minister does not arise from your relation to civil government, from your accrued education, or from your participation in a certain social class. These are incidental to your real authority as a representative of God, of Christ, and of the Holy Spirit. Rather, as Niebuhr says, "Ministers have derived their immediate authority to preach and teach, lead worship, care for souls, and perform their other offices from the church and from Scripture." (H. Richard Niebuhr, *The Purpose of the Church and Its Ministry,* p. 70.) But more basically than this, ministers derive their authority from having experienced themselves the gospel as the good news of God in Jesus Christ and, in a sense, from being eyewitnesses of that which they declare to others.

It is one thing to discuss authority and its sources in the minister's life, but it is another to see this functionally. Just how do you as a minister exercise this authority as a "person of God" and as an "ambassador for Christ"? You do so as a person of faith, who has evidence for things that are not seen, the things which, amid the shaking of the foundations of people's lives, remain as that which cannot be shaken. The actual power of your identity arises, not even from the conferring of status by the church or from some factual knowledge of the Scripture, although neither of these is to be considered lightly or indiscreetly. Rather, as Daniel Day Williams says: "The authority of the Christian . . . to speak and act as a representative of God's forgiveness and his healing power is given only through the actual exercise of the pastoral office. Real personal authority arises out of the concrete incarnation of the spirit of loving service which by God's help becomes present in the care of souls. And this means that ministerial authority can be lost as well as won." (Williams, *The Minister and the Care of Souls.*) This was the witness of our Lord Jesus Christ, the Good Shepherd, when the disciples of John asked if Jesus were "he who is to come." Jesus said: "Go and tell John what you hear and see: the blind receive their sight and the lame walk, lepers are cleansed and the deaf hear, and the dead are raised up, and the poor have good news preached to them" (Matt. 11:3–6). Your very authority as a minister, then, rests in your exercise of your office, and, as with your bodily health, you lose this authority unless you participate in the full exercise of your preaching, teaching, and caring ministries. Let us consider the dimensions of these exercises of the minister of faith.

THE PASTOR AS A REPRESENTATIVE OF GOD

Late one evening a minister received a call to come to a ward in the local hospital. Upon arrival he found an elderly farmer who had just been admitted. The man looked frightened and lonely, but a natural sense of humor welled up from beneath his anxiety. The minister introduced himself, and the patient said: "I heard that you would come if I asked for you. It's mighty kind of you, because I need you. You have heard that story in the Bible about how some fellows was cutting wood one day and the ax flew off the handle and fell in the river. They had to call the man of God to help them get it out. Well, I sure have had the ax to fly off the handle with me. I never been sick a day in my life, and all of a sudden things went wrong and they told me that I have cancer of the colon. I got to be cut on Monday morning. The ax has come off the handle with me, and when the nurse told me that a man of God was close by, I sent straightway for you to help me get the ax out of the creek."

People like this man still search out Christian pastors when they need friendship, encouragement, guidance, reconciliation, and relief from guilt. They seek you—their pastor—because you are the person of God; you symbolize the presence of God as a loving Father and as the center of all moral rightness. People of every condition turn to you, the minister, because you represent the universal gospel of the eternal God. This universality means something more than geographic inclusiveness; it also means that *all* manner of people come to the Christian minister with *all* manner of problems. You as the Christian pastor, therefore, cannot select your clientele; you cannot eliminate those whose plight does not come under the classification of your specialty; neither can you pass hopeless cases to someone else. Regardless of the other ministers to humanity who may be serving your people (whether those servants be physicians, nurses, attorneys, social workers, welfare workers, or public school teachers), you, by virtue of your role as a person of God, can never consider your people as being some other person's responsibility to the exclusion of your own. *You cannot pass your ministry to anyone else.* This is the distinctive difference between the Christian pastor as a servant of people, and others who are also engaged in humanitarian helpfulness.

You as a Christian pastor, then, are a representative of God, commissioned to bring the ruling sense of the presence of God to bear upon the conflict-weary lives of others. You are an apostle of redemption and reconciliation, a practicer of the art of communion with God (II Cor. 5:20). As such, you are concerned with the salvation of the *whole* personalities of your people through an effective relationship to God in Christ rather than with the readjustment of this or that part of their lives.

As a representative of God, you, the minister, are a reminder of all the parental training in the ways of right doing that your people received in childhood. These precepts, regardless of their truth or error, have become incorporated parts of their psychic lives. Consequently, you as the minister may find individuals reacting to you in much the same way they did to their parents, and equating the precepts of their parents with the wisdom of God. You confront the task of disentangling the good gifts of parents to their children from the much more excellent gifts of the heavenly Father that are available through a personal experience of the Holy Spirit. Through this personal experience, religious experience becomes firsthand and intimately personal rather than traditional and customary.

Again, you, the minister, as a representative of God, become a visible embodiment of *conscience*. Therefore many people will draw the fig leaves of respectability over the naked places of their souls lest their minister come to know them as they really are. The minister is a judgmental presence. The fact that a moralistic connotation is placed upon your presence cannot be avoided. You therefore need to avoid the error of thinking that the persons with whom you counsel appear in the same spiritual clothing to you as they do to those to whom they are more closely related. Your task as minister is to discover the real selves of your people and to be the kind of minister with whom they can associate without pretense. The pastor works at transforming blind judgmentalism into compassionate wisdom. At the same time, suffice it to say, the quiet dignity of a minister's own presence is often more of a rebuke to the people than any verbal censure that could be poured upon them.

The strange power of a judgmental presence reminds the Christian pastor of the ever-present temptation to *supplant* rather than to represent God. You as the pastor may easily be lured into substituting your own sovereignty for that of God, "in order that the excellency may be of yourself rather than of God." The matchless insights of Nathaniel Hawthorne in *The Scarlet Letter* and Somerset Maugham in *Rain* are subtle reminders that the minister too is human and not divine. Your relative degree of authority is derived by reason of the One whom you as pastor symbolize; therefore your greatest temptation is to assume that it originated with yourself, to confuse the symbolism of your role with the reality of God.

Within the personality of every individual who turns to you for help is the active tendency to make a god out of you, the minister, with an unconscious need to idolize and desecrate you at the same time. This has been called the "unreal need for a god in human form." (Otto Rank, *Will Therapy; and, Truth and Reality*, p. 63.) One way you may give in to this idolatrous demand is to require strict conformity to your will and to the ideas that you give your people in the form of advice. A very common daydream of ministers is that of seeing their people do just as they want them to do, seeing their own will incarnated in the lives of their people. As Oscar Wilde describes this feeling, "There is something enthralling in projecting one's soul into someone else's gracious form, and letting it tarry there for a moment, to hear one's own intellectual views echoed back; to convey one's temperament into another as though it were some strange and subtle perfume." (Oscar Wilde, *The Picture of Dorian Gray*, p. 38.)

Another way you as a minister may substitute your relative authority for the sovereignty of God in the lives of your people is to use them as means for your own chosen ends rather than treating them as ends in themselves by reason of the fact that they are sacred human personalities "for whom Christ died." Thus you, the pastor, may let your function as administrator, builder of an organization, promoter of a budget, or leader of a crusade come into conflict with your representation of God. You must become a god yourself in order to manipulate your people toward your own predestined goal.

This is simply one form of idolatry. Charles Stinnette has related the problem of idolatry to the care of disturbed and unhappy persons in a precise way. He says: "Polytheism was the conscious problem of the ancient world, and it is the unconscious problem of our age. In the necessity of living through anxiety, man seeks the god of his salvation; and the crucial question is whether he worships idols or that God alone who saves him by restoring him to genuine freedom and selfhood in relatedness." (Charles Stinnette, *Anxiety and Faith,* p. 178.) The bereaved spouse makes an idol of the departed loved one. The couple who cannot have children become obsessed with this inability to the point that the whole organism is out of balance. The person who has been fired from the job organizes life around the failure. Professional persons make their profession their god, spirit, and church. In each case, the life is thrown into shock from the wrongness of its center. Also, the moralistic systems of a legalistic faith can become a possessing idol. To someone with this faith, the minister represents the "seared" or "darkened" conscience.

Also, as a minister you may yield to pressure and make your people's decisions for them; in doing so, you, like Jiminy Cricket, become their official conscience. You take responsibility away from them. You take their freedom from them and enslave yourself with them. Your task is to cooperate in the growth of human personalities that have been born of God. Individuals do not become persons in their own right until they have exercised their free powers of decision, and accepted the responsibility for the consequences of their decisions. As you, the Christian pastor,

stand in the holy of holies of people's souls, they may say
to you, "You tell me what to do, and then I know it will
be right." If you gently but firmly move this responsibility
back to them and increase their confidence in their own
ability to find the way of God, later you may have them
come back and say, "All my life I have had people tell me
what to do, and when they did, it seemed that almost
against my own will I found myself doing just the opposite
from the advice they gave me."

Something strong in human personality reaches out for
an idol, but something eternal in human personality that
outlasts both the idol and the desire for the idol says, "Cast
down imaginations, and every high thing that exalteth
itself against the knowledge of God" (II Cor. 10:5). The
unreal need for a god in human form clutches at the minister's desire to supplant God, but if you yield to this need,
you in turn become an idol cast down when those whom
you exploit discover that you also are human.

Therefore, the Christian pastor's objective is to free persons from bondage to their own self-reflections in the mir-
rors of their chosen idols and to bring them into a life-
giving loyalty to Christ. In this drastic cutting of
affectionate bonds they are likely to shift their idolatry to
you, saying, as did the people at Lystra and Derbe, "The
gods have come down to us in the likeness of men!" All the
while they may still be sitting on their own household gods
just in case they are wrong. Thus a person's own attitude
toward the concept of the sovereignty of God becomes a
continuously thrown down gauntlet before you. If you let
it go unchallenged and accept the dependent worship of
the person, the last state is worse than the one before. If
you accept the challenge and refuse the prerogatives of
God, then you face a struggle with your own childish
desires for omnipotence.

To symbolize the reality of God, therefore, calls for a
unique kind of dedication. As a Christian pastor you know
that you have the treasure of your ministry in an earthen

vessel. Insight into the earthenness of your own humanity prompts you to confess that the excellency of the power is of God and not of yourself. David E. Roberts clarifies the issues confronting the pastor:

> The danger of "playing God" in the lives of people, which certainly must not be minimized, should not blind us to the fact that men can be instruments in the service of healing power. The endowments and skills of the therapist as an individual are immeasurably enhanced by the fact that he is the symbol of something much greater than himself—namely, the drive toward fellowship, wholeness, and honesty which is deeply rooted in human life. (David E. Roberts, *Psychotherapy and a Christian View of Man*, p. 53)

Your security as a pastor arises out of your dependence upon the Chief Shepherd rather than from the completeness of your knowledge, the power of your own personality, or the cleverness of your techniques in dealing with people. You find guidance for your pastoral practice in the Chief Shepherd, "who, though he was in the form of God, did not count equality with God a thing to be grasped, but emptied himself, taking the form of a servant, being born in the likeness of men. And being found in human form he humbled himself and became obedient unto death, even death on a cross" (Phil. 2:6–8).

Just such a renunciation lies at the base of all effective representation of God. Paul describes it best when he says, "We have renounced disgraceful, underhanded ways; we refuse to practice cunning or to tamper with God's word, but by the open statement of the truth we would commend ourselves to every man's conscience in the sight of God" (II Cor. 4:2).

THE PASTOR AS A REMINDER OF JESUS CHRIST

"God . . . has shone in our hearts to give the light of the knowledge of . . . God in the face of Christ" (II Cor. 4:6).

You as a pastor are related to people "as though it were in Christ's own stead." It is your personal motive to have in yourself the mind that was in Christ Jesus. The request of the Greeks when they said, "We wish to see Jesus," is the unspoken need of those people to whom you, the Christian pastor, minister. You symbolize and remind them of Jesus Christ. More recently, the Christological heart of pastoral care has taken precedence in the theological discussions of pastoral care. Daniel Day Williams says that the objective reality "which stands between persons is God made personal and available to us in Jesus Christ." In the pastoral relationship, both pastor and parishioner seek a true knowledge of who they are. As Williams says, "Christ is the person who discloses us to ourselves." More than this, Christ is the New Man "who opens the way to what we can become. . . . Christ is the Third Man in every human relationship." (Williams, *The Minister and the Care of Souls,* p. 67.) He is the One who relates us to our individual and corporate sin, confronts us in our personal decisions about what we are doing with our lives, and separates us from sin, transiency, and disillusionment through the challenge of the power of his death, burial, and resurrection. Christ is the one through whom you as a caring pastor are emboldened to exercise your office. You bear witness, not to your own somewhat meager powers to accept, but to the acceptance you have received and can now communicate to the persons to whom you minister in Christ's name.

The sacrifice of Christ as our High Priest both creates and re-creates right relations between God and persons. Christ's sacrifice removes what wastes away a person's integrity, namely, sin. Because of this forgiveness, you are able to minister in Christ's name. As Hebrews puts it:

> For every high priest who is chosen from among men and appointed to act for men towards God, offering gifts and sacrifices for sins, is able to deal gently with the ignorant and the mistaken, because he himself is ringed around with

weakness. And for this reason he must make offerings for
sins, not only for the people but for himself also. (Heb. 5:1–3,
Williams Translation)

But this affectionate permissiveness does not mean that
there is no serious confrontation, honest criticism, and
appeal to a higher source of judgment. The Christian fellowship, of whatever denomination, rests upon a covenant. This covenant is the horizontal dimension of the
basis of our mutual judgment of one another's acts. Within
this covenant, there is a *ground* of communication for
developing mutually understood personal covenants with
individuals and small groups. These covenants are made,
revised, and renewed through the processes of human life
and interaction. But underneath all of them is the basic
covenant in which we are *bound* to treat one another as
"persons for whom Christ died." Christian love within this
covenant can become cleansingly but not painlessly honest, as the instructions for Christian conversion set forth in
Matthew 18, reveal. But the whole pastoral relationship is,
as Eduard Thurneysen says, "characterized by a movement of accepting and taking away, of comprehending
and apprehending and analyzing the human facts and sub-
mitting these facts to a wholly new judgment surpassing
any human judgment." (Eduard Thurneysen, *A Theology
of Pastoral Care,* p. 132.) And, as Thurneysen says further,
"We accept the facts in the secure knowledge that the
forgiveness of sins through the Word of God must become
effective in these facts." (Ibid.)

Thus we have to become reminders of the Word of God,
Jesus Christ, who is not just an example to be emulated
under vastly different and impossible circumstances, but
a living Christ who has returned to us in the gift of the
Father of the Holy Spirit. Therefore, the central objective
of all *pastoral* care and personal counseling is that "Christ
be formed" in the personality of the individuals who seek
help.

Therefore, the principle of incarnation in continued action requires that you, as a Christian pastor, be a person of faith, "working through love." Hereby you become a permissive shepherd who loves your sheep rather than a pseudo sovereign who rules your subjects. The pastoral task is a voluntary relationship of shared affection and discipline.

Because of this affectionate tie of personal discipline and loving identification, people can trust your motives and confide in you at times when they would be suspicious of their own family, their employer, or their physician. This may be called "the relationship of a trusted motive," whereby you, by reason of the Infinite Love that you symbolize, are given access to the holy of holies of people's confidence. This is an indispensable necessity in your relationship as a pastor to anyone whom you help.

Therefore, you as the Christian shepherd must be continually at the business of examining your own motives for your face-to-face ministry to your people. One cannot hide tawdry motives of greed, love for domination, or erotic concern from those to whom one seeks to minister. The demons of fear, suspicion, greed, hatred, and exploitation know their own kind before they see them coming. Unconscious needs meet unconscious resistances. Nothing is hidden that is not revealed in the intimacy of the pastoral situation. A relationship of a trusted motive prevails only when you as a Christian pastor voluntarily accept and effectively carry through with your power as a representative of the love of Christ. You are a servant of people for Jesus' sake. The effectiveness of all pastoral procedures depends upon the singleness of this motivation, and the ineffective use of the best techniques of counseling can be explained by the adulteration of this motive.

Other names have been given to this relationship of a trusted motive by explorers in the field of pastoral care and personal counseling. Rollo May calls it "empathy," whereby the pastor "feels his way into" the life situation

of the person who seeks the pastor's help. The basic characteristics of a helping relationship are threefold: (1) an
accurate empathy, (2) a nonpossessive warmth, and (3) an
inherent genuineness. However it is named, the relationship of a trusted motive is actually the power of "faith
working through love" to heal a person's hurt, to cast out
fear, and to break down middle walls of partition that
separate a helpless person from sources of divine strength.

The psychological consideration here is called "identification." This is the process whereby one person takes in
the character traits of another because of confidence in,
and love for, the other person, and the desire to be like the
other person. The law of identification on the divine-
human level and in terms of religious psychology is known
as worship. Personality takes the form of the object of its
adoration; therefore it is formed and transformed through
the power of love.

The earliest illustrations of this power are found in the
parent-child relationship, whereby the character of a child
is shaped into a positive likeness or a negative reaction
formation of the actual character of the parents. The character formations of children are largely the result of the
personal behavior patterns of their parents and are only
remotely related to the moral preachments and oral instructions of their parents. As the wisdom of Walt Whitman suggests:

> There was a child went forth every day,
> And the first object he look'd upon, that object he
> became,
> And that object became part of him for the day or
> a certain part of the day,
> Or for many years or stretching cycles of years. . . .
> His own parents, he that had father'd him and she
> that conceived him in her womb and birthed
> him,
> They gave this child more of themselves than that,
> They gave him afterward every day—*they and of
> them became part of him.* . . .

> These became part of that child who went forth
> every day, and who now goes, and will always
> go forth every day.
>   (From *Leaves of Grass*)

The process of identification works in the relationship of pastor to groups and to individuals in much the same way that it does in the parent-child relationship. The Word becomes flesh through the power of faith working through love; insofar as the minister participates in the mind of Christ toward people, the pastoral relationship becomes the transmission line of the character of Christ. Therefore, you as the able minister of the new covenant of the love of Christ do not look upon your work as the scribes did, i.e., as orally transmitting a literal law that is to be carried out legally to the last iota; but you look upon your work as the effective manifestation of the Spirit of Christ. You are a minister "not in a written code but in the Spirit; for the written code kills, but the Spirit gives life" (II Cor. 3:6).

As a pastor you are confronted with the practical task of finding out what is bothering the persons who come to you. You must first be a student of the person in the privacy of the person's own mind before you can be a teacher of the person in the interpretation of the person's difficulties. Also, you must have a certain amount of knowledge of ways of dealing with specific difficulties. In both instances (in your knowledge of the private secrets of your people, and in your knowledge of how to deal with them) you as pastor face the practical application of the principle of the love of Christ.

In the first place, people will not tell their pastor—or anyone else, for that matter—their inmost problems *for fear* they will be condemned. Also, they will not tell those noisome troubles *for fear* they will be exposed to others and their confidences betrayed. These are the two great hindrances to the establishment of a relationship of a trusted motive. The process of reconciliation goes on between you as the pastor and your people as you gradually impress on them that Christian love lies in knowing each other even as they are known of God, and yet accepting each other as they are, because God has so accepted them. Such love casts out fear. Therefore, love has no meaning apart from this personal knowledge of each other and from an ethically severe kind of forgiveness of each other's frailties. Jesus set the Christian fellowship in this framework when he said, "I am in my Father, and you in me, and I in you." Paul aligns perfect love and perfect knowledge in the thirteenth chapter of I Corinthians. In Phil. 1:9 he prays that "love may abound more and more, with knowledge and all discernment."

Furthermore, your pastoral relationship may be impaired also if your parishioners suspect that you are using them as psychological cadavers on which to demonstrate your counseling techniques, rather than your caring for them as you would do as a good shepherd for your sheep —with love and simplicity of motive. Your very knowledge of human nature, if used as an end in itself, may become an impediment to your usefulness. *Every knowledge of the human heart, every skill in dealing with human problems, is as dangerous as it is useful, and ordinarily it is the presence or absence of the love of Christ that makes the difference.*

The knowledge of the inner lives of the persons who seek your care, however, is always imparted to you in the context of the Christian community, not in isolation from it. When you feel that you should be related to persons on a *clandestine* and irresponsible basis, you should peg these feelings as real danger signals of irresponsibility in yourself. On the other hand, when persons seek to develop a relationship to you that is *totally* secret, and which at the same time involves other people—such as spouses, children, parents, and fellow church members—you as a pastor must be realistic about so-called *confidential* relationships. I have learned to make covenants of communication with individuals. This is thoroughly discussed in my book

Pastoral Counseling (Westminster Press, 1974). As minister you build a covenant of communication in which you promise to be fully responsible to the person in your use of facts which that individual gives you. For example, you can promise not to communicate this information without first consulting with the person and working out a plan together as to how the information shall best be used. In return, you can expect and require this same kind of responsible action from the other person: if the parishioner is planning to speak with other persons about what you have said in a pastoral conversation, the parishioner should first confer with you in such a way that everyone concerned can be edified and not torn down by the conversation. The pastoral conversation does not happen in a vacuum but in a dynamic society in which words are a main instrument of helping and hurting people.

Yet the focus of your pastoral identity and the end of your conversation with those whom you would serve is incarnate in Jesus Christ, the Word of God. Both you and those whom you would serve are on a pilgrimage of selfhood, the end result of which is either a self *in* Christ or a self apart from Christ. The encounter of redemption is initiated neither by the pastor nor by the parishioner but by God. This is the thrust of my own effort to portray in detail the nature of Christian selfhood in a serious theological frame of reference. In my book *Christ and Selfhood* the point is made that "by his own decision, God has in Christ chosen to come out on the road of life and meet man where he is. . . . We cannot let the emphasis rest upon ourselves as chosen people but upon God as a choosing God who has decisively acted in Jesus Christ." You as a Christian pastor do not move on the basis of some grandiose feeling that you have been chosen above all others. Rather, you live in steady gratitude for your own association with the living Christ in participation in the body of Christ, the church, and for your instruction in the record of the revelation of God in Christ. As you faithfully exercise your gratitude, you are one who calls Jesus Christ to people's remembrance so that they may be confronted by him.

THE PASTOR AS FOLLOWER OF THE LEADING
OF THE HOLY SPIRIT

"While they were talking and discussing together, Jesus himself drew near and went with them." (Luke 24:15.) Jesus as the living Christ manifests himself vitally in the presence of the Holy Spirit. You as a Christian pastor do well to think of your face-to-face ministry to people as a form of prayer. As you and your people talk and discuss together, or for that matter simply sit in silence together, Jesus himself in the presence of the Holy Spirit according to his promise draws near and goes with all of you. This is a more adequate understanding of the place of prayer in pastoral work than to think of it as being limited to those formal occasions when the pastor reads a part of the Scripture and bows or kneels in prayer with a person or with a group of persons.

Such a feeling of being a continual instrument of the Spirit of God lends reverence to your interpersonal relationships, and naturalness and spontaneity to those special occasions when formal expressions of prayer are appropriate. Ministers who are allowed access to the secrets of human hearts are not immune to developing a raw sense of familiarity with the crudity and frailty of their fellow human beings. Likewise, ministers who are continually called upon for formal prayers are often led to the edge of profaning this holy experience by entering into it lightly, inappropriately, mechanically, and by carrying through with it without depth, sensitivity, or dignity. Furthermore, the seething mass of detail that calls for your concern as a busy pastor often disperses your attention in such a way that your pastoral work becomes corroded with a creeping sense of personal fatigue that brings inattention and boredom.

The promises of Jesus concerning the Holy Spirit dispel all doubt concerning the intention of the Master. He wanted his disciples to depend upon the Holy Spirit's fellowship with them in both the creative and the destructive tensions of their work. You as a pastor often long for a never-failing technique which you can use with success in any situation. Likewise you want to know *one* procedure to follow in dealing with all persons who have a similar grouping of difficulties—such as divorcees or adolescents. But each testing situation calls for different measures, indicated only by the pastor's sensitivity to and grasp of the need of the moment. The appropriateness of the moment determines what needs to be said and how it should be said. But it takes a restful relaxation given only by the Holy Spirit to lay aside all preconceived approaches. This may be a glimmer of the brilliant light that Jesus gave his disciples in his assignment of pastoral duties. Obviously, the tenth chapter of Matthew was written against the backdrop of persecution, for the Lord tells his disciples that he sends them out as sheep in the midst of wolves and that they will be hauled into court and made to testify, with their very lives at stake. Such elements of risk and of jeopardy to life have too often been removed from the sense of identity that reigns in the lives of contemporary pastors. But the conflicts of contemporary life provide a testing arena for the willingness of Christian pastors to witness. Theological disputes, racial strife, far-right and far-left brainwashing attempts, and economic exploitation and graft offer abundant occasion today where, in the privacy of their offices, pastors are in another kind of court. Times of testing are severe, and no rules of thumb are available today. Nor can someone a thousand miles from the scene of action speak with any intelligence as to "what we shall speak." In our own way and in our own day, we too must be suspicious of stereotyped ways of dealing with such crucial situations. We must depend upon the Spirit of our Father speaking in us.

This was the kind of crucial situation in which a certain young minister found himself. His name is not mentioned because he has never sought any publicity for the things he said, nor did he pose later as someone's martyr with special stigmata of his own. But when mobs sought to prevent black children from going to the public school according to the court order, this pastor, a white man, went early in the morning and walked to school with the children. He was beaten by a mob on one morning. But the most significant thing is that he remained as pastor of his church without conflict until years after the incident.

The "middle ground" disappears from many areas of controversy. The intent to be a minister of reconciliation, concerned with the resolution of conflict by effective communication and by the power of the Holy Spirit, is likely to be understood as compromise and cowardice. Mass media of propaganda are used to sharpen and spread biased interpretations of situations, and face-to-face involvement of contending parties is avoided. The Christian pastor, however, is committed to the tutelage of the Holy Spirit and to following the leadership of the Holy Spirit. The Holy Spirit, in the name of Jesus Christ, gives gifts to people, and you as the pastor are committed to the use of the gift of this ministry in the equipment of God's people for the work of ministry for the building up of the body of Christ. This edifying ministry cannot be forsaken in behalf of any pressure group, however worthy the group's temporal objectives.

I have given attention elsewhere to the work of the Holy Spirit. In my book *Christ and Selfhood* full attention is given to the work of the Holy Spirit in the personal and social conflicts of people. The Holy Spirit focuses the conflictual issues of identity at the growing edge of personality, both individual and corporate. This growing edge is often characterized by conflict and suffering. The Christian pastor participates in this growth, and, as Regin Prenter says, "the place where we may learn to know the Holy Spirit is in the school of inner conflict." (Regin Prenter, *Spiritus Creator,* p. 208.)

Furthermore, the Holy Spirit functions as creator of community (as Luke puts it: "All who believed were together") as a result of the action of the Holy Spirit bringing about a sense of belonging and shared meaning between pastors and their people. The Holy Spirit is the comforter who strengthens, given that he might "be with us." The Holy Spirit is the instructor, given that he might "teach . . . all things." The Holy Spirit is the convicter, who convicts "of sin and of righteousness and of judgment." The Holy Spirit is the healer who makes persons whole by bringing to remembrance those spiritual reserves for combating psychological diseases. And finally, the Holy Spirit is the co-worker, who is with us always in the commissioned tasks of Christ.

These powers of the Holy Spirit become the task of you, the minister, under the guidance of the Holy Spirit, in your interpersonal relationships. At one time you are the *understanding friend* who works in the processes of fellowship, creating a sense of community, breaking down the middle walls of partition, and developing a sense of togetherness with an otherwise isolated, withdrawn person who has been cut off from the land of the living. At another time you as pastor are the *comforting strength* of a person in the midst of bereavement, a frustrated or broken love affair, an unbearable pain because of the sins of parents, or the heavy demands of war. The isolating power of suffering is met by the knowledge of the Holy Spirit that gives the sufferer access to "the whole creation [that] has been groaning in travail together until now," and it is the same Spirit that gives expression to those "groanings which cannot be uttered" (Rom. 8:26, ASV). As a pastor, your knowledge of the wisdom and feelings of the ages

that are stored in the Bible will make it possible for you
to express the inmost feelings of your people *for* them.

Again, you, the pastor, function as a *teacher* who informs
an ignorant mind, or who supplies the missing piece in a
confused perspective. Here you accept as a fact the religious illiteracy of the average person and draw upon a
total store of knowledge: the rudiments of personal experience, the patience and comfort of the Scriptures, the example of great personalities, and the systematic knowledge of literature and human nature. At another time you
are the *spiritual confidant* and parent confessor to whom
the fearful and guilt-laden person confesses intimate sin,
who thinks all the time that it is unbelievable that another
human being can look with compassion upon such a sinner, to say nothing of receiving God's forgiveness.

Or, to those individuals who are enthralled by the worship of themselves, you become the one who attempts to
unshackle their experience of God from their concepts of
themselves and set them on the path of progressive
spiritual growth. At even another time you work as the
healer who helps uncover and bring to remembrance
those buried memories of the past which nevertheless create blind spots in the persons' present view of life and
cause them to stumble in their way. Here you, the pastor,
seek to reconcile paradoxical and conflicting desires, and
help your people to assimilate undigested and unaccept-
able past experiences in such a way as to profit by them
rather than become enslaved to them. Finally, you stand
alongside your people as a *co-worker* in the great enter-
prise of the Kingdom of God. You are a "comrade in a
radiant pilgrimage" in which the special relationship between "those . . . of the household of faith" sustains you.
Thus, all your planning, meeting, experimentation, and
ways of doing things become the instruments of insightful
relationships with people. As Paul put it, "What you have
learned and received and heard and seen in me, do; and
the God of peace will be with you" (Phil. 4:9).

These ministries of the pastor alternate with one another from time to time. The spiritual appropriateness of this or that one is largely a matter of timing the needs of each psychological moment. Ecclesiastes has a remark about this time (Eccl. 3:1–11):

> For everything there is a season, and a time for every matter under heaven: a time to be born, and a time to die; a time to plant, and a time to pluck up . . . ; a time to kill, and a time to heal; a time to break down, and a time to build up; a time to weep, and a time to laugh; . . . a time to rend, and a time to sew; a time to keep silence, and a time to speak; a time to love, and a time to hate. . . . God . . . has made everything beautiful in its time; also he has set eternity into man's mind.

And the capacity to fit eternity to time depends upon your total store of accrued knowledge and experience, your intuitive insight into the basic difficulties the individual is up against, and the degree to which you have yielded to the Holy Spirit for spiritual sensitivity and understanding.

Thus the interpersonal relationships of you as a pastor with your people in the times of their suffering become a continuous experience of prayer. In this experience, the inner life of those to whom you minister is continually being opened to the healing love of God as you continually yield to the working purposes of God. Thus the minister of the healing redemption of the gospel goes about the task of bringing its marvelous light to darkened consciences, its fortifying strength to those who are weak and have no might, and its releasing freedom to those who are clutched by fear, consumed in wrath, and enslaved by inordinate affections.

Intensive attention to the work of the Holy Spirit is the wave of the future in pastoral care. In this we can learn much from the mystical frames of reference of men like Douglas Steere in his book *On Listening to Another,* in which he challenges the caring relationship of every kind by saying that any such friendship, regardless of how deep, bears with it "the seeds of tragedy unless both persons have opened their lives to a power that is infinitely greater and purer than themselves." (Douglas Steere, *On Listening to Another*, p. 27.) This power is the Holy Spirit.

THE PASTOR AS A REPRESENTATIVE OF A SPECIFIC CHURCH

"Then after fasting and praying they laid their hands on them and sent them off." (Acts 13:3.) A mixed emotion of uneasy satisfaction comes over most ministers when they realize that they symbolize and represent a *specific congregation of people*. The definite form of a pastor's ministry is affected greatly by the history, the traditions, the personal opinions, and even the passing whims of this group of people. You, the Christian pastor, are called not only to speak *to* this congregation in your preaching ministry but also to speak *for* them in your individual and group counseling. You cannot go "off duty" from this responsibility; it is a twenty-four-hour-a-day, seven-day-a-week ministry. The pastor must represent the congregation to the rest of the community, and occasionally protect members from the rest of the community. You use a staff of guidance on the flock, and quite often must use a rod of protection upon attacks from without. Your problem is to know *when* to use *which* upon *whom!* No veteran minister will call this an easy problem.

Therefore, you as a Christian pastor, being invested with such a responsibility, must have confidence in the congregation; you must believe in their essential integrity. You must be committed with a clear conscience to the major objectives, principal teachings, and operational strategy of the church to which you accept a call. The time to clarify this loyalty is *before* agreeing to become their leader. The wise pastor, upon having received overtures from a new congregation seeking a pastor, will take pains to learn the history, traditions, and practices of the church. You will decide in advance whether or not you can be the community advocate for such a congregation. More care and concern at these formative stages of the relationship between pastor and church will lead to more wholeheartedness of service in the days to come. Such precautions will serve to prevent disillusionment among ministers and confusion in congregations.

This does not mean that as a pastor you should assume that a church must sign a "dotted line" agreement to all your expectations. Rather, it means that you are willing to cast your lot with the people as they are in a loyalty that makes room for the progressive development of their corporate life together. This implies that the pastor needs a working concept of what a church actually *is* as well as an ideal concept of what a church as the body of Christ *can* be.

You as a Christian pastor not only represent the welfare of the Christian community, you also sponsor the individual rights and needs of the persons within the community. One of the unique distinctions of your work as a minister is that you represent *both* the individual *and* the social good of your people at the same time. Individual interests often threaten the safety of the group. The corporate selfishness of the group often oppresses the welfare of the individual. The sensitive pastor is conscious of the power of the church to isolate an individual, and also of the intentness with which some individuals dominate the church until they must be isolated in order that the community may survive. Therefore, you as a good minister repeatedly evaluate afresh the resources and liabilities of your congregation. You understand the dynamics of group behavior as well as the motives of individual conduct. The opportunities for personal counseling will arise most often in connection with groups with which you have met. And, too, the structure of your relationship to an individual is greatly determined by the kind of affiliation that person has with the church that you, the pastor, represent. (See Howard Clinebell, *The People Dynamic;* also, Howard Clinebell, *Growth Counseling: Hope-Centered Methods of Actualizing Human Wholeness;* Larry L. McSwain and William C. Treadwell, Jr., *Conflict Ministry in the Church;* and Clifford Sager and Helen Kaplan, eds., *Progress in Group and Family Therapy.*)

A pastor, by virtue of personal as well as economic dependence upon the congregation, ordinarily gives preference to persons and groups who belong to that fellowship. The next group are the close relatives and friends of members of the congregation, regardless of their connection with the church. You as a pastor are most often criticized in this connection for being absent from the pulpit and community in order to do this or that service for some other church or organization. You may also be attacked for spending so much time in individual counseling with a few persons who may or may not be concerned with the life of the church that you neglect the needs of the large number of people who are members of your church. The ethical decisions that you must make as to the use of time and energy along these lines are legion in number. But the way you make these decisions is the streambed along which your usefulness to your people either flows or evaporates.

THE PASTOR AS A SHEPHERD OF THE NON-CHRISTIAN

You as a contemporary pastor do not care only for those who are safely within the confines of your church, or of Christendom as a whole, for that matter. You are a shepherd to those on the outside as well. You are a powerful symbol, an interpreter, and an evangelist. The persons with whom you associate may be apathetic and indifferent to the Christian faith. They may be suspicious and distrustful toward both the Christian community and the Chris-

tian faith. They may be directly hostile toward and reject
the Christian faith. Yet you as a minister are responsible,
as a witness to the gospel, for relating in some challenging
and dynamic way to these persons.

The pastor is a powerful symbol to the non-Christian.
You symbolize authoritarianism and dogmatism to many
who are hostile toward any authority, especially that
which their religious parents exercised over them. In dealing with persons who are hostile, you must meet the
stance of atheism. The persons may insist, in a more passive kind of rejection, that they are not atheists but devout
agnostics. In either instance you, the Christian pastor,
symbolize the domination and dogmatism of which the
persons want to be free. Such people are stereotyped in
their reactions, and *all* ministers are alike to them. If you
can be permissive enough to establish a dialogue with this
type of person, warmth and acceptance begin to flow, not
necessarily for the Christian faith, but for you yourself as
an exception to the rule the person has made about ministers. However, this blanket judgment of *all* persons as
looking upon *all* ministers as authoritarian is in itself a
stereotyped kind of thought. Seward Hiltner and Lowell
G. Colston made a careful contrasting study of counseling
done in a psychological counseling service with counseling
done in a local parish situation by a pastor. They arrived
at a startling conclusion:

> The psychologically sophisticated person might predict that
> the person coming to the church for counseling would ex-
> pect authoritarian guidance while he who came to the coun-
> seling center would be democratic and expect to work out
> —with help—his own problems. This was not our finding.
> Whatever religious or pastoral authority may mean to peo-
> ple these days, with our parishioners it did only rarely carry
> authoritarian overtones. And whatever the actual objectiv-
> ity of science and psychology, the prevailing aura over the
> counseling center, it did not prevent many people from
> expecting it to produce answers in what they would be
> shocked to hear called an authoritarian fashion. Religion

must continue to work on the problem of authoritarianism, but our experience suggests that science and psychology have it in even larger proportions. (Seward Hiltner and Lowell G. Colston, *The Context of Pastoral Counseling,* p. 37)

Therefore, the Christian pastor today may be in a position to explore with the person who is hostile toward the Christian faith the personal spiritual history that lies behind a need to rebel against Christianity. You as a pastor may find that the gospel has been communicated to the person with such heavy distortion that even you yourself would reject the caricature of the Christian faith that the person has thrown overboard as invalid for living.

In the second place, you as a minister may symbolize insincerity and hypocrisy to the person on the outside of the Christian fellowship. All professing Christians may be "phonies" to the suspicious and distrustful person. From Carl Sandburg's "Contemporary Bunkshooter," to Sinclair Lewis' Elmer Gantry, to J. D. Salinger's Holden Caulfield, the Protestant pastor has been made uncomfortable by the implication of phoniness, insincerity, and dissimulation. You as a pastor, on the other hand, are burdened with a sense of guilt for having to play a role, wear a mask, and be "nice" to everyone. But the Biblical image of the shepherd is that of a person who is disarmingly honest. You are forthrightly freed by the grace of God in Christ to activate your identity as a pastor through confrontation as well as through the solicitous comfort and support of those both inside and outside the church. Consistency and candor supply security once the shock of the first encounter with such a minister subsides. People suddenly realize that such a minister's yea is yea and nay is nay, and that much more than this is evil.

But more subtle than either the hostility or the suspicion is the fact that you as a minister command commitment. You are a person whose mind is made up and fixed. You will be asked by persons who are outside the orbit of the

Christian community: "Where is it that you will not bend?" At the same time, commitment itself removes the luxury of indecision which is often mistaken for open-mindedness. Commitment removes the spiritual bachelorhood that majors in uninvolvement and detachment from any durable relationship. As a pastor you represent this kind of decisive commitment and durable covenant of a faith community. Your efforts to establish a durable relationship to persons whose way of life is detachment and avoidance of responsible involvement may be met with an intricate number of rebuffs, unfulfilled covenants, and unproductiveness. The detached person finds responsible involvement with any committed person, regardless of what the commitment may be, to be an uneasy friendship. As Mr. Faithful said to Christian concerning Mr. Talkative in John Bunyan's *The Pilgrim's Progress*, "He would rather have done with your company than to change his ways."

The atmosphere of contemporary culture is such, however, that it may cause you as a pastor to assume unwittingly that those on the outside of the church are invariably hostile, suspicious, or uncommitted as far as the Christian faith is concerned. One reason for this is that you are likely to be institutionally oriented to people rather than personally related to them for their own sakes and not as a means to your institutional and "churchly" objectives.

Genuine Christian evangelism is not recruitment of members for an institution as an end in itself. It is the persistent intention to introduce *a* friend to *The* Friend, Jesus Christ, and to trust that friend into the hands of Jesus Christ. For example, the purpose of a pastor's visitation may be first, last, and always to get the persons to be more active in the church. Even when you visit them when they are sick, you may use the situation to promote the church. When you have once caught the vision of caring for people as ends within themselves, of losing yourself in the center of their "thrown situation," then you discover them to be less hostile, suspicious, and detached. You find at the core of countless numbers of individuals an estrangement, a loneliness, a feeling on their part that no one cares for their soul, and a querulous sense of strangeness that anyone would genuinely take time to listen to and understand them without having some "sales pitch" or ulterior motive in mind. That someone would is such good news that it is unbelievable! In fact, even when they begin to believe it, you as pastor have to call upon the independent action of the living God to help them believe it! When we see people from this perspective, we as Christian pastors take a new look at the internal meaning of hostility, suspicion, and detachment. We have begun to be schooled in the kind of compassion that only the Good Shepherd can generate, because it was he of whom it is said: "When he saw the crowds, he had compassion for them, because they were harassed and helpless, like sheep without a shepherd" (Matt. 9:36).

Chapter III

The Personal Qualifications of the Pastor

The representative of God, the ambassador of Christ, the follower of the leading of the Holy Spirit, the emissary of a church, and the shepherd of non-Christians needs much spiritual equipment and emotional stability.

The writers of the New Testament were enthusiastic when they spoke of the necessity of a pastor being called to the ministry, but they were equally exacting in their requirements of those who were chosen for the task. In the early churches *many* were called to the task of being an overseer of souls, but few were chosen.

Early Christians were not vague in their statement of the personal qualifications of those into whose hands was committed the care of the flock of God. They did not leave this important decision entirely to the sentimental whims of persons who aspired to the office. The responsiblity was laid upon and taken seriously by the churches themselves. The writers of the pastoral epistles and of I Peter felt it necessary to describe in minute detail the qualifications that they themselves sought to incorporate into their own way of life. They held high standards for those who became their fellow workers. They were convinced of the nobility of their task.

Consequently, pastors today have at hand in the New Testament (I Tim. 2:11 to 3:7; Titus 1:5-9; I Peter 5:1-4) the standards whereby they may judge the fitness of a pastor. Churches and aspiring candidates for the ministry may judge themselves.

WOMEN IN SILENCE?

At the outset of these Scriptures, women are prohibited from teaching, speaking, or having authority over men. When I originally wrote this book in 1950, as well as when I revised and enlarged it in 1964, the passage in I Tim. 3:11–15 was not even mentioned. However, in the last two decades of the twentieth century, reality does not permit this—albeit benign—assumption on my part. Women today are not silent, not even in the public visits of the Roman Catholic pope, John Paul II. They are tired of being ruled over by men. They expect, demand, and, I think, deeply deserve the recognition, consecration, inclusion, and financial support of their historic function as caring ministers. The historic participation of women in Catholic teaching orders, Protestant missionary circles, and overseas service demonstrates that women have been in the formal ministry of the churches for many decades and even centuries. I can recall as early as 1954 participating in the ordination of a woman pastor, Virginia Kreyer, who has since served the cerebral palsy population of Long Island, New York, for twenty-seven years. Therefore, I am articulating here a rationale that is more than changing the grammar on a page. Several issues need to be noted.

First, John Calvin, in 1556, commented on I Tim. 2:12, saying that the Scripture does indeed say that women "may not take it upon themselves to speak in public," nor are they permitted to teach. Yet Calvin makes an exception for exceptional cases. He says the appointment of Deborah is an example. Yet he sees this and other like examples to be extraordinary events: "Extraordinary acts

done by God do not overturn the ordinary rules of government, by which he intended that we should be bound.
. . . He who is above all law might do this; but because 'it
is a peculiar and ordinary case,' this is not opposed to the
constant and ordinary system of government." (John Calvin, *Commentaries on the Epistles to Timothy, Titus, and
Philemon*, p. 67.) Even Calvin in the sixteenth century
could permit Biblical, if not contemporary, exceptions to
the rule. Today, I would challenge the rule itself and do
not just confirm it with yea-saying an exception. The state
of the art of *Seelsorge* or pastoral care in the next two
decades faces the adventure of building a larger ministry
in which there is neither male nor female in the opportunity to actualize the call to be a pastor.

Second, the formal, professed basis for the defense of
the rule against including women is that Scripture explic-
itly forbids it. Thus, we are subtly shifted from consideration of women in ministry to a defense of the legal observation of specific sentences in the Bible. We find ourselves
in the cul-de-sac of literalism. Yet we ignore other specific
commands, not of Paul, but of Jesus (Matt. 18:15–20), and
justify our doing so by saying that ethical confrontation for
wrongdoing in the community of Christians is simply unwise and impractical. I resolve this dilemma by recognizing that all Scripture is written for our instruction, but all
Scripture is not equally wise. There are levels of wisdom.
The apostle Paul recognizes this when he says: "Now concerning the unmarried, I have no command of the Lord,
but I give my opinion as one who by the Lord's mercy is
trustworthy." (I Cor. 7:25; see also I Cor. 7:6.) Also, Jesus
revealed a higher level of understanding when he
rebuked his disciples for wanting to call down fire from
heaven as Elijah had done. (Luke 9:51–56.) You see the
dramatic difference of levels of wisdom when you read I
Tim. 2:12: "I permit no woman to teach or to have authority over men; she is to keep silent." Now read Gal. 3:27–28:
"For as many of you as were baptized into Christ have put

on Christ. There is neither Jew nor Greek, there is neither slave nor free, there is neither male nor female; for you are all one in Christ Jesus."

Hence, I conclude that the apostles were following their own Jewish customs which predated their relationship to Jesus Christ when they "placed" women in "silence." In the Gospels, I read Jesus *asking* women to speak. Jesus Christ is the Light which causes Moses, Elijah, and even the apostle Paul to cast very deep shadows in what they have to say. Yet the apostle Paul himself recognizes the difference between an opinion and the word of the Lord. In not recognizing this ourselves, we make new laws out of legal precedent. I refuse to do this and prefer to give women a due place in ministry, as indeed did our Lord. (See Evelyn and Frank Stagg, *Woman in the World of Jesus,* for an extensive and detailed discussion of the exegesis of Scripture on this issue.) Consequently, throughout this book, I assume that women indeed *are* called to be pastors; that they do, as they have for centuries, the work of the ministry; that they are uniquely gifted and responsible to God and congregations even as are men. They are not exempt from the disciplines of the ministry and are called to take them as seriously as do men. Being a man pastor is no picnic, romance, or exemption from temptation, vanity, or foolishness. Neither is being a woman pastor.

Yet the critical issue for women in ministry in the next two or three decades is whether or not they will be financially supported for their endeavors as are men. My own estimate is that they are being called to develop new forms of ministry in the care of neglected populations of the handicapped, the aged, the poor, and women of all ages who are abused, incestuously violated, raped, and trapped in the commercial exploitation of their femaleness. My prayer and hope is that the churches will awaken to the support of these ministries. Yet I doubt that the churches will do this in any wholesale way until they affirm women as leaders of worship, interpreters of the Word, and ministers of the broken body and shed blood of Jesus Christ. I pray that I may see this in my lifetime.

"ABOVE REPROACH"

If you are a pastor, you have earned the respect of your community; that is, you are above reproach. You have not been laid hold of for disorderliness, indecency, and immodesty. This is not merely a matter of having kept up appearances before your neighbors, but rather that you have tested your own work before the community and actually have the approval and acceptance of those about you.

Especially important is it that you have the respect of non-Christians. First Timothy states it: "He must be well thought of by outsiders" (I Tim. 3:7). The purpose of this requirement is made plain: "In order that he may not be publicly exposed to abuse and affliction and fall into the snare of the slanderer." You who are to bear witness to those who are outside must live convincingly before them, be above their reproach, and have their respect if you are to have any influence over them. This requirement points not only to the positive witness of the church to those outside but also to the need for protecting the flock of God from those on the outside.

Of course, it is a common saying that unless you are maligned by sinners, and persecuted by the unrighteous, you do not truly have the firstfruits of being called to the ministry. The "persecutory passages" of Scripture and the fact that the Chief Shepherd was criticized for eating with publicans and sinners are cited as supporting evidence. Nevertheless, it was the religious people of Jesus' day who criticized his behavior, and not those who believed on him or those who were publicans and sinners. Those who were on the outside, the lost sheep of the house of Israel, never accused him of being one of them. Among these groups he was "above reproach."

The ever-present fact of gossip and slander in a community hovers like humidity over the face-to-face ministry of a pastor. You may be unaware of it, but you are never free from its influence. It necessitates your being above reproach. You must have brought your whole life under a finely balanced discipline lest you yourself become a castaway.

Not a New Convert

The New Testament says plainly that you should not be a new convert, a novice, a neophyte. Rather, you are a veteran of the Christian way of life. No specific length of service as an active Christian is stated, but experience taught these early churches that a "newly planted" Christian had to be put to the test of time before being given the responsibility of the care of others.

One clear reason for this requirement was stated: "In order that he may not become puffed up with conceit and fall into the condemnation of the false accuser." The literal phrase for "puffed up with conceit" is "to be wrapped up in a cloud," or "beclouded with conceit." This word is used again in I Tim. 6:4–5: "He is puffed up with conceit, he knows nothing; he has a morbid craving for controversy and disputes about words, which produce envy, dissension, slander, base suspicions, and wrangling among men who are depraved in mind and bereft of the truth, imagining that godliness is a means of gain."

Accordingly, then, the course of experience through which a novice goes in the work of a pastor is after this order: You first are overwhelmed by the new sense of importance of the role into which you have been cast. You get the same sense of competitive victory that made Paul feel he had advanced beyond many of his own age, and caused him to become "extremely zealous." Then you

begin to realize your inadequacy and become very inse-
cure in trying to discharge the new responsibilities. This
prompts you "to put up a front," and to try to cover your
ignorance with high-sounding words and obscure intellec-
tualisms that confuse your listeners and hide the simplicity
of the gospel. This cloud of confusion brings on divisions
and wranglings among people who are also babes in the
way of Christ. Party cries begin to be heard. The more
unstable people of the community begin to use the situation of godlessness to see who can gain their own personal
ends.

Such Biblical understanding merits the conclusion that
one of the explanations of "split churches" and a multiply-
ing number of rival sects in Christendom today is the
spiritual immaturity of carelessly chosen pastors and leaders. They are cakes not turned, burned on one side and
raw on the other. Attempts therefore to unite Christendom without getting back to this source of its divisions are
futile indeed. These groups are set into motion by spiritually adolescent leaders with a thirst for power. These leaders can do more to shatter the unity of churches in a short
while than mature leaders can undo in a long time.

This does not mean that a person's age should be the sole
determinant of selecting a pastor, for the Scriptures do not
refer merely to chronological age, but to spiritual maturity. It does mean, however, that you should have
achieved a sufficient degree of full-grownness as a Christian not to get lost in the cloud of personal conceits.

"THE HUSBAND OF ONE WIFE"

Two of the pastoral epistles (I Timothy and Titus) require that the pastor be the husband of one wife. This may
be interpreted several ways.

First, if, as we said before, the church of today and of the
future is to affirm women as pastors, we must assume that
women are, as wives, not exceptions to this same expecta-

tion of men as husbands. Through the centuries, religious people have been party to the sexual exploitation of women. Consequently, sex may be an instrument of hostility and aggression in women as well as in men. Similarly, men who are pastors are like women in that when men become depressed and angry their means of "acting out" their anger is too often in sexual behavior. Consequently, the expectation for you as pastor is that you pay close attention to fidelity to marriage as a means of being sexual in an exemplary and disciplined manner. No double code of morality can be used by pastors of either sex.

David Schuller, again, in the *Ministry in America* study says that the three most negative criticisms of ministers "do not deal with the lack of any particular skill but rather focus on the minister as a person. . . . The harshest criticism centers on what people describe as undisciplined living, a construct centered on being involved in illicit sexual relationships and other self-indulgent actions that irritate, shock, or offend." (Schuller, "Identifying the Criteria for Ministry," in *Ministry in America,* pp. 19–20.)

Second, polygamy and concubinage were prevalent practices in the communities of which the early churches were a part, and the writers of I Timothy and Titus evidently were insisting that their leaders be an example of the Christian principle of monogamous marriage. They looked upon singleness of devotion to one marital partner as essential to the integration of personality alongside the necessity of singleness of devotion to one God. These two distinctives, in glaring contrast, set the Christians apart from their neighbors who practiced both polygamy and polytheism.

Third, this passage may be interpreted less directly to mean that the early Christians preferred a married minister to a single one. Later, ascetic development of a celibate ideal challenged this. Social pressures among Protestant churches today almost demand that a minister be married. So universal is this demand that occasionally theological

students depend upon this external motivation for the
selection of a mate rather than upon inner devotion to the
person they marry. The pressure for choosing a mate with
an ability to be a sort of "assistant to the pastor" occasionally dominates the marital choice of ministers to such an
extent that affection becomes a secondary consideration.
Nevertheless, the main intention of the Scriptural requirement seems to be that a pastor *needs* a mate as a companion in the work of the gospel, as a partner in the enjoyment
of mutually expressed sexual powers, and as a comrade in
the adventure of parenthood.

As we move into the last two decades of the twentieth
century, the issues of husband-wife co-pastor teams, as
well as sole women pastors, put this Scripture in a new
light. We no longer can assume a "cryptic" pastoral demand of the spouses of pastors to function as "unpaid associate pastors." We are being pressured by women, by the
economy, and by law to think in terms of "equal opportunity employment." Also, when this issue is not squarely
faced, pastors' wives, especially, are in large numbers developing their own careers apart from their husbands' pas-
torates. Even so, some churches and denominations *assume* that their pastor's wife will be gainfully employed
outside the church and use this as a reason to pay the
pastor less.

Fourth, this passage may be interpreted in the light of
another prevalent social problem at the time of the writing: divorce. The application becomes most pertinent to
present-day practice. Divorced persons are, in increasing
numbers, applying to theological seminaries for admission, in order to prepare for the active pastorate. This
poses a thorny ethical problem for the individuals involved, for theological faculties, for ordination councils,
and for churches in need of pastors.

The statements of Paul in I Corinthians 7 indicate that
the early churches were very tender and sensitive to the
plight of people who became involved in pagan marriages

prior to having become Christians. They most certainly did not consider divorce or even remarriage as an unpardonable sin for which they would break fellowship with an individual Christian. The New Testament ideal for all marriages is complete chastity prior to marriage and complete faithfulness to one's marital partner after marriage until death. This ideal is implicit in the statement that a minister shall be "the husband of one wife." The New Testament does not hold forth a double standard, one for ministers and one for other people. But today, one divorced minister (anonymous to this author) was right when he wrote: "The minister certainly does have to face up to many risks resulting from divorce that other men do not have to face. Whether we like it or not, there is a sort of double standard, one for the minister and one for the nonminister, in the public mind." This poignant statement needs to be set against the New Testament times when the cleavage between standards for ministers and other persons within the church was not nearly so great. It is an open question as to how much of a paid, professional ministry existed at the time of the writing of these pastoral epistles. The ministry as an employment situation did not exist as we have it today. Another divorced minister said: "I did delay my decision [to be divorced], not because I doubted the need for a divorce, but because I was not prepared to do any other kind of work and I hated to give up the ministry."

This is vastly different from the situation that existed at the time of the writing of the pastoral epistles. Yet this double standard does exist today. Some ministers who are divorced are able to carry through with a ministry that is effective insofar as their churches allow it. Others are completely closed out of the ministry. All sorts of casuistic explanations of these differences can be developed. None of them succeed in equating the New Testament situation with present-day conditions. Nor do present-day conditions remove the validity of the New Testament ideal for marriage for all people. The main ethical issue that the problem of divorced ministers presents is the way in which the church, especially American Protestant denominations, neglects the spiritual guidance of the whole church in terms of educational preparation for marriage among Christians. Pastoral care of couples at crucial junctures of their marital pilgrimages was nonexistent in at least 80 percent of the cases.

From a Biblical and theological point of view the problem of the divorced minister is not materially different from that of the divorced Christian generally. Yet the divorced minister spotlights the timidity and pastoral neglect with which Christian denominations approach having clear expectations and providing preparation for the marriage of all Christians. In the absence of this kind of ethical seriousness, the church shifts from one stance of sentimentality and unrealism to another of harshness and unreasonableness in dealing with ministers who themselves become divorced. Consequently, the minister as a public figure is dependent upon a vote of confidence of a given congregation that in one week can spend several hours in adulation of film heroes and heroines who practice the consecutive polygamy sometimes mistaken for divorce and yet at the same time expect their minister to be completely untouched by such cultural fallout in the ethical atmosphere. The attitudes of congregations toward divorced ministers vary from one educational level to another, from one part of the country to another, and from one denomination to another. The ethical relativism of Christians validates the need for a reaffirmation of the Christian ideal set forth in the New Testament for the marriage of all Christians. At the same time, the compassion of Jesus Christ makes imperative the necessity for careful clinical study of a given divorced minister's situation as each seeks the guidance of the Holy Spirit for the minister's calling under God.

A final consideration of the married life of the pastor is

to underscore the qualitative difference between the celibate priest, who is totally committed to the church, and the Protestant pastor, who has a spouse whose relationship is primary. A considerable number of Protestant pastors *seem* to be married to the church, leaving their spouse to a second place in devotion. This skews the priorities of these pastors in such a way that the marriage tends to go into crisis again and again. The fallacy of this skewed set of priorities would not be so if such pastors would rethink the basic theological unity of their spouse and/or children as being primary before God.

Good Manager of Own Household

The New Testament writers seem to assume that if a pastor is the "husband of one wife," he will also be the parent of children. One of their criteria for judging the fitness of a person for the ministry was his effectiveness as a parent. They required that pastors have a finely balanced control of their own home, because "if a man does not know how to manage his own household, how can he care for God's church?" (I Tim. 3:5). Today, when women are becoming pastors also, a special burden of the traditional expectations of mothers is upon them. If a husband-wife team, for example, become co-pastors, it is imperative that *both* of them share and share alike in child care and domestic duties.

Many pastors have interpreted this to mean that they are to rule over their children with an iron hand, the clutching authority of which is never to be relaxed. Such parents are often embarrassed to find late in life that their children rise up in rebellion at the tyranny of their parents and reject not only them but their religion. Certainly the writers of this passage of the New Testament meant something more than and different from this interpretation. The larger Biblical context reveals a more adequate understanding.

In the first place, the patriarchal type of family organization in which these early Christians participated had its beginnings in the early Hebrew period when the father of the family was the only priest of the family. He was the representative of God to the family, and all that has been said concerning the pastor as a representative of God applied also to the Hebrew father's relationship to his family. Accordingly, the exhortation found in I Peter 5:2-3 may be paraphrased and applied to the relationship of pastors to their children without doing violence to the total Biblical context: "Act as a shepherd to your children, not as lording it over them, but as an example before them." In other words, the power whereby you as a minister maintain control over your children is the strength of the child's natural need to become like the parents. A wise parent depends more on the persuasive pull of this need than on the coercive demand of an infallible parental authority.

Again, the Greek word for "to manage" is derived from a word that means literally "to stand over." It is followed in the text by a term that is translated "with all gravity." This word is derived from another word which means "to worship." The interpretation of the law of identification set forth earlier is applicable here. On the human level, the character of the child is shaped by the tie of identification with the parents. If this goes either to the extreme of stark fear of the parent or to abject servility, the parent, for all practical purposes, becomes the god, the object of the infantile worship of the child. Therefore, the child is instructed by Paul, "Obey your parents *in the Lord,* for this is right" (Eph. 6:1). You rule over your children as a representative of God and "in the Lord," not capriciously and by virtue of an assumed infallibility. In so doing, you serve as a "molding influence" upon the life of the family. You depend more upon affectionate management of your relationship to your children than upon "pulling rank" as a preacher.

Not only do you exert a molding influence over the family by maintaining a loving tie of identification between you and them, but you also serve as a "sieve" to protect your family from destructive outside influences. The children of a pastor can very easily become confused by the many voices of the congregation who seek to direct their path. The possibility of their own choices may be purloined by the social pressure of the group that you represent. Your protective function, therefore, as a parent often has to be applied to the congregation as well as to people who are not Christians. Always stand *between* your family and the church both as a protector from many well-meaning "authorities" on child guidance and as a mediator of the more desirable graces of the Christian fellowship.

A third meaning of the requirement of effective parenthood that is laid upon a candidate for the ministry is embodied in the instruction to Timothy: "If a man does not know how to manage his own household, how can he care for God's church?" (I Tim. 3:5). The word translated "care for" is used only one other time in the New Testament. In Luke 10:34–35 the word describes the way the good Samaritan treated the wounded man whom he found. Actually, then, it means in this context that you care for the church with a *healing carefulness.* You care in the same manner for your children, supplying their economic and bodily needs as well as their spiritual ones. In another place, Timothy is instructed: "If any one does not provide for his relatives, and especially for his own family, he has disowned the faith and is worse than an unbeliever" (I Tim. 5:8).

This is not to say that you are to let luxury and extravagance determine your ministry. It is to say, however, that a real question may be raised as to the sincerity of candidates for the ministry who use the Christian calling as an excuse to neglect the basic physical and emotional needs of their children. If you neglect your own children's needs for affectionate tenderness, spiritual instruction, and economic security, you will have no basis for a genuinely pastoral care of the flock of God.

The letter to Titus connects the soundness of one's teachings to the quality of one's behavior. Persons who "teach what befits sound doctrine" can control themselves, show integrity, and be a model of good deeds. Your basic assumptions about life can either hold you together or let you fall apart. Sound convictions, then, produce sound minds. Where do you "take a stand" as a Christian, and at what points are you steadfast and immovable?

An acid test of your fitness for your work as a minister is whether you are such a parent that your children can look up to you and want to be like you and the Lord. This test reveals the connection between family maladjustment and the use of religion as an escapism from what would otherwise be an impossible home situation. Your face-to-face ministry to people calls for the skills and patience of a successful parent. By and large, people react in most subsequent groups in much the same way they learned to react to their mothers and fathers, brothers and sisters. They carry these established patterns with them into the rest of life. In the church, more often than not, the other members of the family are present also. This requirement of successful parenthood, then, is as old as the New Testament and as contemporary as some of the most recent research in psychology.

SANE, SENSIBLE, OF A SOUND MIND

The mental health of a person who aspired to the office of an overseer of souls was of concern to the early churches. Jesus himself was vitally concerned with people being "clothed and in . . . [their] right mind." He gave himself to the healing of those who were demented and stimulated the compassion of his disciples then and now to bring the therapeutic power of the Christian gospel to bear upon life situations. But when he had healed such persons, though they "begged that . . . [they] might be with him, . . . he sent . . . [them] away, saying, 'Return to your home, and declare how much God has done for you' " (Luke 8:38f.). He expected their own home community to nourish them back to a creative place of service. He expected them to put their newfound wholeness to work with the people whom they knew best.

The letters to Timothy and Titus use the same term, which may be translated variously as "sane," "sensible," or "of a sound mind," "self-controlled," "sober-minded." Those words from which the term is derived, and those words to which it is related, refer to the relationship of the beliefs of a pastor and to the emotional stability of the candidate for the ministry. The writer specifies the several different ways by which the mental health of a candidate is to be judged.

First, you as a candidate must be a person whose moral sensitivity has not been dulled and gapped by the use of alcohol. You cannot be a person who "spends time sitting by a bottle." The lowered threshold of moral sensitivity, the shaken loss of physical precision, and the aching emptiness of unresolved anxieties characteristic of the person who solves problems with alcohol are all counterindications of fitness for the ministry to other people. Such persons stand in need of a physician themselves. But a minister who becomes the victim of alcohol addiction is no moral failure beyond repair. The same resources of healing available to the Christian who is not a minister are open to the pastor also. The same reluctance to seek help is the pastor's temptation as well.

With such help available through pastoral counseling, psychotherapy, and effective participation in Alcoholics Anonymous, the minister may then turn and strengthen others. The ideal of sobriety is not equivalent to Christian redemption, although it may seem so to a person who is in the grip of alcohol or drug addiction, or even more so to members of the family. Rather, if you are overtaken in this fault, you should be cared for with gentleness and responsible realism, whether you are an ordained minister or not. No double standard can exist here without doing away with the Protestant principle of the priesthood of the believer.

Secondly, you as a candidate must also have control of the desire for money. As John Calvin says, the minister of Christ cannot be "a slave to his own stomach and his purse." (John Calvin, *Commentaries on the Catholic Epistles*, p. 143.) You cannot serve two masters, God and mammon, nor can you bypass as of secondary importance the primary concerns of human need and the edification of the mental and spiritual lives of people in order to achieve your own financial ends. Yet the laborer is worthy of hire and you can and should be candid and forthright with people about impossible demands for penalizing your family. The tension between avarice for money and improvident neglect of your family must be maintained, not set aside.

Thirdly, you must have control of your desire for power. The prestige-seeking impulse can be so out of proportion to other spiritual hungers that one feels that one must "lord it over" the flock and squelch anyone who dares compete with or oppose oneself. You cannot push your own needs for independence of your people so far that you do not recognize any dependence upon them for that reasonable degree of approval which makes for mental health and social usefulness. You cannot succeed in such a manner that you cause one of Christ's "little ones" to fail.

Fourthly, most emphasis, however, is placed upon the degree of mastery you have over your own anger. Paul says that a person should be a "master of himself." This implies that you have great strength and power of spirit, but that you know how to express your aggressions in a positive and healthy manner. You are not "arrogant" and self-pleasing, inclined to orgies of bad temper in which you deliver yourself over to your own meanness of spirit. You are not "violent but gentle," not "quarrelsome" and continually searching out something over which to start a fight. You may be described also as a "noncombatant" in the fights that persons around you choose to start. In a word, you do not label your own lack of self-control as "prophetic ministry." You are keenly conscious of the fact that you "prophesy in part." A woman pastor may have been "programmed" to express her anger in tears rather than in clearly thought out words. Her "wavelengths" for getting angry demand an agonizing self-appraisal. Tears in the heat of controversy are a luxury for many women but not for the one who aspires to be a pastor.

The absence of these negative factors does not attest to the mental health of a person unless certain positive values live in their place. Therefore the writer specifies that you need a well-balanced sense of moderation, rather than to be given to extremisms. A sense of fairness and an appreciation of fitting behavior appropriate to each occasion reflect the precision of your self-control. Paul calls this "being just," or "rendering to every man his due because of his own uprightness." Matthew Arnold most aptly described this fine mental balance as "sweet reasonableness." If you are a mentally healthy person, you have a reasonable degree of insight into your own weaknesses and have learned to turn them to the best advantage. You have the capacity for bearing a reasonable amount of frustration of your own desires, for sensing other people's privations before deploring your own, and for accepting responsibility for your own thoughts, decisions, and actions.

The New Testament writers tend to interpret mental stability in terms of self-control. This is something very different from repression, which means rejecting or keeping something out of consciousness. Repression consists of an unawareness that one even has inordinate aggressions, in which case the person may feign humility in such a way that it angers other persons. But self-control consists of the frank recognition of hungers and impulses and the acceptance of the personal responsibility for their management. The minister is not exempt from the demands and satisfactions of personal discipline.

Contemporary steps toward promoting a high standard of mental health for candidates for the ministry are heartening. Yet there is a real need for younger ministers to conduct a voluntary search for guidance. If you are preparing for this noble task, you are wise to systematically set about the business of removing emotional weights that so easily can beset and render you ineffective or positively harmful in your personal ministry to people. The most natural way of accomplishing this is that of turning to older ministers and theological professors who have devoted their lives not only to their own active ministry but also to the careful training of other ministers. Another way is that of serving an "apprenticeship" alongside spiritually healthy ministers from whom you can learn. Then, too, the growing facilities for the clinical training of theological students provide controlled conditions whereby you can face the hidden anxieties in your own personality as you minister to large numbers of institutionalized people.

If as a prospective minister you discover that you are using more energy fighting your inner conflicts than in doing the work of the Lord, if you sense that your personal relationships to your family and associates are such that they prevent you from being an "able minister of the New Testament," you should feel no embarrassment about searching out a qualified and ethically serious physician who can render whatever therapy is needed. A good majority of personality handicaps are learned behaviors that *can be overcome,* given a spirit of teachableness on the part of the suffering person. You as a minister-to-be should not expect to solve all your personal problems *before* you attempt to deal with those of others. This is a fantasy in itself. You do well to have dealt adequately with your major handicaps by the time you start an active and full-time ministry.

Niebuhr, Williams, and Gustafson, in their study *The Advancement of Theological Education,* analyzed the various categories of theological students in terms of their reasons for coming to a theological seminary. These have a timeless quality about them. Although they were written about men, they also apply to women who aspire to be pastors:

> With all the risks involved, at least ten kinds of men who come to our seminaries may be described. 1) There is the student who is in seminary because his parents, pastor, and home congregation have decided for him that he will make a good minister. 2) A man may be suffering from deep wounds in himself and seek through theological education to heal his own disturbed mind and spirit. 3) A student who functions well in interpersonal relations and anticipates the prestige and success that will be forthcoming from a ministerial career will find his way to seminary. 4) A person who has prematurely tasted the fruits of success in a church career as a boy evangelist, dynamic youth leader, or student movement executive must complete what are to him often only *pro forma* requirements for ministerial status. 5) The man who decided for the ministry at an early age, frequently out of a sense of alienation in the world, and who enjoyed the protection of the pre-ministerial group in college will find his way to seminary. 6) A zealous spirit characterizes the student who has found a gospel and knows its saving power. He wishes to share his good news with the world. 7) Religion and theology present themselves as objective intellectual problems to a searching mind, and the theological school seems to be the place to pursue a study of these problems. 8) An experience of a tragically disorganized society, or of disordered minds, often leads a student to study for the ministry. He sees the Church as an institution out of which flow healing processes for the social and personal evils of our time. 9) Frequently found in the present generation is the man seeking for a faith adequate to bring order into the intellectual and moral confusions that have characterized his previous personal and academic experience. 10) Finally, there is the rare student of mature

faith who lives in the knowledge that it is God who saves and
justifies. He is seeking to become an adequate servant of his
Lord. (H. Richard Niebuhr, Daniel Day Williams, and James
M. Gustafson, *The Advancement of Theological Education*,
pp. 146ff.)

These categories point to an ancient piece of wisdom to
remember in all statements about the ideal qualifications
of ministers: Ministers are human beings and not God.
Ministers have illnesses, too. The presence of illness is not
necessarily a disqualification for the ministry. On the contrary, illnesses have to be distinguished from one another.
Is the illness a way of life for the minister, or is it a gate
to a new life? Illness may be the sum total of the failure
of an inadequate, poorly grounded way of existence. It
may be the "opening" for the reconstruction of a more
realistic, solidly grounded way of life. Charles H. Spurgeon, the stellar preacher of nineteenth-century London,
was plagued with stage fright. He said that it was painful,
"but this weakness has been an education for me."
(Charles H. Spurgeon, *An All Round Ministry*, pp. 207–
208.) Men like Frederick W. Robertson, H. Wheeler Rob-
inson, Harry Emerson Fosdick, and Anton Boisen are examples of ministers who, with far less medical and pastoral
help than is available to the average minister today, found
their way through emotional breakdowns to a powerful
witness for Jesus Christ. With the comfort with which they
themselves had been comforted of God, they in turn became a comfort to others. This kind of disclaimer has to be
entered in discussions of mental health among ministers.
Otherwise, the canons of mental health will become a new
legalism whereby you, by your own efforts, struggle for
some imagined perfection. This, like all other legalisms,
destroys your own sense of need for grace and renders you
helpless to exercise grace in relation to those who seek
your help.

Churches seeking pastors and lay leaders, such as deacons, elders, vestry persons, and stewards, are in need of

education along the line of choosing people who are spiritually healthy. A person's size and the sound of the voice are not adequate standards by which the person should be judged. The New Testament, as has been seen in this context, speaks with definiteness and accuracy on the things that are to be looked for in a minister's personal stability. The churches are under obligation to "try every spirit" to see whether it is of God, because there are many false prophets gone out into the world. As a true prophet you need all the fiber of personality you can muster to stand the test of the pastoral relationship. False prophets often find their way most easily into the affections of their people by reason of their "standing head and shoulders above the rest," their speaking "in the tongues of men and of angels," or their compulsive zeal that "scours land and sea." Only when churches demand something better will ministers be chosen who are capable of bringing health as well as goodness, soundness of mind as well as strength of zeal, and wholesomeness of direction as well as intentness of purpose to the life of the body of Christ.

MUST HAVE A FIRM HOLD ON THE SURE WORD

Your emotional stability has a great deal to do with the quality of your beliefs and largely determines the manner in which you seek to impart these beliefs to other people. Therefore the New Testament writer insists that you have a firm hold on the sure word of the gospel. You must have a sense of certainty about the truths you teach and the Person whom you represent. As John Chrysostom says, such competence in the Word of God is the means of healing grace we use:

> Save for good example, there is but one means and method of cure: the spoken word. This is the sole instrument, the only diet, the finest climate. It takes the place of medication, of cautery, and the knife. If it is necessary to burn or cut, this is the instrument which must be used; and if it fails, all else

is useless. By this means we raise up the prostrate soul, and
cool the fevered; we cut away its excesses and supply its
defects; and we do everything else which is required for the
health of the soul. (Saint John Chrysostom, *The Priesthood:
A Translation of Peri Hierosynes,* by W. A. Jurgens, p. 70)

You need competence to give your people a sense of
certainty about their life in relationship to God, because,
as Paul has said: "If the trumpet give an uncertain sound,
who shall prepare himself to the battle?" (I Cor. 14:8). Two
evident reasons support placing such a demand upon you.
First, people depend upon you for confidence, security,
and certainty, amid suspicion, insecurity, and doubt. As
Goethe appealed, so do they: "Give me your convictions;
I need them. Keep your doubts; I have enough of my
own." Secondly, every congregation has a legitimate need
for authority in its minister. You must be able to speak as
one having authority from your own personal experience
with Christ, from the thoroughness of your knowledge of
the record of revelation, from the firsthandness of your
own understanding of human nature, and from the intimacy of your own acquaintance with grief and pain. Such
an authority meets a group's needs, whereas the traditions
of the scribes leave the group thirsty.

A HEALTHY TEACHER

You are expected not only to have a firm hold on your
beliefs as a Christian but to have laid hold of a healthy
quality of teaching. You need to be mature in Christ, no
longer "tossed to and fro and carried about with every
wind of doctrine, by the cunning of men, by their crafti-
ness in deceitful wiles" (Eph. 4:14). You are to have a firm
hold on the sure word that is taught in order that you may
give instruction "in the health-giving doctrine." New Testament writers were aware of the fact that many congregations do not want pastors of stability. They prefer the
unstable pastors: "Having itching ears they will accumu-

late for themselves teachers to suit their own likings, and will turn away from listening to the truth and wander into myths" (II Tim. 4:3–4). Creative teaching is the church's most effective means of producing spiritually healthy people. It plays the same part in the life of those who are whole that healing plays in the life of those who have need of a physician. This gives a vital significance to the original meaning of "orthodoxy." From the point of view of the pastoral epistles, orthodoxy is that kind of teaching which creates wholeness of life in an individual's relationships to self and to neighbor by reason of a firmer hold upon the reality of God in Christ. From the point of view of the individual, the soundness of a teaching may be determined by its influence upon the forces of spiritual growth within the individual's life. From the point of view of the group life of the church, the soundness of a teaching may be determined by whether or not it contributes to the "edification of the church." If a teaching confirms childish irresponsibility in an individual, and justifies that person in remaining as is with no need for teachableness and no confession of the need for growth, it can be justly called unsound. If a teaching or a practice divorces a group of people from a Christlike spirit and alienates them from one another and from the larger community of Christians, genuine questions may be raised as to the soundness of the teaching.

Yet, less than one twentieth of the active minister's time is spent in actual teaching relationships, as such. The ministry of pastoral care has, however, taken on new diversity and strength since 1956, when Blizzard's work was done. More attention is being given to small-group and teaching ministries of the pastor. However, careful studies of the extent of this are few, if not nonexistent. The dramatic success of the disciplined groups of Alcoholics Anonymous suggests that a part of the lost radiance of the churches has been the power of a small learning group to change human life. The priesthood of all believers and the minis-

try of the laity, if you believe this way, shape your ministry
to be a teacher of the laity, as one who equips the fellowship of believers for the work of ministry. This, furthermore, shifts pastoral care from a sacramental mold in
which the ministry is a confessional type of the care of an
individual in isolation from the community. Instead you
develop an instructional pattern in which the pastoral care
is done in the context of a caring fellowship. You do not
operate under a seal of the confessional as much as you
work within the context of a covenant of responsible communication. You may *need* to talk with other responsible
persons about the individual with whom you are working.
You covenant with the individual, however, not to do so
without the person's full knowledge and consent. The relationship of the members of the community to each
other, in turn, becomes the "content" of the pastor's instructional approach to both the individual and the community in the light of Christian truth.

AN APT TEACHER

The New Testament writers expect of us as pastors, not
only that we be sure of our teaching and that the quality
of our teaching be sound, but that we be capable of making these teachings come alive to our people. We are "apt
teachers."

Your aptitude as a minister for your task is one sure
evidence of God's intention in your life, because God does
not call you to do something without reference to your
own creative gifts in the first place. Colloquially, the word
"apt" has a curious double meaning. It is often used to
mean "likely to come to pass." In this context, the question
could be asked concerning a candidate for the ministry:
"Are you likely to become that for which you are being set
apart?" In its other sense, the word "apt" is often used to
mean "capable, or possessing the ability" to do a task—in
this case, to teach. Much research needs to be done and

clear instruction given by already active pastors as to the specific skills necessary for competent action as a minister. The Spirit of God always takes the form of the vessel that it fills, and the specific form that the sense of mission takes in an individual's life is largely determined by that individual's basic intelligence and vocational aptitudes.

This matter has been left to chance and to the competitive struggle for existence among the churches and among ministers. A natural law of selection works in weeding out incompetent pastors, but it works apart from the loving intelligence of Christian people and is often a cruel thing in its operation. Because of prayerless and careless vocational choices and irresponsible spiritual guidance on the part of pastors who counsel young people about entering the ministry, there have been bitter disappointments in wasted human lives. The sight of a thirty-year-old man who has spent half of his life in school preparing for the ministry and finally ekes out a living selling encyclopedias would frighten his earlier spiritual guides. Many are called into the ministry without a full knowledge of its demands. The blight of disappointment sets in when they, by their own word, conclude that they will never be capable of doing the work of a pastor.

Wise counsel suggests that spiritual appeals for life dedications to Christian work be made in such a way as to allow room for the processes of time, growth, and spiritual instruction to fit the intentions of the consecrated people to the realistic objectives that they are actually capable of achieving. The rigorous requirements of the ministry as *both* profession and calling should be made clear. Some on-the-job observation of the minister at work in preaching, teaching, caring, leading, worship, organizing, and administering will demonstrate the realities of the ministry to a prospective candidate. This would involve a deepened and broadened understanding of the glory of God in the Christian calling. It would also involve a step-by-step path of preparation and decision rather than a one-leap approach. Some sensitive spirits find their place in the world in a moment, in a twinkling of an eye, but they are the rare ones rather than the customary ones. To make a wholesale, detailed, specific dedication which you find out later you have neither the ability nor opportunity to realize may actually do you harm. To move under the sealed orders of our Lord may call for equally as much faith and reward us with equally as much adventure.

WORKING NOT BY CONSTRAINT BUT WILLINGLY

The standard that is set forth in I Peter for you and me is that we be spontaneously happy in our work. This is one sure test of the call of God to a work: the degree of peace and satisfaction we have in doing the work. We are enjoined in I Peter 5:2–4 to do our work not out of a dull sense of necessity and morbid compulsion but of our own free will and desire. This cuts across the grain of much conviction that you must have "fought the call" to be a minister, and that you would be doing something else if you had had your own choice in the matter.

Then too, we are encouraged to maintain a sense of spiritual anticipation and eagerness in our work. We do not look upon our work as a "service rendered" for which the congregation "owes" us our pay. There is a vast difference between the shepherd and the hireling. The one enters into a creative fellowship with the Chief Shepherd. The other is counting the hours until payday and wondering whether those who came in later are getting as much pay. The one has a sense of mission and the other has a job.

However, let us face ruefully a hard fact about ourselves as Christian pastors. We tend to hide slovenly work and a lack of spiritual discipline under a proud claim of being free of "professionalism." At the same time, we are uneasy and feel inferior in the presence of people of other professions such as medicine and teaching who are subject to distinct professional requirements and disciplines for their tasks. I have discussed the tension between the ministry as a gift and as a professional discipline in which we are competent in my book *Pastoral Counseling* (pp. 79–99). Let me say here that the gift of the ministry is a call to the practice of the presence of God in prayer and to the study and interpretation of the Word of God. Further, it is the call to understand and heal the hurts of people in the name of Christ. These are *competencies,* and to do them *well* is to activate our *profession* in a disciplined way. To do them in a careless, incompetent, and sloppy way is to be *unprofessional.* If we are supported financially for doing so, we *do* what people covenant with us we will do when they agree to support us. *Not* to do so is *unprofessional,* i.e., to fail to act in good faith. I say these things because too many people equate being a professional with greed for money. This needs setting straight here.

The neotraditional understanding of yourself as professionally trained, dedicated, and disciplined in your identity has done much to rescue the meaning of "professional" from unsavory connotations of "money-getting." The reverse side of the coin for you as a professionally paid religious worker is that you are responsible for doing the things for which you receive money. You are to be a good steward of your time. Side issues cannot be allowed to pull you from the main center of your working day. For example, if you do not learn to limit the demands that interfere with your preparation for teaching and preaching, you will soon jeopardize the opportunities to perform central functions. This is one sturdy reason for thorough clinical pastoral education. In this training you learn to measure your time and strength according to the real needs of your parishioners instead of according to your own need for approval. You handle your time and energy in a disciplined and purposive way, i.e., as a professional and not as an amateur. Thus you do more effective pastoral care and counseling and conserve your time for other tasks as well. In these senses, your "aptness" as a teacher and shepherd

portrays you as one who knows what you are doing. You
do not do a "hammer and hatchet" kind of patchwork. You
do a genuinely professional work. You profess faith in Jesus
Christ. You commit yourself to fellowship and discipleship
with Christ. You remove the option of being either known
or not known as a Christian from your decisions. You set
yourself to the commission of caring for people. Your responsibility for them as persons is an ethical imperative. As
such, you are "professional" in the highest sense of the
word. You make all who are "professional" in the lowest
sense of the word uncomfortable in your presence. You
are an *apt* teacher and shepherd.

The absence of such discipline and commitment underlies the servile attitude of a hireling. Naturally following
this comes an increasing necessity to "lord it over" the
flock. Then there is no spontaneous joy in a pastor's work.
When there is a fleecing attitude on the pastor's part, the
people soon begin to rebel. That pastor becomes anxious,
irritable, and unhappy, because few dictators can be otherwise. The love of power, no less than the love of money,
is the root of the evil of crass commercialism in the ministry. Such ministers are always afraid lest their authority be
questioned, challenged, defied, or betrayed. Such pastors
have to depend upon a "gestapo" that cannot be trusted
to enforce commands. If you are a serene pastor, though,
you depend upon affectionate ties with people for the
force of your leadership. You depend, not upon the love
of power, but upon the power of love for the achievement
of results—not as "domineering over" those in your
charge but as an example to the flock.

Your love, however, is not sufficient. That cannot be
your crown of glory. Rather, the consummate requirement of the pastor is that you depend devotedly upon the
Chief Shepherd for your own spiritual sustenance and live
in the buoyant expectation of the Shepherd's continual
manifestation of himself. Paul calls this being "holy" and
"a lover of goodness." These terms of endearment of the

life of a pastor lay the emphasis upon your consecration and devotion, without which all other qualifications are in vain and usually are consumed in their own vanity. Søren Kierkegaard has called this "purity of heart," by which he means the power "to will one thing, and that is Christ."

You cannot safely haggle with halfheartedness, partial-izing of desires, reservations of mind. Having brought all mixed emotions and ambivalent feelings to consciousness, you have brought them to a positive conclusion. The mul-tiplicity of selves that cast a vote in the congress of your destiny must have cast their "Yes!" in favor of the noble task of the pastor. Then you are ready for your work as a good minister of Jesus Christ, capable of standing, and, having endured all, of remaining. You can say with Walter Rauschenbusch: "I have found a task apart from which nothing I have ever learned or done is foreign."

"Who Is Sufficient for These Things?"

The apostle Paul disavowed the identity of one of the "peddlers of God's word." He rejected what we today call "phoniness" in order to be a man "of sincerity, as commis-sioned by God, in the sight of God" to speak in Christ. The fragrance of the knowledge of God in Christ was an aroma of life to those who participated in redemption, but a fragrance of death to those who willfully remained es-tranged from God. The basic qualifications of the Christian pastor set forth here were developed through the experi-ence of the early church in implementing this sense of commission of which the apostle Paul had earlier spoken. When the apostle Paul compared himself with the claims of the gospel of Christ, he asked: "Who is sufficient for these things?" When you compare yourself with these ideals, you feel a contrast rather than a comparison. As one student commented: "Even in the New Testament, you can draw out some less than exemplary illustrations of pastoral care." Other students have asked: "Who, then, can be a minister of Jesus Christ if these are the qualifications?" Thus we are confronted with the ambiguity between a Biblical statement of ideal expectations and life as it is. Humanly we realize that these ideals produce tension in and of themselves in the effort simply to approximate, much less achieve, them. The genuineness of the conflict that such ideals create in the best of ministers cannot be ignored.

Furthermore, these ideals can be taken as legalistic maxims. Taken apart from the grace of Jesus Christ and the power of the Holy Spirit, these maxims give those who imagine they have achieved them a basis for pride, rejection of others, and a means of punishment of others. Therefore, these ideals should instead be light and guidance to you and me in our continual confession of sin and search for forgiveness, grace, and mercy. Then our ministry becomes a pageant of gratitude on the part of one who, as Paul and John Bunyan both said of themselves, is the chief of sinners. The fellowship of believers is not a company of perfect people. It is a communion of sinners who accept one another. They have covenanted together to bear one another's burdens and so fulfill the law of Christ. As such, we are the chief of sinners who offer sacrifices not only for the people's sins but for our own as well.

Demands upon the minister are stressed in this chapter. These demands cannot be allowed to obscure the succor and support offered you by your community of faith and by the God and Father of the Lord Jesus Christ. The ease with which sources of strength are obscured in the average community makes it all the more imperative that ministers, as spiritually called and professionally trained persons, learn how to sustain one another in times of stress and frailty. Small groups of ministers can do much for one another in this way. In retreat centers and day-to-day support groups, these groups can be a vital part of the continuing theological education of the minister. A willingness to accept one's humanity and frailty without denying the validity of the ideals of the Christian ministry set forth in the pastoral epistles is a paradoxical tension inherent in the nature of the ministry. To do this with inner sincerity and in fellowship with other ministers both clarifies your identity and rests your integrity in the awesome goodness of God.

Chapter IV

The Identity and Integrity of the Pastor

You as a pastor are justified by your faith relationship to God in Christ, to yourself, and to your faith community and not by the tasks you perform. Therefore, this is a shift from a task-oriented, work-centered meaning of your existence as a Christian pastor to an identity-centered and *being*-centered integrity.

The overall shift of emphasis between the Niebuhr, Williams, and Gustafson study of the ministry done in the middle 1950's and that of Schuller, Strommen, and Brekke in 1980 reflects a shift both in the expectations that the laity have of ministers and in the ministers' own expectations of themselves. That shift is from a task-oriented group of functions and "doings" by the pastor to the integrity, personal commitment, and faith of the minister. They center upon you as a priest and a person. This study in *Ministry in America,* as we have already noted, places your personal integrity as the second agreed-upon expectation of ministers across 47 denominations.

With clarity of identity and integrity of being, you as a Christian pastor do and do not do many things. *What* you do is not determined by the other-direction of the most recent demand laid upon you. Your functions are determined by your inner sense of identity and integrity or lack of it. The major thrust of your dialogue in prayer with God, in conversation with yourself and your family, and in interaction with your faith community of the church is, then, the clarification of your identity and the focus of the integrity of your "personhood" under God. From this you draw your guidance as to the nature of your task. By means of this you resolve conflicting expectations of yourself by others.

You search for a unified perspective of your calling under God that issues in a joyous participation with the people whom you serve. If you are to do your work well, refreshing strength must be afforded you from a coherent vision of your identity. Instead, Christian pastors are often confused in identity. They seek to find the way between the divided camp of the contradictory social demands and personal ambitions that beset them, knowing neither who they are nor where they are going. A vision of his identity both challenged Jesus to lay down his life and at the same time gave him satisfaction that "the world knew not of." The vision must have been renewed daily in our Lord Jesus Christ through his worship in intimate communion with the Father, through his powerful interchanges with the expectations of his disciples, and through his responses to the shepherdless multitudes who sought his ministry. It can hardly be different for the Christian pastor today who, as undershepherd of the Good Shepherd, is an authentic person under God, not just a walking job description.

In 1956, Samuel Blizzard consulted six hundred active Protestant ministers. They were asked to describe, from three different vantage points, their own self-image concerning whom they considered themselves to be. First, they were asked what they thought was *most important* in their calling; second, they were asked in which identity they considered themselves *most effective;* and, third, they were asked in which identity they were happiest and from which they received the *most enjoyment.* The following ranking of the six functional identities of the minister was found:

IMPORTANCE	EFFECTIVENESS	ENJOYMENT
1. Preacher	1. Preacher	1. Pastor
2. Pastor	2. Pastor	2. Preacher
3. Priest	3. Teacher	3. Teacher
4. Teacher	4. Priest	4. Priest
5. Organizer	5. Administrator	5. Organizer
6. Administrator	6. Organizer	6. Administrator

Considerable internal contradiction prevailed in these ministers' self-images. They felt that preaching was their most important function and that they were most effective at preaching. But they received more satisfaction from their work as a pastor, which they ranked next in importance and in personal effectiveness. Thus they probably allowed less time for preparation of sermons, and neglected that which they, for one reason or another, felt was more important than pastoral care. On the other hand, their sense of effectiveness as pastors was less than that as preachers. Ranking fourth in importance and third in effectiveness and enjoyment was the work of teaching. The pastor's identity as a person of prayer and worship was third in importance but fourth in effectiveness and enjoyment. At the very bottom of the scale in importance, effectiveness, and enjoyment were organizing and administering the life of the church. The internal integrity of the identity of the pastor at that time was perplexed, confused, and frustrated, according to Blizzard's initial findings. (Samuel Blizzard, "The Minister's Dilemma," *The Christian Century,* April 25, 1956.) Though these findings are twenty-five years old, they still are a helpful schema for assessing your identity in relation to your multiple tasks. A valuable and imaginative discussion is to be found in Seward Hiltner's *Ferment in the Ministry: A Constructive Approach to What the Minister Does.*

Blizzard sought some objective basis for measuring the

actual decisions of the same group of ministers regarding what their identity is in fact and function as well as in their idealizations. He asked these ministers to analyze their use of time, as ministers, on ordinary working days. The use of time is one candid criterion of a person's internal sense of identity. In the same article cited with reference to the previous data, Blizzard published the following information on the ministers' use of their time. He combined the priest and preacher categories because of their close affiliation in the preparation and participation phases of ministerial work.

THE MINISTER'S WORKDAY

Rural: 9 hours, 17 minutes

Urban: 10 hours, 32 minutes

Administrator	8/20
Pastor	5/20
Priest Preacher	4/20
Organizing	2/20
Teacher	1/20

Average time per day spent in sermon preparation:
34 minutes (rural), 38 minutes (urban)
Stenographic tasks: 1 hour, 4 minutes

Blizzard's study revealed that the particular tasks that the ministers in their own self-concepts valued least, felt least effective in performing, and received the least satisfaction from—i.e., administration and organizing—occupied exactly half of their time. Their identity as a pastor came more nearly to having the same place in their output of time that it did in their personal values, taking one fourth (five twentieths) of their time. The priestly, preaching, and teaching functions consumed the other fourth of their time. Teaching, as such, was the most neglected dimension, receiving only one twentieth of their time. Stenographic tasks occupied more time than did the teaching ministry of the pastors.

Blizzard was careful to note in his studies that these impressions were derived from the ministers themselves, not from their parishioners. Charles Y. Glock and Philip Roos of the University of California studied twelve Lutheran congregations in order to get the parishioners' view of how their ministers spent their time, and what kinds of performance on the part of the minister received the greatest and least approval from the congregation. (Charles Y. Glock and Philip Roos, "Parishioners' Views of How Ministers Spend Their Time," *Review of Religious Research,* Spring 1961, pp. 170–175.) Their study was based on 2,729 questionnaires received from a sample of the membership of twelve churches. The persons were asked what two kinds of work they thought their pastor spent the most time on, and what two kinds of work the pastor spent the least time on. The table on p. 133 represents their replies.

Glock and Roos concluded that parishioners formed their opinions on the basis of *visibility,* i.e., the importance of an activity was determined by the number of members who directly saw the minister in action at this particular kind of work. As a result, the parishioners felt that pastors spent most of their time at (1) sermon preparation, (2) work for the church at large, (3) attending church meetings, and (4) office work, in that order. They felt that the pastors spent the least amount of time in (1) personal recreation, (2) visitation of members, (3) visitation of nonmembers, and (4) giving advice and counsel to individuals, in that order. Glock and Roos compared this information with Blizzard's studies. They concluded that the wide margins of difference between ministers' self-images and their actual reports of time use, on the one hand, and the parishioners' perceptions of these same things, on the other, reflect a serious failure of communi-

PARISHIONERS' RANKING° OF TIME
SPENT ON EIGHT ACTIVITIES
BY MINISTERS IN TWELVE
LUTHERAN CONGREGATIONS

| Activity | Ranking | | | | | | | | Mean rank |
| | Most time | | | | | Least time | | | |
	1	2	3	4	5	6	7	8	
Sermon preparation	8	2	2	–	–	–	–	–	1.5
Work for church at large	2	5	3	1	–	1	–	–	2.6
Attending church meetings	2	2	5	2	1	–	–	–	2.8
Office work	–	–	–	5	2	2	3	–	5.2
Giving people advice	–	–	1	2	6	2	1	–	5.0
Visiting nonmembers	–	1	1	1	1	5	3	–	5.4
Visiting members	–	2	–	1	2	2	5	–	5.4
His own recreation	–	–	–	–	–	–	–	12	8.0

°Ranks were based on scores for each activity computed by subtracting the number of "least" responses from the number of "most" responses and dividing by the total number of responses, "n." "Don't know" responses, which ranged from 27 percent to 52 percent of the parishioners in the twelve congregations, were omitted in the computation of this table.

cation on the part of the church and its ministry to interpret to its membership "just what the ministerial role entails in practice."

Although Glock and Roos do not say so, the main avenue of communication between the leadership and the membership of the church, namely, effective teaching, occupies only one twentieth of the pastor's time. From these data the hypothesis can be drawn that the failure of communication may lie in the devaluation of a teaching ministry by both pastor and congregation. If pastors were involved in more give-and-take discussion with small groups of their church, possibly the level of communication could be effectually improved. Apart from some such face-to-face encounter in which minister and people can communicate on a common ground with two-way interchange, the hypothesis of Glock and Roos will hold unchanged: "The image of a profession will be largely informed by what is visible in the professional activity."

Glock and Roos then asked additional questions of the parishioners as to their evaluations of what their ministers ought to be doing with their time. The parishioners were asked whether they felt that their pastor spent too much, too little, or about the right amount of time on each of eight functions. The study revealed that the majority of the parishioners were uncritical of their ministers. The following table represents the opinions of those who did express an evaluation:

INDEX OF PARISHIONER APPROVAL
OF EIGHT MINISTERIAL ACTIVITIES
ACCORDING TO PARISHIONER CONCEPTIONS
OF TIME SPENT ON THEM

Activity	Approval score° for parishioners who perceive their ministers as spending:		
	Most of their time on an activity	Least of their time on an activity	Neither most nor least of their time on an activity
Sermon preparation	.65	.05	.80
Work for church at large	.25	.55	.70
Attending church meetings	.45	.50	.55
Office work	.00	.85	.65
Giving people advice	.60	.10	.80
Visiting nonmembers	.80	.10	.65
Visiting members	.85	.00	.65

°Scores should not be interpreted as representing proportion of parishioners approving an activity. In fact, a majority of parishioners were uncritical of their minister. ["His own recreation" omitted by the authors of this article.]

Two activities—visiting members and visiting nonmembers—were most approved by the members. Although the members perceived their ministers as spending most of their time on sermon preparation, the members believed this to be of only moderate importance. These members considered attending church meetings and doing office work as of minimal importance or insignificant in their approval of their minister. When we compare these parishioner expectations with Blizzard's estimates of what ministers themselves consider to be most important, the expectations of both are almost identical. The preaching and pastoral functions take precedence in the minds of both the pastor and the parishioner. A positive conclusion can be drawn from these two studies: Delegate some of your clerical tasks. Reject the compulsion to attend *all* the meetings both in and out of the church. In turn, concentrate the time saved in this way upon a more effective teaching ministry of your own. Thus, you create a situation in which the basic truths of the Christian faith can be communicated in depth and detail. Some of the failures of communication between you and your congregation could thus be overcome. At the same time, you would have natural group situations for developing lay ministers for preventing and remedying some of the problems that consume your energies in individual counseling work.

When you draw such a conclusion, however, your defenses begin to mobilize. You perceive yourself predominantly as a preacher. You think of yourself as most effective here, and, next to your pastoral work, you actually enjoy the pulpit ministry most. In your education and in the church at large, you have been both taught and encouraged to think of your ministry of teaching as something any willing lay person can do. You feel, therefore, unfaithful to your call to be a prophet if you do not strictly define your ministry to groups in the formal preaching situation.

These data suggest several pertinent ideas concerning

the diffusion of your identity. The task of administration takes far more time than you feel is important, uses you most effectively, or provides you with the most meaning and satisfaction. Niebuhr's attempt to enrich this focus of the minister's identity by calling the minister a pastoral director really has not taken root in the ensuing twenty-six years. You as a minister are an "overseer" of a particular congregation. You are a shepherd and cannot divorce your pastoral ministry, in which you do get such real satisfaction, from your creative oversight of the fellowship of believers as a community. Contemporary systems analyses on concepts have much more to offer you than simply giving the task the name of pastoral director.

Again, your best strategy is to assert and activate your own identity as a teacher. If you are fortunate enough to have the additional services of an educational director, the duties of this person can be reshaped to include more actual teaching and less administrative and clerical work.

However, if your *pastoral* instruction as a Christian shepherd is activated, you can equip many lay persons to be pastors to one another. An effective perception of yourself as a teaching pastor enables you to develop an appropriate background for many of the things you preach from the pulpit. Two-way communication in teaching groups creates a healthy dialogue between the person in the pew and the message being preached.

A mistaken sense of prophecy pervades much of the contemporary ministers' conception of themselves as preachers. Many pastors directly identify themselves with Old and New Testament prophets and apostles in their forthrightness of utterance. However, pastors neglect to note that the system in which these prophets and apostles preached was an open, not a closed one. Rarely did they preach under the highly formal circumstances of the typical Sunday morning audience of today. They could be interrupted, asked questions, and disagreed with by their hearers. The conditions of prophetic and apostolic preaching were much more akin to the two-way group teaching situations of today. The pastors of today have neglected these opportunities and ruled them out of their working day to such an extent that little of their time is spent in this way. As a result, pastors attempt to prophesy in a preaching situation in which response, retort, and resonance are improbable, if not impossible. The members of the audience have no way of expressing their feelings except by compliments or by personal hostility, withdrawal from attendance at church, the use of the telephone at home, and personal head-knockings with the pastor. These reactions must, then, be dealt with through personal diplomacy. This consumes the time of pastors and leaves them with the feeling that they dare not speak their minds fully in the pulpit. The end result is insipid preaching and bored listeners who endure silently while the pastors have their say.

The point of the suggestion here, then, is that the identity of yourself as a pastor can be integrated most effectively around your sense of being a teacher. The *Ministry in America* study indicates a high expectation of you that you have "clarity of thought and communication," that you be alert to the world around you, sensitively using a broad base of information to stimulate people to become thinking Christians, and to do so as a "service in humility, relying on God's grace," without seeking personal fame or deliberately agitating controversy. Teaching is a situation in which this can happen. You do not do all the talking, as in preaching, or most of the listening, as in counseling. Rather, teaching is a communication "halfway house" between preaching and counseling, providing background for and entrée into either preaching or counseling. Yet in Blizzard's earlier findings, he discovered that only one in twenty-five ministers perceived themselves as being an educator, an identity around which all the other dimensions of their calling were integrated. Let us see how pastoral care as practiced by parish ministers can be focused in their identity as a teacher; and also how their work as a preacher and as a leader of worship can be similarly focused in their function as a "teacher come from God"; and finally, how their identity as an administrator and an organizer can be focused in their identity as a teacher.

PASTORAL TEACHING AND THE CARING FELLOWSHIP

The group life of the church as a teaching agency of the community is intimately related to the pastoral care and personal counseling that the pastor does. You as a pastor cannot relegate the teaching ministry of your church to assistants without doing violence to both your preaching and your pastoral relationship. The education that a congregation receives through the church school provides the background of understanding with which the people hear a pastor preach. This education serves as a front line of preventive defense against those conflicts which cause people to seek pastoral counseling. The reasons for this are not so evident and need clarification, however.

When you as a pastor take your parishioners' personal problems seriously, you find yourself overwhelmed by the many individuals both within and without your congregation who seek help. You cannot possibly get to them all. You find yourself in need of arranging persons with similar difficulties and needs together in groups in order that you may serve them more adequately in those needs which can be dealt with on a group level. Also, they need to know and learn from one another. A large measure of their distress is caused by their isolation and loneliness in suffering. For instance, many pastors have discovered that a wholesome group life cushions the shock of retirement for older people and keeps them from becoming ingrown in their later years. Group work with and pastoral care of older people are complementary ways by which the church and you as a pastor minister to those in later maturity. You need not choose between those two methods.

You use both. This could be said also of the other age groups and interest groups of the church.

Again, the teaching ministry of the church gives you access to the families of the individuals who seek your counsel. The taproot of the unhappiness of the individuals with whom a pastor counsels is in their family relationships. A pastor spends great parts of each week in marriage and family counseling. To conduct such a program of pastoral care and personal counseling without an adequate curriculum in family life education, with which to prevent such difficulties and to do away with some of the need for counseling, is pastoral nearsightedness. The training of young people, not only in the dramatic story and ethical imperatives of the Bible but also in the preparation for and participation in Christian marriage, is an indispensable part of the pastoral care and personal counseling of a pastor.

Furthermore, an adequate teaching ministry provides both an inlet and an outlet for pastoral care and personal counseling. For instance, from two contacts with a discussion group on the subject "Learning Spiritual Values in Family Living" a pastor received three requests from individuals attending the group for counsel concerning their family problems. One was an impending divorce situation, another a case in which a marriage had been consummated under false pretenses, and another a family in which the presence of the parents of both the husband and the wife in the home was gradually stifling the growth of the children. Likewise, in this same group were several couples with whom the pastor had already counseled in premarital guidance, two of whom had invited the pastor to perform their wedding ceremony for them. The fact that instructional groups serve as an inlet through which people may come to you the pastor for individual help and an outlet with which you can conserve the results of your personal counseling makes your own teaching ministry of primary concern to you. To neglect this center of your calling in the church or to relegate it to others without concern is to lose touch with one of the main sources of counseling opportunities.

Furthermore, you are largely responsible for the selection and equipping of lay leadership in the teaching ministry of the church. At this point your counseling function and your work as an educator converge most meaningfully. Whatever methods the churches of various denominations have for recruiting lay workers in the educational life of the church, one need remains constant: *these persons should be emotionally healthy and carefully instructed in addition to being willing to serve.* Religious work meets many inner needs of persons: relief from guilt, escape from home tensions and conflicts, relief from boredom, and other security needs. These needs, however, should be secondary to the welfare of the persons whom a Sunday school teacher seeks to guide. Quite often the parishioner who is most eager to gain or to retain a church office is the one least competent to do the work.

Therefore, choose leaders carefully and give close attention to the personal adequacy, emotional stability, and basic construction of persons who volunteer for a given task. This can be done tactfully through home visitation, personal counseling, and specialized groups taught by professionally skilled persons. I know of one church that consistently follows this practice, and the result has been a healthy church with a minimum of inner conflict and friction among its organizations.

Finally, the family life of parishioners and their group life in the church are psychologically and educationally separate facets of the same experience. The marital and parental happiness of the leaders of the church becomes a contagion for good or evil in the younger members who follow their patterns of living. Therefore, you as a pastor need to work for the selection and training of leaders who have adequately succeeded as parents and as participating members of families. Such leaders can sponsor a strong curriculum in family life education. Healthy leadership and an adequate church school curriculum become bonds that tie the pastoral task and the educational work of a minister together in an inseparable union. You can bring new life and disciplined instruction into the whole life of the church if you use the time you spend in attending meetings and doing clerical tasks for preparation for and leadership of "equipping sessions" in which you yourself are the teacher.

However, one of the reasons pastors do not do this is that they are ill at ease in small groups. They want a crowd. They are defensive about groups in which they do not do all the talking but are open to being challenged by varieties of opinions. They are more secure in the lecture-sermon situation than in a workshop group. But you can overcome these inhibitions. You can develop your skills and insights for small-group teaching ministries. When you do so, you have the instruments for releasing the powers of a congregational fellowship that the monotones of one-way preaching and the isolation of private counseling with individuals cannot touch.

PASTORAL TEACHING, THE PREACHING MINISTRY, AND PASTORAL CARE

The vitality of the small-group ministry provides a fellowship of people who know one another. You teach them how to care for one another and for those on the outside of their fellowship. The atmosphere created by these two-way communication groups makes your preaching ministry more than mere speechmaking. You become an articulator for the single-heartedness that the Holy Spirit has produced in the small groups. You have already dealt with heavily controversial subjects in situations where listeners can have their say. In the interaction between the members of the group and between the group and the leader, definite understandings and new insights have been developed. The combined witness and wisdom of the group as a whole can become the basis for your development of sermons. In turn, the sermons can be starters for new directions of thinking in the groups that you teach and lead. This gives you more freedom in dealing with controversial subjects. It provides a medium for the expression of feeling and opinion that may be contrary to your own. Such teaching groups are in themselves preaching opportunities in the sense of dialogue as over against the monologue of formal pulpit situations of preaching. On the other hand, the group members who listen to the formal pulpit sermon feel that they have had a part in "the making of the sermons."

Contemporary preachers often find themselves in a complaining mood because, for instance, "they cannot preach what they know about the Bible" in the pulpit. They look upon their technical training in the historical method of Biblical study, the literary approach to Biblical interpretation, and the results of modern scholarship concerning the Bible as something that they cannot communicate to lay people. They convey just enough of this knowledge to make both the congregation and themselves anxious, indecisive, and suspicious of one another. The pulpit situation provides them only twenty to thirty minutes a week in which to preach to the majority of the congregation. The lay-taught church school provides another thirty to forty minutes a week of instruction in the dramatic story and moral truths of the Bible, with all too little attention to the context and basis for Biblical interpretation.

Furthermore, as I have indicated in my small volume entitled *The Bible in Pastoral Care,* many of the personal problems of family conflict, sexual temptation and deviation, hostility, and community distress presented to the pastor in personal counseling reflect distinct misinterpretations of the Bible at one or more significant turning points in the counseling relationship. These misinterpretations amount to gross superstition at times. They represent the failure of the teaching ministry of the church in the clear communication of the Word of God. Similarly, William Oglesby, in his book *Biblical Themes in Pastoral Care,* has related the Bible to the broken relationships, wounds of loneliness and grief, and the need for forgiving and being forgiven that pastors meet in their pastoral care.

Thus the absence of an effective teaching ministry of the church and its pastor actually creates hindrances to preaching. On the other hand, some of the need for counseling grows out of the sheer ignorance and misinterpretation of the Scriptures. The falling away of young people from the church and from the stability of the Scriptures is just one of the many results of this lack of effective teaching. Therefore, pastors who activate their identity as teachers of small, face-to-face groups where they "leap the gap" between their own education and that of their congregation in the Bible, theology, church history, Christian ethics, and pastoral care find a coherent center for both their preaching and their pastoral care. They will find a fresh, new kind of preaching in which they can be open, candid, and spontaneous with people. They will cease to curse the darkness of their people about the Bible. They light the candles of a teaching ministry. Even if at first they can get only two or three persons to take the time to be with them, these pastors have the leaven that may spread to the whole congregation.

More specific attention, however, must be given here to the interaction of formal preaching with the pastoral ministry to individuals and families. Historically, the renascence of concern with the intimate, personal ministry of a pastor to individuals in distress began with the emergence of a kind of preaching which Charles Kemp has rightly called "life-situation preaching." As early as the ministry of Horace Bushnell, there was a studied effort of ministers to begin with the human situation and derive the message of the pulpit from the dilemmas of their hear-

ers. Bushnell preached such sermons as "Unconscious Influence" and "The Moral Use of Dark Things," which even
now are used as models in homiletics classes. Later, Harry
Emerson Fosdick became the main exponent of this kind
of preaching and is said to have measured the effectiveness of his sermons by the number of persons who sought
his personal guidance in the following week. Of course,
this was not new with Fosdick, for Jonathan Edwards had
himself done much of his most effective work with individuals who sought him out after his sermons. This indicates clearly that this approach to preaching does not necessarily presuppose a particular kind of theology.

Vital contrasts distinguish the preaching ministry from
the pastoral task. Elaboration of each of these distinctives
will add strength to this meaning. The preaching ministry
is a public one; the pastor's access to the crowd is emphasized. But the pastoral task is ordinarily a private and personal ministry, and the relative anonymity of the service
is emphasized. This difference is accentuated when a parishioner fears that what has been said to a minister in
private may become topics and illustrations for the minister's preaching in public. You may discover as you counsel
with a parishioner that the person feels singled out in
certain statements you may have made in a sermon.

Therefore, as a preacher-counselor you do well to ask for
the permission of a given individual before you refer to
the person or to what has been said in a public address of
any kind. When you do refer to the person, it is better to
do so in a two-way communication group where the person can respond if need be. But if the reference does
happen to be in a formal, pulpit situation, then let it be
done only in such a way that the integrity and dignity of
the person is enriched and not destroyed. For you to hold
individual persons up for ridicule, disdain, or as "horrible
examples" should be strictly forbidden, *tabu, verboten,
interdict*—i.e., unlawful in any language! The Bible and
classical literature are replete with such bad examples. For

you to use acquaintances of your personal ministry in this way indicates laziness in preparation and ad-libbing in delivery. Therefore, before you make any reference to individuals, observe the rules of advance preparation, ask for their permission, and make reference in a way that will edify them and not ridicule them.

Furthermore, many people prefer to talk with a minister whom they do not see every Sunday and who does not know all their friends, rather than with their own pastor. This may be true even though these persons have no fear of or lack of confidence in their own pastor. The chaplain in the hospital observes this in remarks that patients make about their pastors. As one woman said: "I could never tell my pastor these things. He knows me too well. But I can tell them to a chaplain, because he is detached." The pastoral relationship, in its deeper reaches, requires a considerable degree of anonymity in order that the persons may be aided in the difficulties that matter most to them.

This calls for extensive cooperation among ministers of the same community in referring persons who are too close to them to other pastors who can maintain a more detached and objective relationship. It also necessitates a close cooperation between the parish pastor, physicians, and specialized pastoral counselors. In larger communities, pastoral referral centers and pastoral counseling centers have been and will continue to be established. Specialized help of skilled psychologists of religion and pastoral counseling is becoming a felt need in an exceptional number of communities. You can locate these by writing or calling the American Association of Pastoral Counselors: 3000 Connecticut Avenue, N.W., Suite 300, Washington, D.C. 20008. Their telephone number is: (202) 387-0031.

The second distinction between the pastoral and the preaching situations is the time element. Pastoral work is difficult to control in terms of the extent of time needed for each individual and the number of persons who seek the pastor's help. Your pastoral care and personal counsel-

ing ministry can so encroach upon your time that you will
have none left for anything else. This overloading in turn
becomes a barrier to effective pastoral counseling. People
will feel so guilty about taking your time that their qualms
of conscience will prevent them from using wisely the
time that you do give them. Conversely, the time element
enters again when you, pressed for the preparation of the
sermon for Sunday, are interrupted by a person who needs
immediate attention. You may have difficulty listening to
the person's story. You may even be tempted to preach to
the parishioner what little of the sermon you have prepared.

Again, the preaching-pastoral relationship proposes a
paradox in the approach you use to meet the needs of the
same people. As a preacher, you approach their lives in
terms of goals, ideals, objectives, and purposes for living in
the Kingdom of God. But in pastoral care and personal
counseling, you approach each person not merely as one
who is unswervingly loyal to the absolute ideals of Jesus
but also as one who understands when people miss the
mark of the ideals of Jesus. As a pastor, you have the wisdom of the serpents concerning the frailties of human
nature, and an affectionate tenderness that will "lift up the
fallen." This gentleness grows out of the forgiveness you
have received for having missed the mark yourself. Pastoral leadership casts its light in the arc of these two poles
of influence: the devotion of a pastor to the absolute ideals
of Jesus and the patience of a pastor with human imperfec-
tion. The preaching task is primarily that of challenging
people with the distant and flickering but unquenchable
lights of the City of God. The pastoral task is primarily that
of being able to identify with people just as they are, "to
sit where they sit," even in their "haunts of wretchedness"
in the cities of persons "where cross the crowded ways of
life." The two functions are coalesced in the worship of
God as you learn to participate with your congregation in

the processes of growth in the covenant of the loving ideals of Jesus.

Enough of the distinctions between your preaching function and pastoral task have been named. However, some startling parallels between the two relationships ease the adjustment of these functions to each other. The similarities outweigh the difficulties.

The good preacher depends upon the same laws of personality as does the good pastor for effectiveness. The dynamics of preaching, teaching, and healing are much the same as far as the pastor's relationship is concerned. For instance, in pastoral care and personal counseling, you must establish a "relationship of a trusted motive," before you can help the person. You must be able to put yourself in the place of the individual with whom you are counseling. In turn, that person must be able to identify with you as a pastor, i.e., to trust your motives, appreciate your way of life, and even desire to be like you. The establishment of this rapport takes time and patient relaxation of suspicions and defenses of all kinds.

This is equally true of the relationship of a preacher to a congregation. A bond of honor and shared feeling transmits the message of a preacher to a people. Some pastors can establish this more quickly than others, but the sense of togetherness must be there before the sermon becomes a reality to the hearers. The congregation tests the reality of a person's utterance without planning to do so, and the sermon becomes an "I-Thou" relationship, a personal encounter involving both candor and comfort.

Preaching as a personal encounter becomes the careful and devoted management of a growing understanding between you and your congregation rather than merely an oratorical demonstration. The theological professor who has been a pastor and blended with a congregation finds occasional preaching in first one pulpit and then another to a group of total strangers to be a tasteless experience in comparison. Pastoral care and personal counseling lend feeling and meaning to preaching. Preaching becomes the spiritual preparation for counseling.

As such, the preaching of a sermon becomes an inlet into counseling with individuals, an important source of precounseling contacts. Also, the ministry of comfort and reassurance, instruction and interpretation, can often be done more powerfully through preaching than through individual counseling, because it is done in the presence of the larger community of worshipers. Furthermore, individuals can more easily accept or reject a given interpretation when they are in a group or a crowd. On the other side of the pulpit, too, you can give guidance that applies to "all mankind" and carefully avoid being too stringent on a given individual. Having done this, you, in private conference with parishioners, can spend your time listening to their side of the story. Such a reciprocal relationship between pastoral care and preaching will go far in alleviating the feeling that many lay people express when they object to not being allowed to answer the preacher back or to ask a question. A listening pastor makes an understanding preacher.

The pastor who maintains a consistent counseling ministry will move in the direction of life-situation preaching. By definition, life-situation preaching "begins with life situations and is aimed at them. . . . It starts where people live. Such preaching must, of necessity, have a close relationship to pastoral work." (Charles F. Kemp, ed., *Life-Situation Preaching*, p. 16.) The characteristics of such preaching are fourfold: (1) the *interpretation* of human experience in the light of Biblical truth rather than the exhortation of people to the observance of certain moral precepts, as such; (2) the development of personal *insight into the motives of personal and group action* rather than the condemnation of this or that kind of behavior; (3) the *encouragement* of the congregation toward faith in God, in one another, and in themselves as means of gaining control over behavior that they themselves discover to be alien to the mind of Christ; (4) the growth of a *sense of comradeship with God in Christ* and the changing of personality through this "transforming friendship."

Contrary to some opinion, life-situation preaching may be thoroughly Biblical and even exegetical. However, the approach to the Bible itself is a life-situation approach. The studied effort of the exegesis is to reconstruct the "situation that was" at the time of the writing. The interpretation, however, is not simply paralleled with a similar contemporary situation-in-life. Instead the timeless elements of both situations are identified and become the outline of the sermon. The end result is a meditative interpretation of Scripture in the present tense. This was my intention when I wrote the book of sermons, *The Revelation of God in Human Suffering,* which was published in 1959. Similarly, Charles Kemp has edited a book of life-situation sermons entitled *Pastoral Preaching* (1963). A more recent thesaurus of such sermons is *The Twentieth-Century Pulpit,* edited by James W. Cox (1978).

Of course, certain aspects of the life-situation approach are immediately identifiable as "the psychological approach" to homiletics. Such an approach implies a *conversational, eye-contact, extemporaneous delivery* rather than a more impersonal, formal, and oratorical delivery. It rules out histrionics and other appeals to the more superficial emotions. Yet, being united to the sense of touch, to sound, and to rhythm makes the message more concrete. It calls for a personal inventory, a confrontation of the self, and a reordering of the deep emotions of family love and hate, vocational intention, and the fundamental desires that drive human action.

You as a preacher, through the processes of sympathetic imagination, empty yourself of your own frame of reference and take upon yourself the condition and cries of the people's inner lives. You seek to articulate their prayers for them. In so doing, you are their spokesperson before God as well as God's spokesperson before them. In this

150 _The Christian Pastor_

kind of preaching prophetic and priestly functions are
blended into one act of preaching. No artificial dichotomy
separates these. For as a prophet at one and the same time
you declare yourself to be both a person of unclean lips
and a person dwelling in the midst of a people of unclean
lips. Therefore, you can sit where they sit.

Naturally, life-situation preaching produces relief from
a sense of guilt and rest from tension through the resolution of conflict. It stands over against the type of preaching
that creates unrest through the introduction of conflict
into a complacent mind and the development of a sense
of guilt in people who are "past feeling" a given moral or
spiritual value. As such, a sermon based on life itself qual-
ifies as an act of worship in itself. The people of God are
refreshed on their way. As Seward Hiltner puts it: "The
preacher is a living human organism, as are the other
people to whom the Word is also life and salvation.
Preacher—Word—people: these are all alive. Discourse—
Book—behavior: these are all, in a significant sense, dead
because they are nonorganic. But life, [the image suggests
to us,] is never to be apprehended with simple directness,
alone and in itself. The order of the Word is 'no angel
visitants, no opening skies.' It is, instead, through death to
life, through the nonorganic to the organic, through the
Book to the Living Word, through the three dead
homiletical points to just possibly a receptive heart or two.
Homiletically speaking, in the midst of life we are in
death; and only if we learn to tolerate death—a Book and
not an angel, an idea and not just a feeling, a conviction
and not merely a charitable impulse—can we approach
life." (Hiltner, _Ferment in the Ministry: A Constructive
Approach to What the Minister Does,_ p. 56.)

WORSHIP: THE LIFE'S BLOOD OF THE PASTOR

The relationship of a pastor to individuals, groups, and
congregations undergoes a metamorphosis in the act of

worship. Consciousness of the pastor's presence fades out and awareness of the real presence of God reaches its zenith. The quantitative differences of character between the pastor and those to whom the pastor ministers become as nothing as the eternal qualitative difference between all persons and God becomes more evident.

Worship, as Gaines S. Dobbins has said, is the "interruption of our daily routine" and of our involvement in the transitory things of life "to recognize the supreme worth of God, to praise him for his goodness, to meditate on his holiness, to renew devotion to his service," and to sever our idolatries. (Gaines S. Dobbins, *The Church at Worship,* p. 35.) The act of worship, therefore, has a wealth of connotations for the pastoral task of the minister.

Informal worship, where two or three are gathered together in the spontaneity of the shared knowledge of the presence of God, is the true atmosphere of the face-to-face relationship of a minister to an individual. The reverent care of living persons is a type of worship in its own right. This has been the primitive foundation of many religions, and, with all its limitations, is the extent of the worship of the vast majority of the people of the world. However, even in the Christian experience of worship, the reverence for God and the reverence for human personality are inseparable. The acute appeal of a suffering person is the medium of revelation most often promised by Jesus. "When did we see thee?" is the question of both true and insincere worshipers. "As you did it to one of the least of these my brethren, you did it to me" (Matt. 25:40).

Although the face-to-face ministry of a pastor to individuals should be, and often is, an Emmaus road form of prayer, it does not become such without personal discipline on the part of the pastor. The question regularly comes to a pastor: "To whom do you go when the worries of other people become too heavy for you?" The answer to this question in a pastor's private worship life is the beginning of your own response to "a serious call to a devout and holy life." As Thomas a Kempis said: "No man doth safely speak, but he that is willing to hold his peace. No man doth safely appear abroad, but he who can gladly abide at home, out of sight. No man can safely command others but he that hath learned willingly to obey." The transforming power of Jesus came through prayer and self-discipline, and you and I cannot expect it to be otherwise with us.

When you consider your interpersonal work of caring for people as a form of prayer in itself, you find personal resources that keep your confidence in people strong, prevent you from losing patience with them, and undergird you with a steady calmness in the presence of acute pain and unhappiness. Without this sense of worship, you become threadbare in the wear and tear of the emotional tension of your task. Fatigue sets in, irritability increases, aggressiveness and defensiveness are the next to follow. In order to allay your own sense of guilt, you then become overconcerned and overprotective toward those to whom you minister. Consequently, you will spend more and more time with fewer and fewer people, and lose your perspective of even their needs.

Another connection between informal worship and pastoral work is apparent. Your capacity to listen to people is dependent upon your reverence for them and your own teachableness. You cannot give such concern unless you have received it yourself as an act of grace from God and those persons who nurtured you. The surplus of God's grace abounds to meet the needs of others. You as a Christian shepherd are one whose "cup runneth over." Without this awesome sense of gratitude, without this sense of the abundance of the fullness of God in the satisfaction of your own needs, you yourself become demanding. You feel misunderstood and imposed upon. You feel like telling your own troubles to the person who is seeking your help. You become more talkative, and, with this, your capacity to listen has failed you. You become inattentive and insensitive to the subtle feelings of the person who seeks your help.

The third tie that binds worship to pastoral calling and counseling is the expectancy and need of people. If you do not share in worship with those with whom you work, you soon begin to lose their respect. They begin to suspect your motives and to doubt your sincerity. A prayerless relationship between you and your parishioners gradually relegates you either to the familiarity of all the rest of their social companions or to the atmosphere of an interviewer-client relationship. Both of these latter relationships have their intrinsic values, but they are peripheral to the central function of the minister as a representative of God.

Public worship, as indeed is true of private worship, likewise affords necessary resources for the conservation and multiplication of your pastoral effectiveness. One of the main distinctives of your role and function as a Christian pastor is that you are related to those whom you help both individually and socially, both privately and publicly, both on horizontal planes of fellowship between persons and on a vertical plane of communion between persons and God. The place of public worship is where all these lines of influence and relationship meet. Therefore, you have at your disposal the resources of the community of worship to meet the needs of the individual for worship and relief from isolation. The resources of the individual are at your disposal, also, to guide you toward the beautification of worship and the strengthening of the moral fiber of the community.

The chief end of worship is "to glorify God, and to enjoy him forever." The church at worship is celebrating the joy of the resurrection of Jesus Christ. The people are jubilant over the redemption of their lives from destruction, the steadfastness of their relationship to God, and the inseparableness of the fellowship they have in Jesus Christ.

The results of public worship are by-products of this fellowship. In these results, the fruits of teaching, preaching, and caring are multiplied. *Rest, the renewal of strength and energy through relaxation, is one of the shared objectives of both pastoral work and public worship.* The release from nervous tension and the discovery of new reserves of power for living through worship is a neglected emphasis in the activism of many Protestant churches. "Even youths shall faint and be weary, and young men shall fall exhausted; but they who wait for the LORD shall renew their strength, they shall mount up with wings like eagles, they shall run and not be weary, they shall walk and not faint" (Isa. 40:30–31). This need for rest prompted the institution of the Sabbath, sustains the continued practice of public worship, and vitally relates that practice to your caring ministry as a pastor.

The quest for community in a sense of the shared meaning of life with others is also a common venture that prompts people both to participate in public worship and to seek your understanding counsel as their pastor. You are the chosen representative of that specific community. To converse with you personally is a private way of approaching that community. The relief from isolation through public worship with the people in Christ is the heart hunger of the worshiper's motive.

Sin and guilt isolate people from those of their own community. They are accompanied by a longing for restoration "by those who are spiritual," for a sense of belonging again to the group whose approval is most important to the sinner, as well as for restoration to God, who insists upon clean hands and a pure heart in those who "worship him in spirit and in truth."

The private confession of sin has very little meaning apart from the corporate worship between imperfect people and the God and Father of the Lord Jesus Christ. These persons in turn are people of unclean lips also, and the individual lives "in the midst of a people of unclean lips." All sin is shared guilt as well as being an individual responsibility before God. Corporate worship is God's remedy for corporate sin. Here a person realizes that one is not alone in sinfulness nor in dependence upon the forgiveness of God. "All we like sheep have gone astray; we have turned every one to his own way" (Isa. 53:6) is an accurate description of the path toward isolation, self-centeredness, and loneliness in a person who is burdened with sin. The ingathering of corporate worship leads to the unification of persons who have a common experience of the forgiving grace of God. The outgoing of the worshiping community is a witness of the joy of fellowship. This witness is the most convincing form of evangelical outreach. "That which was from the beginning, which we have heard, which we have seen with our eyes, which we have looked upon and touched with our hands, concerning the word of life— . . . that which we have seen and heard we proclaim also to you, so that you may have fellowship with us; and our fellowship is with the Father and with his Son Jesus Christ" (I John 1:1, 3).

Thus the values of personal insight and the beginning of a lasting community are created, conserved, and then multiplied in public worship. The radiation of gratitude and self-acceptance lays the foundations upon which Christian worshipers can agree as to common goals and objectives for concerted Christian action. At this point, the work of a pastor, in the secret places of personal counseling to change people's attitudes privately, becomes manifest in public work and social action as these individuals set about righting glaring social wrongs in the community.

THE PASTOR'S INTEGRITY AS A SPIRITUAL OVERSEER

The center of your integrity rests in your own faith in God and your identity as "a teacher come from God." The circumference of your identity is the body of Christ with which you live in worshipful fellowship. This parish of yours is not an "administrative fiction," but, as Georges Bernanos called "the face of his parish," the church is "a living cell in the everlasting church." In your perspective of yourself as a "spiritual overseer," you find the integrity to sustain yourself in your identity as "a teacher come from God." Some ministers who read this description will feel that it is not in keeping with the realistic problems of time and quantities of work with which the average pastor must grapple. Such a concept of pastoral work in the context of the identity and integrity of the minister, however, implies radical departures in the underlying philosophy of the oversight of the church.

American churches have been schematized according to two secular patterns of administration: (1) mass production in business, which depends primarily upon volume rather than discipline of quality for profit, and (2) promotional advertising techniques, which depend upon the unpersonal media of publicity, correspondence, telephone, and bulletins for results. Churches and denominations have more or less unconsciously fallen into these same patterns by insisting upon the largest congregations possible and relying upon the cleverest techniques of propaganda possible for the recruitment of members. All this moves preaching and the sacraments to the center of the church life. It insulates you as pastor from personal contact with people, making of you an executive and administrator of a corporation rather than a shepherd of a flock.

The end result of this has been that the participation of the individual church members has decreased in proportion to the increase in the size of the congregation. The church members accept less and less personal responsibility for participation in the Kingdom of God. They shift more and more of it to paid workers. They give less and less money to the causes of the church, and the paid workers must depend more and more upon small gifts from larger and larger numbers of people. The early churches were in a reversed position. They were disciplined rather than inclusive in their membership. They emphasized personal discipline rather than promotional values. They exerted influence and gave gifts all out of proportion to their numbers and wealth, because they "first . . . gave themselves."

Consequently, the position taken here is that numbers, whether large or small, are not the criterion for effective church life, pastoral ministry, and Christian outreach. The mere fact of largeness does not predestine a church and its minister to carelessness in the oversight of the flock. In fact, the church may have by reason of its larger numbers a wider variety of services, potential leadership, and professionally trained ministers to perform the work of ministry. Yet, maintaining a disciplined fellowship presupposes face-to-face relationships of people who know each other, regardless of the numerical size of the church.

A large church, however, must have a conception of the ministry as a group effort in which the pastor is not a soloist, assisted and accompanied by others. Rather, the pastor is a more experienced person with more seniority and historical wisdom in the given parish. Such a pastor functions as a quarterback of a working team the members of which stay in close and unbroken communication with each other. A multiple ministry of four pastors served on an equal basis in a certain church—equal in status, salary, preaching, etc. The experiment was a gratifying success in terms of what the ministers learned together about human nature and their interactions with each other. The experiment ended abruptly when the four ministers, it was reported by one of them, were unable to work out their differences at one point. The reasons for this were listed: No two, much less four, ministers are equal! Decisive action should be taken by one member of the team, especially in time of crisis. The decision as to who does this should be based upon experience, seniority, and historical wisdom of the person so designated, and determined by the congregation itself. Plenty of theological reason underlies the importance of taking into account both diversity of talents and proneness to self-regard, pride, and hidden motives in ministers themselves and the importance of realizing that no one member of the team is free but each is bound to Jesus Christ to act in behalf of the church as a whole and not for themselves alone. More positively, I would recommend that ministers who work together on a large church staff build a covenant of communication with one another and consider a part of each week as a time to share their faith and theology in freedom, acceptance, and trust. The objective would be to deepen their relationship with Christ and with one another. Such an approach has possibilities for transmuting the organization of a large church into an organism of fellowship of the staff members with one another with concern for people other than themselves, either individually or corporately.

On the other hand, the mere fact of *smallness* in numbers is not a guarantee of effective pastoral care and personal concern on the part of members for one another, much less for those on the outside. Many small churches expect only that the minister be the "preacher" in the strict sense of the word. The church members will assume that they must handle their personal problems with no regard either for the church or for the minister. The exceptions to this would be socially acceptable problems such as acute physical illness, death, and bereavement. Then, too, a small church can be a mere extension of two or three families and their employees, tenants, or servants. As such, the patriarchs and/or matriarchs of these families exercise the overseeing functions. The pastor serves only in the strictest formal sense as an "overseer of the flock," responsible primarily for preaching at formal services, officiating at funerals, and occasionally performing a wedding ceremony. The family "ingroup" may exclude by silence anyone who is "outside" and almost automatically "rank" those who are on the "inside." A small church, therefore, can become a colony of hell much more easily than it can become a colony of heaven in which the church is a self-transcending fellowship, disciplined by obedience to God. Lewis J. Sherrill has said that in a spiritual community every other dimension of the community—cultural, family, personal—is transcended in that "God is present in this community; . . . the Spirit of God is forthgoing into, and present in, every relationship within the community." (Lewis J. Sherrill, *The Gift of Power,* p. 50.)

Therefore, the conclusions and hypotheses that have been reached here are simply stated: whether the church is large or small numerically, it should be a *disciplined church.* By "disciplined" I mean an *instructed, committed, self-aware, self-transcending, and self-forgetting church.*

These five dimensions of the disciplined church all center upon the first one, *instruction.* The minister and the church place primary value upon *openness and teachability* as a prerequisite for membership in the church. Granted that the person has either been brought up in the church or comes new to the church seeking membership as an adult, the point of discipline at which to begin is the willingness of the person to enter upon a thorough program of instruction and guidance as to the meaning and direction of the individual's own history, calling, and destiny as a Christian.

In the second place, the disciplined church is a *committed* fellowship. Commitment involves an explicit and definite covenant of faith based upon the knowledge of the Biblical account of the revelation of God in Jesus Christ, the witness of the church throughout Christian history, the bond of ethics that holds Christians together with one another and makes their witness distinctive among others, and the kinds of responsibilities that Christians have for caring for distressed and broken persons about them. For example, when the Christian fellowship participates in the joyful celebration of a wedding, this is an act of worship and commitment of two persons to each other and also to

the church. They disavow their previous sins and commit
themselves to Jesus Christ as Lord of the home they are
about to establish. Becoming Christians is not just in order
to keep the marriage together in the same social group. It
is a commitment to the fellowship of faith that will sustain
the couple in the same way of life in Jesus Christ as Lord.
When, by whatever means a church does so, the fellowship baptizes a person, this is done with explicit knowledge, previously arrived at by the individual and observed
by the fellowship of believers, of the meaning of the Christian faith. The church becomes an instrument of confrontation for prospective marital partners, new parents, and
new Christians. These people are confronted as to what
they know of the Christian faith and whether they are
genuinely committed to what they know. The church is a
"company of the committed," as Elton Trueblood has elo-
quently said.

In the third place, the disciplined church is the *self-
aware* fellowship. Members do not worship in isolation
from one another. They are aware of the nature of their
relationships to each other. For example, students in theological seminary classes often attend them as "courses to
be passed," "requirements to be met," and "notes to be
taken." They are often rudely awakened to the fact that
a professor expects them to become aware of the other
members of the class around them, to become acquainted
with them, and actually to learn from them. Only slowly
do they take hold of the awareness that they have a responsibility to one another in the learning process. In turn,
members of their churches are similarly individualistic in
their relation to the church and its minister. Church members are startled to become aware of the church as a powerful, interacting field of varied and exciting human relationships. The disciplined church has a "we consciousness"
in Christ and among the separate members. I saw this
most vividly when I thanked a widow for her ministry to
an unwed mother in New York City, a girl about whom my

wife and I had been concerned and to whom we committed ourselves to minister. This widow had provided a room in her apartment for the girl. When I thanked her, she said: "Oh, I haven't done anything. You see, I am a member of Riverside Church!" She saw herself as a part of the living organism of Riverside. She saw what was done as the ministry of her church. This self-awareness of a group and its members is what Anton Boisen has called "the group whose approval one considers most worthwhile." The disciplined church is the one that has made its approval that which its members consider most worthwhile among persons.

Again, the disciplined church is the *self-transcending* church. This is not just a mutual admiration society. The community judges itself not by itself but transcends itself in the worship of God. It is not religiously shy about mentioning God. On the contrary, the transcendent light of the Father beams brightly upon this fellowship, and the members are aware of both the light of God's love and the shadow they cast when that light falls upon them as a people of God and as individuals within the "we conscious" group. The petty idolatries of family, causes, programs, pressure groups, trivial ambitions, etc., are brought into serious confrontation with the Lordship of Christ. This is the heart of the meaning of worship.

The disciplined church comes to the pinpoint of the caring ministry in its *self-forgetfulness.* The church has to lose its life if it is to keep it. The pastor who represents the church becomes weary, for example, of "badgering" people into coming to church, being more active in the church, giving more money to the church, etc. A pastor must discover deeper and richer reasons for visitation than these. If not, visitation will be a chore to which you as pastor go "like a quarry-slave" and from which you return as if "scourged to [a] dungeon." Sooner or later you forsake visitation of this kind as sheer boredom. Conversely, the perception of the church as an organization which is in the world to be ministered unto provides most of the excuses for those who are opposed to, indifferent to, and suspicious toward the church. Those people are completely disarmed when the church and its ministry forgets itself, ceases to devise ready-made answers for criticisms, and becomes genuinely interested in the persons themselves for their own sakes.

The discipline of the church to outsiders, then, becomes the intention to build a durable, trustworthy relationship to them and their families as persons, quite apart from whether they attend all the meetings, listen to all the sermons, or give money. The church must in this way seek first the Kingdom of God and his righteousness, and all these other things will be added by God. To be self-forgetful in this way requires an act of faith on the part of the church itself, for faith is not just an individual matter. Groups of people have a corporate faith, too. It must be something rooted in God, and not in the human desire to get prospective members in the community before some other denomination—or, God forbid, before some other church of your own denomination—does.

One may rightly ask: Where has this call to instruction, commitment, self-awareness as a people of God, self-transcendence, and self-forgetfulness been tried recently? Gordon Cosby returned from World War II, in which he had served as a paratroop chaplain. In the unrelenting stress of battle, he saw even active church members torn away from their spiritual resources. After the war, he returned to Washington, D.C., and established the Church of the Saviour. The fellowship of this group extends to people of all races, denominations, and creeds or creedlessness. The requirements for membership are stringent. Those who want to join must have completed satisfactorily an extensive program of instruction in Biblical studies, church history, the study of great devotional literature, the arts of caring for distressed people, etc., before they are considered for membership in the church. Members are pledged to tithing and to giving time to specific tasks in the service of the church. Each member belongs to a small group dedicated to vital Christian outreach. The whole exciting story of this church has been written by one of the original members of the staff of the church. With anecdotes, specific program descriptions, and her own gift of the Holy Spirit, Elizabeth O'Connor challenges most of our major presuppositions about church life and the Christian life in her book *The Call to Commitment*. When you read this story, you will be convinced that one positive example of a disciplined church outweighs all the negative evidence.

Finally, these conclusions all imply that the church must have an aggressive missionary strategy for its own community. New churches must be formed in order to localize and personalize the ministry of both the pastor and the churches themselves. Individual churches cannot live on a competitive basis in relation to one another, therefore, but must devise plans for a cooperative missionary strategy in which the total life of the community as a whole is the primary concern of each group. This implies a cooperative rather than an organic relationship, in order that the autonomy of each face-to-face group may be conserved. At the same time the effectiveness of the social outreach of the whole Christian community can be increased.

PART TWO

PASTORAL METHODS

Chapter V

The Pastor's Understanding and Assessment

You as a pastor receive a telephone call, or someone requests a visit, or you are visited at church, at your office, or at your home, or you are simply stopped for a conversation by someone whom you know or who is a stranger. What happens between you and that person that does not ordinarily happen when a person similarly approaches any other friend or any other educated or disciplined professional person? Let me suggest some things that either happen of themselves quite spontaneously or can and must be catalyzed by you as a "teacher come from God."

AN UNDERSTANDING DEVELOPS

You are a person of *understanding.* You are and are becoming what the Old Testament Hebrew calls a *tebunah,* a person of perception, understanding, with powers of discernment. Proverbs 20:5 says it best: "The purpose in a man's mind is like deep water, but a man of understanding will draw it out." Much of people's conversation with you is *not* like deep water. It is "splashy" and superficial, noisy and filled with pleasantries, small talk, and even good-natured banter.

Out of the pitter-patter of this superficial chitchat, however, more profound "soundings" are connected to the trivial matters being discussed. A person tells you that the

wind last night blew over a tree in his yard. Thank goodness (not God) it did not fall on the house! You can either
continue to be superficial by saying: "Luck (not Providence) was on your side." After all, you don't want to be
a pious God-talk person *all* the time. Yet you notice that
the person is quite preoccupied. Therefore, you, *understanding* the undertow of feeling that eddies around the
topic, say: "How long have you had that particular tree in
your yard? Was it a special tree to you?" Then he says: "My
oldest son and I planted it when he was five. You know—
George—he was the one killed in Korea." Then you cease
to be superficial; you say: "Then you lost not only that tree,
but another beloved memory of George. How did you and
your wife find talking about it?" "Not too easy; but we did
anyway." "Good," you say. "Would it mean something to
Mary if I wrote her a note, called her, or dropped by?
What do you think?"

You as a leader of small groups and larger worship congregations, if you have experiences like those I have, become fatigued wearing a fixed smile, and get bored to
distraction hearing the stereotyped, banal things people
say to you after a group meeting or a worship experience.
It is not enough for them to say: "I am glad I came." They
have to say: "I *enjoyed* it." In your fatigue and boredom,
you steel yourself and say to yourself: "If I am a person of
understanding, something more profound is going on
here." Out of the corner of your eye, you notice that a shy
person is waiting until the rest of the crowd leaves. You
make note. Another person in the group wants to ask a
detailed question.

Accurate Empathy and Repentance

As you can readily see, pastoral understanding is human
empathy on its way to being informed, to becoming accurate. Undisciplined empathy is nonchalant about anything
except the feeling for or with another person. Yet senti-

mental good feeling may eventuate in that person feeling that you are a well-intentioned person (at best) but that you really do *not* understand. Therefore, *discipline* your empathy. Submit superficial goodwill and fond good intentions to the tests of accurate information and perception. One of the first barriers to this accuracy is your own "assumptive world," your own preconceptions, your own biases. What are you to do with these?

Edmund Husserl suggests that a "disciplined naiveté" is a royal road to the accurate perception of other people. Disciplined naiveté means the suspending of—at least for the time being—your own values, biases, convictions, etc. This does not mean that you abandon, forsake, or deny these. Rather, you *suspend* them. Husserl calls it "bracketing" them. Your values and mine, when we are listening others, "blurt" into our listening process. Consequently, the other persons feel we have heard *our opinion* of them, but *not* their understanding of themselves. Yet if you *practice* deliberately bracketing or suspending your judgment, you will find *them* giving you *their* judgments of themselves. As you do so, the process of rethinking or *repentance* goes on within them, stimulated by the indwelling power of the Holy Spirit. Pay close attention to how they revise, amend, or even strongly disagree with their own thoughts! This is repentance going on before your very eyes.

The most succinct and clear description of transference and countertransference can be found in Karl Menninger's book *Theory of Psychoanalytic Technique* on pages 78 to 98. Especially helpful is his discussion of the ethics of the counselor in this respect. These phenomena do not occur merely in the relationships of pastors with the persons they are counseling. You will find these phenomena more active in your administrative interactions with members of your official board and their spouses, with church musicians, secretaries, etc. The Christian community has yet to have the courage or wisdom to identify a *positive* ethic for the intimacy between members of the opposite sex who are not married to each other. All we have is a harsh negative ethic interspersed with much subterfuge. Yet, as disciplined pastors we get some real ethical leadership from these words of Sigmund Freud. He speaks of the erotic involvement of a physician with a woman patient. The same could be said of a pastor's involvement with a person of the opposite sex, or of the homosexual relationship as well:

> For the doctor, ethical motives unite with the technical ones to restrain him from giving the patient his love. The aim he has to keep in view is that this woman, whose capacity for love is impaired by infantile fixations, should gain free command over a function which is of such inestimable importance to her that she should not, however, dissipate it in the treatment, but keep it ready for the time when, after her treatment, the demands of real life make themselves felt. . . . She has to learn from him to overcome the pleasure principle, to give up a satisfaction which lies to hand but is socially not acceptable, in favour of a more distant one, which is perhaps altogether uncertain, but which is both psychologically and socially unimpeachable. (Sigmund Freud, Papers on Technique (1911–1915 [1914]), "Observations on Transference—Love" (Further Recommendations on the Technique of Psycho-Analysis III) (1915 [1914]), *The Standard Edition of the Complete Psychological Works of Sigmund Freud,* Vol. XII (1911–1913), tr. and ed. by James Strachey, pp. 169–170)

The main issue at stake is that your ordination to bear witness to the release from bondage by Jesus Christ takes precedence over all other passions. The critical question for you and me is: How passionately guardful and devoted concerning our ordination are we?

Nonpossessive Warmth and Personal Commitment

Repenting persons need to be encouraged and enhanced by your provision of a nonpossessive, nonadoptive warmth in your relationship to them. You can be ever so attentive to people, yet they do not feel you are an understanding person. Nonverbal cues of being in a hurry, being preoccupied, simply "doing what you are being paid to do," being a spokesperson for your church or other agency, etc., speak volumes. These persons struggle to "get through to you," become more and more demanding and shrill, and leave all the more frustrated. All they want to do is "get out of there."

If the person feels *welcome,* is "given hospitality," and if what the person says is taken seriously, you have begun to show warmth. It may be sometime before the person shows warmth to you. Yet it appears more quickly than you ordinarily expect it. Psychotherapists often name the warmth "the transference," by which they mean that these persons unwittingly transfer to you the affection or the hostility they had for their parents or siblings in an earlier time. They react sometimes strangely and both you and they are bothered by it. Similarly, you "countertransfer" feelings from your family of origin to them. Both you and they interact accordingly.

A "warm" relationship, in these senses, means two things. Warm can mean positive, loving, and even sexual feelings. In the Bible, this is true. (See I Kings 1:1–4.) Or warm can mean anger, wrath, etc. This is true in the Bible also. (See I Kings 18:36–40.) Yet warmth has another dimension than affection or anger. It also can mean *care,* i.e., that this person matters to you; you care what happens to the person. You are committed to the person's well-being, best interests, and personal worthfulness. You are *steadfast* in your devotion to the person. Consequently, you are related to the person as a person and not using the person as a means to your ends.

All this adds up to your understanding these persons. Your best pastoral intentions are to form and maintain a durable relationship that can absorb anger, frustration, and disappointment. You successfully resist erotic or financial exploitation. You nurture mutuality, which in turn

generates hope, when other relationships fall by the way-
side. These relationships participate in the Eternal. They
are the stuff of which the Kingdom of Heaven is made.
They may move in time without much verbal chatter
about God or Christ, the church, or the Holy Spirit. However, when such specific God consciousness comes to pass
in the fullness of time, the relationship itself is the exegesis, the witness, the concrete instance of what God is about
in the world, why Jesus Christ died and was buried and
was resurrected in order to effect, and how the church
thrives by the power of the Spirit through good report and
evil report now in our time.

What I describe here as "the clarification of the understanding of your relationship" is spoken of in much counseling literature as "contracting" with the person. I appreciate the meaning but find that the word "contracting" is either misunderstood, passively resisted,
or outrightly rejected by many religiously oriented people. A much more useful word with them is "covenant-
ing," "forming a covenant," etc. This is a Biblical and
theological concept of great depth, richness, and persuasion. Consequently, I suggest that you as a pastor use this
term to describe your clarification of your relationship to
your counselee.

The pastoral understanding, then, is the context for pastoral diagnosis and treatment of persons as individuals,
groups, or families. You may be working with people who
are being served by physicians, lawyers, nurses, social
workers, psychologists, teachers, and persons from a variety of other disciplines. One or more of them may be a
Christian, a devout Jew, a Hindu, etc. Many of them may
have a reverence and respect for the person that puts a
careless, balky, and uncommitted pastor to shame before
God. However, if you have read this book this far, *you* are
not that kind of pastor. You, therefore, will always be
loathe to confuse your responsibility for a *pastoral* under-

standing of the person with anything that others of these professions may be doing. You are, as Paul said in Gal. 6:4, putting to the test your own work. Then you will have reason to boast in your own work and not in either a sense of intimidation or arrogance in relation to the work of others.

PASTORAL ASSESSMENT OR DIAGNOSIS

The apostle Paul prayed: "And it is my prayer that your love may abound more and more, with knowledge and all discernment" (Phil. 1:9). The kind of relationship and understanding we have just been discussing must grow and abound in more knowledge and more discernment. As Isaiah says, without discernment we cannot expect to enter into the compassion of the Lord for people, nor expect to enjoy the Lord's favor (Isa. 27:11). The word *discernment* is rarely mentioned as a central responsibility of the pastor. Please take a close look at its New Testament meaning with me. Discernment is the process of proving by testing, of determining what is essential. When you discern something, you put it to the test and examine it. This process is diagnostic in nature. It is the same experience in a medical setting in which a person goes through some tests to verify health or its absence.

This is the same responsibility of the pastor of "testing the spirits" urged in I John 4:1. A command to *disbelief* precedes it: "Beloved, do not believe every spirit." The most stultifying stereotype of you as a pastor is that you are a naive, gullible do-gooder who is a soft touch for every manipulator that comes along. Rarely is a skeptical spirit commended, even by your most cynical counterparts in the ministry. However, this passage of Scripture does so. It says that many false prophets have gone out into the world. You are to be as wise as serpents and as harmless as doves. What a paradox! This section of this chapter, therefore, aims to suggest some specifics in how you can realistically appraise, assess, or diagnose the *spiritual* condition of those to whom you are pastor. Your discernment grows as you do so. May this discernment result in a growth of your compassion, an improvement of the accuracy of your empathy, and a mellowing and maturing of your judgment in your human ministries in the name of Jesus Christ. May you avoid the fate of becoming a cynic, a manipulator, or a crass secularist in the process.

The Station in Life

Your parishioner has a certain place or station in life. You too have a station in life. The two of you "pause for station identification." The person to whom you minister has a right to know who you think you are in relation to that person. If the person doesn't know your name, that you are a pastor, and where you work, then *tell* the person what *your* station in life is with as little anxiety and fanfare as possible. When you are traveling or are on vacation, your privacy is valuable to you and it is not necessary to do this. However, if you wish to *be* a pastor to someone, then tell that person who you are. People's memories are poorest in remembering names. Tactfully use your personal name more than once in a conversation. If the person is ill and in a hospital, indicate more than once that you are a pastor so that the person does not confuse you with many other strangers who visit at the bedside.

The Life-Support System

Your preliminary diagnosis of the life needs of a person begins—correspondingly—with a gentle inquiry into *the person's station in life.* What is the person's name? Where does the person live? How long has the person lived there? Who are the other members of the family and who lives in the household? What is the person's work and that of those the person loves? *Has the person lost anyone close:* e.g., Has someone (*a*) grown up and left the home; (*b*) gotten married and moved out; (*c*) gone to college, into the military, etc.; (*d*) moved to a nursing home, as in the case of the handicapped or elderly; or (*e*) died? Who is left? Thus you get an overview of the immediate and extended family support system. As well, you learn whom the person has lost and is bereaving.

The life-support system extends. The church relationship of the person is of importance to you, but you are interested in its importance to the person. A studied nonchalance on your part is needed. What is the person's church connection and the *history* of the relationship? Have there been changes along the way and how routine or dramatic were these changes? Who have been influential pastors, Sunday school teachers, youth leaders, military chaplains, college youth ministers, etc., in the person's life? Have there been alienating, hurting experiences that disenchanted the person? Was the person at any time involved in a paid religious vocation and is the person still involved? Has the person a significant religious leader now, or is the person isolated, alone, a "lost sheep of the house of Israel"?

Your primary assessment concern is not to badger the person into going to church or into a forced, premature religious commitment. You may be, in doing so, "sewing a new piece of cloth on an old garment" that is a poor foundation for it. You may alienate the person further. The religious assessment has only well begun.

The Present Plight of the Person

Your assessment of the immediate situation of the person to whom you are ministering consists of three things: an inspection of the events at hand, a clarification of the mutual expectations you and the person have of each other, and a commitment to a mutually agreed upon plan of action or treatment of the situation. You do three things well:

1. Inspect
2. Clarify
3. Commit

Your major pastoral calamities, when examined closely after the fact, usually can be traced to your having made unwise or impossible commitments to people without having inspected the facts or clarified your relationship. You probably promised a lot of things you neither had to give nor could have wisely done in any event.

The Inspection

A careful inspection of many pastoral requests is usually done initially by telephone, although this is by no means always true. Several demands are made of you at the outset. "I need to see you as quickly as possible!" Or, "I would like to set up an appointment with you tomorrow when I can come to see you." Or, "Can you come over here to our house right away? We need you badly." Or, "Do you mind if I stop by your house or office in about an hour?" Etc.

You note that none of these requests tell you *what* the persons are eager, in a hurry, upset, or under pressure about. They have an *agenda,* but they do not share it with you. Some clarification is needed. Therefore, you slow the process down as gently and tactfully as possible. Then you begin a detailed inspection of what is happening.

You may ask: "Before we make a plan, please tell me what is happening to you and then I can make a better plan with you." Or, "What kind of situation are you in there? Are you able to talk with me without others hearing you or do you mind their hearing you?" Or, "Can you give me some idea of what is on your mind so that in the meantime I can be thinking and praying about our visit together?'"

Another factor inheres in the inspection of the situation. What is *your* responsibility for seeing *these* persons? Are they members of your church? Are they members of the church of another pastor? Are they not members of any church at all? Are they residents in your community? Are they transients? In the privacy of your own mind, you need to ask yourself: "Am *I* the person who can best meet their needs or do I know 'just the person' who can do so better than I can?" Further, you need to ask yourself: "What kinds of unrealistic promises am I being prone to make here and can I indeed fulfill those promises?" Ordinarily, furthermore, you as a conscientious pastor are likely to try too hard, do too much, and substitute your motivation for theirs. Jesus often asked those whom he helped to exert an act of faith of their own: "Take up your bed and walk!" "Go show yourself to the priest." "Stretch forth your hand." "Go bring your husband here." Do such yourself.

You know enough about the situation now and are therefore able to clarify your relationship to the person and to make sensible promises. In the process you have quietly and steadily reduced the person's shock, panic, and hysteria. You are called and consecrated to bring order out of the person's chaos through the discipline of your inquiry. Several options are now available to you to bring the person's situation into a controlled pastoral care situation. The options turn around three major factors:

1. *Time.* You should have enough knowledge to know whether you are dealing with an emergency or a situation that has been and will be in progress for some time. If the person immediately tells you that a child has been hit by a car and the parents are distraught, you say little more except that you are on the way and need directions as to where the event has taken place. In situations like this, as

my philosophy professor in college said, "you go twice when you go immediately." Pastors in a community can serve better in emergencies if they join with the local hospital emergency departments, provide "on call" service in return for disciplined workshops in such things as first aid, coronary pulmonary resuscitation, and disaster strategy sessions.

However, the majority of situations you face as a pastor are *not* emergencies. They only seem to be to the panicked, hysterical people who are alarmed. Marriage conflicts are one of the most recurrent examples. When you make a detailed inquiry you will find that many of these persons are actually appealing for a thoroughly disciplined telephone conversation with you. Fifteen to thirty minutes on the telephone may—for the time being—be what is needed. In any event, you can accurately assess the need for a longer conversation. I do not advise telephone conversations of much more than fifteen minutes unless the person's distance from you—it may be long distance—or a physical handicap, etc., objectively requires it. In other instances I prefer to make an appointment for a home visit, an office visit, or a hospital visit. More *time* requires different *space*.

2. *Place and Initiative.* The place of meeting has embedded within it the factor of initiative. Where you meet a person has a high symbolic value. For example, for you to meet an estranged wife at a restaurant for lunch to converse with her about her husband's suspicion of her having an extramarital affair would seem to be the height of foolishness on your part as a pastor. However, it has happened! To the contrary, to meet her at your place of worship in a room prearranged and at a time when a secretary, a trusted lay leader, or your spouse is in the building and aware of what is happening is the height of wisdom and care. You stabilize her life situation by such considerateness. The Lord Jesus Christ seemed in his earthly ministry to *assume*

that we are sinners and to have much patience with our frailties. However, even his infinite patience was taxed when men and women played the fool!

The wisdom with which you engineer the timing and placing of your pastoral conversations is a way of being thoughtful and considerate of people. It symbolizes your dedication to them. Expecting them to come to you at your place gives you a chance to return some of their hospitality to you. It gives you control over the interruptions, the telephone, and the time of conclusion of your conversation. More strictly, it is one way of testing their real desire to do something about their own plight and of stimulating such motivation all the more.

Yet there are people who are depressed, reproaching themselves for their assumed worthlessness, humble in their poverty in this world's goods, or angry and at total odds with the people of God. A full-scale and even unannounced visit to them may be the dramatic breakthrough that has long been needed.

3. *Identity.* Another subtle factor inheres in the demands laid upon you that call for assessment: *Who are you to these people anyway?* Are you just another curious onlooker in their lives? Are you a neighbor *no different from any other neighbor?* Are you a sort of social worker who manages, takes charge, makes contacts with resource people, and is supportive and even psychotherapeutic? Are you an educated person who "has studied psychology" and can help them "figure out" the crazy things going on around them? *Just who are you anyway?*

Do not leave this to chance. Take hold of the situation and make it clear that you are *a pastor,* that all of you are in this together but none of you is alone. God is with you and with all of you together. You are searching together for God's help and guidance. There is a way through it and you are going to help them find it. Now, if you are a *woman* pastor, you will be doubly tempted to be a friend, an older sister, a mothering one, an advocate for the rights of the oppressed women in the situation. Some chauvinist man or chauvinist woman may seek to write you off. Do not let this deter you. Let them know that you are there in the name and power of God and not to debate such issues when they need so many other ministries more. Ask them to debate that with you later when things are not so intense and their needs for a caring Christian are not so pressing. Just remember that men who are pastors don't handle these situations with much ease, either!

FACTORS IN THE PASTORAL DIAGNOSIS

Let us assume now that your parishioner, your church member, your counselee, or—as an esteemed physician colleague calls the pastor's people—your supplicant is with you in a discreet and secure place of privacy. Let us assume that a considerable degree of distress or desperation besets the person.

You are concerned about the *whole* being of the person, not just the religious life. However, the *center* of your concern is the religious life. All else is integral to this, but this is the *raison d'être* of your relationship. Why? Because if you leave this unattended, you cannot expect other people to take it seriously. This you cannot with integrity refer to others. Your concern, though, is that the spiritual inquiry into the person's life before God be natural and not contrived, personal and caring and not mechanical and freighted with propaganda for this or that institution, however dearly you hold that institution. You are *not,* as Paul says, a huckster or peddler of religion. You have nothing to sell or buy. You are a prophet in the heritage of Isaiah. You can say:

> Ho, every one who thirsts,
>   come to the waters;
> and he who has no money,
>   come, buy and eat!

Come, buy wine and milk
without money and without price.
(Isa. 55:1)

Consequently, *your* conversation links even the trivial
chitchat about a cup of cold water to profoundly interpersonal problems and to the sources of divine nourishment
and hydration of their lives by the living God. How does
this happen? Can it be repeated in more than one instance?

Contributions to the actual mechanics of your own pastoral appraisal of persons whom you serve have been
made by Edgar Draper, M.D. He is a psychiatrist who also
has his degree in theology. (Edgar Draper, M.D., et al.,
"On the Diagnostic Value of Religious Ideation," *Archives
of General Psychiatry,* Sept. 1965, pp. 202–207.) Also,
Paul Pruyser, a clinical psychologist and author of *A Dynamic Psychology of Religion,* has made a lasting contribution in his book *The Minister as Diagnostician.* My own
discussion of this is found in my book *The Religious Care
of the Psychiatric Patient.* For our purposes here I want
to summarize and, it is hoped, enlarge upon and enrich
further these contributions. However, for the last two
decades of this century, I hope these patternings of pastoral relationships will deepen, if not replace, the popular
psychologies that enamor many pastoral counselors today.

The work of Edgar Draper started with a thirteen-ques-
tion interview schedule. These are open-ended questions
and can be answered in an individual interview or in written form, or they can be used as the basis of a group
discussion. You do best to submit them to memory without
too much regard for the order in which they appear. Then
let them emerge in your natural conversation as the "heat
of the moment hatches them." Be easy. Be natural about
it. With some people, though, you may find that they
rather enjoy going through the interview outline quite
formally. Psychiatric patients find its familiar language a
refreshing diversion from all the medical language that is

foreign to them. Contrary to even your apprehensions, they do not ordinarily respond to it as an authoritarian inquisition. However, it does give specific religious substance and center to your conversation and it implements the body of knowledge you feel most informed and secure in using.

Some of my esteemed colleagues who spend their full time in what they describe as pastoral psychotherapy are likely to misunderstand and even misrepresent me at this point for narrowing pastoral counseling to *only* religious subject matter. Please do not project that misunderstanding into what I am suggesting. Rather, I am saying that if you enter people's lives through the *religious* avenues that Draper suggests, the wide experience of many of us who use this approach assures you and them that they will raise all sorts of other issues about their families, their intimate sexual lives, their conflicts and burdens about their work, their hallucinatory and/or delusional formations, their fears and/or intentions to divorce their mates, their malpractices in their businesses or professions, their fear of impending death, their alienation from the church, and all the thousand mortal ills to which the flesh is heir.

Yet they do the things *in the context* of your firm identity as a Christian pastor who is informed about the ethical and religious life of persons. They do have few fuzzy ideas as to who you are unless you yourself are dodging the issues of your pastoral identity.

Draper's inventory focuses on the intimate personal, rather than the institutional, aspects of religious living. The questions are as follows:

1. What is your earliest memory of a religious experience or belief?
2. What is your favorite Bible story? Why?
3. What is your favorite Bible verse? Why?
4. Who is your favorite Bible character? Why?
5. What does prayer mean to you? If you pray, what do you pray about?

6. A. What does religion mean to you?
   B. How does God function in your personal life?
7. A. In what way is God meaningful to other people besides yourself?
   B. How is God meaningful to your father or mother?
8. What religious idea or concept is most important to you now?
9. What is the most religious act one can perform?
10. What do you consider the greatest sin one could commit?
11. What do you think of evil in the world?
12. What are your ideas of an afterlife?
13. If God could grant you any three wishes, what would they be?
    (Draper, "On the Diagnostic Value of Religious Ideation," p. 203)

My own clinical application of Draper's projective questions suggests several important areas they do not cover. For example, Martin Luther and Dietrich Bonhoeffer would put *temptation,* or *Anfechtung,* as an important issue for exploration. It could be phrased this way:

"In the face of the frustrations, injustices, and hurts you have felt, what are the most persistent, recurring temptations you struggle with?"

People tend to feel more pain and suffering with temptations than with sins they have committed. They feel guiltier about them. Their despair and hopelessness is more evident here. As Martin Luther says, "Without temptation *(Anfechtung)* no man can rightly understand the Holy Scriptures or know what the fear and love of God is all about. In fact, without *Anfechtung,* one does not really know what the spiritual life is." (C. Warren Hovland, *"Anfechtung* in Luther's Biblical Exegesis," in *Reformation Studies* [Essays in Honor of Roland H. Bainton], ed. by Franklin H. Littell, p. 46.)

Furthermore, I find that people's experiences of influence by religious leaders is not covered in Draper's inventory. Therefore, I suggest a question like this:

"Who has been the most influential religious leader, teacher, or friend in your life?"

This often opens up stories of strong people who may still be accessible to them in their times of stress. People who have let them down, alienated themselves from them, and may be continuing harassments to them also come to the fore in the conversation. You begin to learn what to avoid, nurture, and correct in your own relationship. Bear in mind that you are relating to these persons as a Christian. They form, change, and/or reform their understanding of the Christian ministry in the course of your dialogue. The discipline of being an example, of teaching by precept *and* example, will not be abrogated or repealed in the twenty-first century; it can only be ignored and neglected. But you as a faithful pastor will not be one of those who do so.

Another lasting contribution to the diagnostic assessment of a pastoral situation has been made by Paul Pruyser of The Menninger Clinic. He also insists that you as a pastor do your work with individuals, families, and groups on the basis of distinctly theological and pastoral "ordering principles," not psychological, medical, psychiatric, or sociological ones. These are data in which you have been educated. As my colleague Curtis Barrett, Ph.D., also a clinical psychologist, says: "We should *unabashedly* formulate on the basis of whatever organized body of knowledge we are said by credentials to have mastered." He perceives a pastor as a "man of understanding" who has mastered theology, ethics, Biblical knowledge, and the historical liturgy and confessional practice of Christendom. He would also heartily affirm those women who have done so and are "women of understanding." Our ordinations are our primary certifications to this effect. Paul Pruyser, then, would want us to know how to translate these languages, but they should be our native tongue.

Thus, when you as a pastor present an assessment or a diagnosis, as Pruyser says, it should be readily recognizable by theologians and other pastors. Yet these conclusions should be based upon *observed* behaviors and eyewitness accounts of people themselves. They are not surmises, fantasies you have imagined, or farfetched theories you have spun.

If they are thus "empirical differentiations," they will make sense both to you and your parishioner, church member, counselee, supplicant, etc., as you choose to identify them. For an outsider, they will yield a vivid picture of what the person is really like and generate concrete suggestions as to strategies for helping the person and those who care about the person.

With this background, Pruyser suggests the "stuff" of which a genuinely pastoral conversation and assessment is composed. I commend his seven steps of inquiry to you with a whole heart, because I find them dramatic issues that are the intimate personal concerns of all manner of people, both in and out of the church, rich and poor, educated and ignorant, articulate and inarticulate. Let me present Pruyser's sevenfold dimensions of the pastoral diagnostic process. He suggests that you have these in the back of your mind and bring them into your pastoral conversations:

1. Explore the person's awareness of the *Holy.*
   (As background study, read Rudolf Otto's *The Idea of the Holy;* Oxford University Press, 1958.)
2. Explore the person's awareness of *Providence.*
   (For an intimate exploration of this, read Myron Madden's *The Power to Bless;* Broadman Press, 1979.)
3. Search with the person the person's subjective experience of *faith.*
   (Enrich your own appreciation of faith by reading Lewis J. Sherrill's book *The Struggle of the Soul;* Macmillan Co., 1951.)
4. Probe the person's sense of *grace* or *gratefulness.*

(Examine David Roberts' classic discussion of grace in his book *Psychotherapy and a Christian View of Man;* Charles Scribner's Sons, 1950.)

5. Meditate with the person about times of *repenting* that the person may have been through.

(You will find your own perspective of repentance enriched if you read William Barclay's *Turning to God: A Study of Conversion in the Book of Acts and Today;* Westminster Press, 1964; and article on "Metanoia" in *The Theological Dictionary of the New Testament,* Vol. 4, ed. by Gerhard Kittel; Wm. B. Eerdmans Publishing Co., 1967, pp. 975–1008. An older, yet very helpful volume is William Douglas Chamberlain's *The Meaning of Repentance;* Westminster Press, 1943.)

6. Get in touch with the person's sense of *communion.*

(For the dark side of this need, read Clark Moustakas' book, *Loneliness;* Prentice-Hall, 1961.)

7. Explore the person's sense of *vocation.*

(How does the person see his or her life "turning out to be"? What are the main things that "keep the person going"? Elizabeth O'Connor's book *The Call to Commitment* [Harper & Row, 1976] is excellent for enriching your concern for the person's reasons for living.)

You may rightly wonder *why* in relation to this diagnostic design suggested by Pruyser I have urged you to read such books as those listed here. I have learned a particular way of studying the experience of my counselees from watching my physician colleagues do their work. When a patient presents a particular syndrome of suffering to them, they will consult their basic texts, articles, and recorded experiments about the particular problems of their patients. I have taken up the habit myself and find it a way of continuing my own education.

Then, too, in teaching ministers in the care of severely disturbed individuals and families, I have noticed that they tend to "discount" at best and discard at worst all the results of their theological education. My objective, therefore, is to urge you to "reprocess" all you learned in the classroom through constantly rescrutinizing it in the light of the questions and dilemmas presented to you by people you serve.

As you can see, I am suggesting that you develop an understanding relationship with the person whom you are seeking to help and that you then follow Draper's and Pruyser's patterns of spiritual inquiry. You will be astonished at the simplicity and ease with which most people will let you come to know them in depth as you do this.

Over behind the positive religious themes that Pruyser suggests is the "dark side" of the themes. The sense of the Holy has its darker counterpart in the sense of the devil, the uncanny, the eerie, and the weird. The awareness of Providence is beleaguered with the feeling of fate, bad luck, Kismet, or being cursed. The experience of faith is stalemated by the loss of courage, the fretfulness of fear and anxiety. The experience of grace is set over against legalism, perfectionism, and compulsive guilt. Repenting experiences are frustrated by a spirit of unforgiveness and hardness of heart. Loneliness is a blight that militates against the sense of communion. Laziness will affect and outwit the sense of vocation when fine resolve and fantasy of total success keep a person from risking the adventure of the high calling of God.

By no means does Pruyser's pattern assume a Pollyanna view of the human condition. Rather, you are a harbinger of hope and are committed to the power of the gospel to reach into the possessive grasp of these dark portents of the human heart and to call out the healing responses that will usher the person into a pathway to redemption from destruction, comradeship with other fellow strugglers in the Christian faith, and full access to the power of God in Jesus Christ through the Holy Spirit. (Pruyser, *The Minister as Diagnostician.*)

WHAT OF THE BEHAVIORAL SCIENCES?

I have presented to you a distinctly *pastoral* and *religious* understanding of your relationships to persons you seek to help. You have a right to ask me: "What of the diagnoses and treatment plans of other professional people among the behavioral scientists?" As a professor of psychiatry and behavioral sciences, let me answer you. You will find that a conversation based on the above diagnostic pattern, held with a person who has been examined and treated by a therapeutic team, reveals dynamics of personal struggle that their instruments do not present. Your data will be easily assimilable by them into a *distinctly human* view of the client, patient, counselee, or whatever they call this person.

Furthermore, you will find that the language you use is assimilable into *their* understanding, too. It is religious language, but it is not religious "ingroup" language. It is easily translated into a commonsense, "bread-and-butter," understanding of personal faith. It avoids the clanging of the conflict-ridden language of religious controversy. For example, note that such terms as "millennialism," "liberalism," "higher criticism," "infallibility," "excommunication," etc., do not appear.

One important ingredient is missing, however, as far as the behavioral sciences of social work, psychology, psychiatry, and other medical specialties are concerned. Little or nothing appears in these formats to implement the historical and sociological knowledge of religious subcultures such as denominations, belief systems, sectarian movements, cults, and popular television and radio forms of religious entertainment and propaganda.

These affect people's behavior profoundly and these effects appear in the hospital rooms, offices, and clinics of the behavioral scientists. They, in many instances, have specific health teachings, such as the excellent health laws of the Seventh-day Adventists about nicotine, alcohol, cholesterol, etc. These result in less obesity, lung cancer, heart disorder, and alcoholism in their population. Jehovah's Witnesses' attitudes about blood transfusions have resulted in new techniques of heart surgery without blood transfusions. Many religious groups are exploring the power of their faith to create communities that reduce unemployment, divorce, delinquency, and welfare addiction.

In my book *The Religious Care of the Psychiatric Patient* I have sought to add this sociocultural dimension to the diagnostic and therapeutic appraisal of a distinctly pastoral kind. In addition to this reference, you as an active pastor will sharpen your assessment acumen by taking courses in American religious history. Reading Sydney Ahlstrom's *A Religious History of the American People* will be a tonic, an eye-opener, and a sermon starter for you. If you are a student in a seminary and hope to be a *pastoral* counselor, get with it! Learn as much about American religious denominations, sects, cults, and movements as your curriculum will provide.

In a day of experts and competence, remember you are the expert on religion, the competent counselor whose love is growing in all manner of knowledge and perception.

One more perspective is imperative in your demeanor throughout the whole process I have described: Are you there to fix blame? Are you rushing in where Jesus refused to tread to become a "judge or divider" over people? Don't do it! I think this is a better way: Hold in your care of families a multilateral rather than a unilateral partiality. This means that you avoid the "blame frame" of families in conflict as they seek to fix blame upon each other or to "gang up" and scapegoat *one* member of the family. Instead of this unilateral partiality, use a multilateral partiality in which you seek to be accurately empathic of *each* member. No one is to blame; everybody is responsible. Thus, the "black sheep" or the "identifiable patient" cannot so preoccupy your attention that other members of the family will go unattended.

Chapter VI

The Levels of Pastoral Care

Christian pastors care for people on many different levels of relationship. At one and the same time, you may be the personal friend, next-door neighbor, pastor-preacher, pastor-counselor, and golf or fishing companion of the person to whom you minister. Furthermore, you do not, unless you are a pastor in an unusually large city, spend much time with people whom you never see again after finishing a series of three or four interviews. You are related to the same persons over a period of years, during which your relationship moves from one level of formality and informality to another and back again, depending upon the variety of crises endured.

These are the facts that make it unwise for you to carry over *in toto* the office techniques of professional counselors of any kind. It is true that hospital chaplains, professors of pastoral psychology in seminaries, specialist pastors in pastoral counseling centers, and other persons do much very formal counseling. Some exceptionally large churches have placed clinically trained pastors on their staffs to do mostly formal counseling of people who are referred to them. Churches, associations of churches, and councils of churches have developed counseling services in which exceptionally well trained ministers have a full-time responsibility as counselors. They are increasing rapidly. Every pastor needs to know what to do when called upon for more complex and detailed pastoral counseling which might be characterized as one of the "nonmedical forms of psychotherapy." At the time of this writing there are well over two hundred different kinds of psychotherapy. Pastoral counseling, in this book, refers to the multiple-interview counseling done by a parish pastor, a teacher in a college or seminary, a service chaplain, etc., i.e., a *generalist.* Pastoral psychotherapy refers to specialized and controlled therapy done by exception rather than the rule in the pastorate. Today this is a highly disciplined subspeciality of the ministry. These ministers are thoroughly educated in both theology and psychotherapy. They have paid the price in time, energy, money, and personal discipline to do so. They are competent in nonmedical forms of psychotherapy. An increasing number of them are educated, ordained, and certified in medicine. Their consecration must be incorporated into any full-fledged understanding of the ministry of the gospel. I myself am one of these. However, my primary commitment in counseling, teaching, and writing is to equip *generalist,* nonspecialized pastors to do well their daily care of the flock of God. Yet, at the Ph.D. levels of my work, I seek to equip a pastor to be either a generalist or a specialist or both. Nor do I as a specialist feel that the intrinsic tasks of preaching, leading public worship, performing weddings, conducting funerals, and consistent pastoral visitation in homes should ever be deleted from even the specialist's day's work.

Furthermore, the research findings, the proven data base, and some of the demonstrated methods of the specialist minister go far in making the work of the generalist pastor more skillful and application of the gospel more prescriptively exact and specific. A bibliography of such materials is at the end of this book for your reference.

One basic principle, however, operates in the work of both the pastor and the pastoral psychotherapy specialist. One of the major difficulties underlying the problems of both parishioners and patients is the individual's inability to establish and maintain durable relationships with significant people. Whether it is a physician suggesting longer-term, multiple-interview psychotherapy, a full-time pastoral counselor initiating a formal, multiple-interview kind of counseling, or the generalist pastor seeking to get this person to be a faithful, regular churchgoer, the issue tends to stand or fall on the individual's ability and willingness to link a covenant with a significant person and carry through with it on a sustained basis over a period of time.

You, therefore, do best to study and to evaluate the specific level on which you have access to personal encounter with people to whom you are related in a helpful way. On what basis *is* this person able to sustain a durable relationship? On that level you can begin work where you find yourself. You must be flexible enough to adapt yourself to a person on *that level of relationship at which you can best serve the person.* When you do this, you discover several different levels on which individuals react to you as another human being to whom they can reveal themselves. You will also find different levels of the individuals' personal insight into their own problems and willingness to do something about them before God. In this respect, you have more than one kind of relationship on which to meet people on different levels of formality, informality, and combined formal and informal relationships. Your major discipline is keeping the relationship clarified and unconfused in both your own and the parishioner's mind.

These areas of action may be called *the levels of pastoral care.* Another way of describing them would be to call these levels *types of pastoral care.* I prefer to call them levels for two reasons. First, these levels tend to appear in any given relationship of pastoral care in something of the order in which they are to be described in the following pages. Therefore, the character of a relationship may change perceptibly within the scope of a single hour or from one conference to another with the same person.

Secondly, the existential psychologists have been sufficiently convincing that you can learn from them. A knowledge of the more subtle and complex areas of personality reveals that the most important forces that determine behavior are quite often out of the field of the clear level of awareness of a person. In the pastoral relationship, as it grows with time and acquaintance, "deep calleth unto deep," and "in the hidden part" people are made to know wisdom. Thus the pastoral bond is more than a mere "telling" of things by one person to another. It is the provocation of wisdom through an especial relationship. This is essentially a Hebrew concept in which a distinction is drawn between the Hebrew word that means "to tell" in the sense that one would be taught from reading a book, and another word that means "to cause to know," in the sense in which one comes to realize something by immediate, firsthand experience. It is something of what the men of the Samaritan village meant when they said, "It is no longer because of your words that we believe, for we have heard for ourselves, and we know that this is indeed the Savior of the world" (John 4:42).

Furthermore, you might use the working model of personality that is used by what has come to be known as "phenomenological psychology." These "levels of pastoral care" represent the different contexts or "frames of reference" in which a pastor encounters fellow human beings. At one time the field of relationships focuses most meaningfully in these varying identities of the minister—as a friend, comforter, priestly confessor, teacher, and counselor. These are different foci for the caring identity of the pastor in the light of the parishioner's frame of reference. (See Donald Snygg and Arthur Combs, *Individual Behavior.*) However, the symbolism of "levels" of pastoral care still presents to this author the most effective basis for describing the vitality of pastoral relationships, although the phenomenological approach yields what Seward Hiltner calls a "perspective" of human relationships too important to be ignored, depreciated, or left unused as a way of thinking.

Christian experience, when seen from the vantage point of levels of feeling relationships, moves from hearsay *about* Christ to the level of personal acquaintance *with* Christ and personal dependence *upon* Christ, to the level of learning *from* Christ, to the level of confession *to* Christ, to the level of healing *by* Christ, to the level of reconciliation *with* Christ, and finally achieves spiritual usefulness on the level of comradeship *alongside* Christ to witness *for* Christ.

You, as an "ambassador for Christ" by your own spiritual maturity, must at least be on your way to comradeship with and witnessing for Christ. As you do this and people seek your personal counsel by reason of your accurate representation of Christ, you work "on behalf of Christ." Then, you work in accord with the example of Christ and the nature of Christian experience on *five different levels of pastoral care* of people in terms of their movement toward spiritual maturity. These levels are: the level of friendship, the level of comfort, the level of confession, the level of teaching, and the level of counseling and psychotherapy. On every level you are a witness to the good news of the grace of God in Christ. Your ultimate objective is the development of a co-worker in the Kingdom of God. You as a pastor are not primarily committed to symptom removal or even health for health's sake. You are concerned with the long-range vocation of the person and the removal of the person's impediments to genuinely caring for and ministering to other people.

THE LEVEL OF FRIENDSHIP

If you and I are worth our salt as pastors, we rely on basic friendship as the very soil of our relationships with people. However, friendship is more than merely having people's goodwill at heart in your ministry. For people whom you serve are not always friends with each other. They are at odds with each other often. Many people demand of you that if you are their friend, you *must* be their enemies' enemy. Woodrow Wilson, in a speech made on April 20, 1915, said: "The test of friendship is not more sympathy with one side or the other, but getting ready to help both sides when the struggle is over." We are indeed called to be peacemakers, ministers of reconciliation, always searching to realize that we are children of God.

If you are a Protestant pastor, you most aptly come to your people in the role of friend. The term "brother," which many church people use for their minister, reflects the democratic friendship they have for one who is "first among equals." You mingle as a friend and neighbor with the people whom you serve. You go to wedding gatherings, all-day meetings, young people's social gatherings, and many kinds of men's and women's social clubs. However, as we have seen earlier, your people do not expect this of you as often as you think. Your being "given to hospitality" is an asset to you. It is soon sensed if you are hard to get to know and do not mingle well with people.

On social occasions, timid, isolated, and withdrawn persons can come to know you as a minister. Their confidence in you can be established so that they will later say, "It was at the 4-H cattle show when you stopped and said hello that I decided that if I ever got courage to tell this to anybody, you would be the kind of person I could talk with." This establishment of rapport is the gracious making of yourself accessible to people, rather than the compulsive falling over yourself to "win friends and influence people." This latter attitude springs more from the fear of not being approved by others than it does from an easy sense of affection for people for their own sakes. Through your ministry of casual friendship, you avoid the fate of being seen as *only* a person who appears at crises. Pastors who during wars delivered telegrams advising their members that a relative had been killed or was missing in action know that the minister can be a sign of bad news. Fortunately, chaplains and other ministers do not do this now, but are called in later. If you participate in the simple joys of life, you offset the perspective of a minister as a bearer of bad tidings.

The ministry of friendship is the indispensable necessity for all other deeper levels of pastoral work. It is the seedbed of most fruitful services to people. As Washington Gladden said, "To do good to all men as he has opportunity will be the impulse of the pastor's love." (Washington Gladden, *The Christian Pastor and the Working Church.*) Furthermore, a great portion of the real help that comes to people in crises is through persons whom they would term "just a good friend" and not through professional people or "full-time Christian workers." Some of the most effective pastoral care in churches has been done by lay persons who have had rich experience as parents and who are masters at the simple business of making, meriting, and keeping friends, i.e., they are "given to hospitality." Someone has called this "back fence" counseling. Ways of teaching this rudiment of the Christian life should be devised through the teaching ministry of the pastor. Martin E. Marty, the eminent theologian and historian, has given you and me a *required* text for this teaching ministry in his intensive and warmly personal book, *Friendship.* He says that "having friends and being a friend must take place in a climate of change."

However, friendly confidence with a person who comes to you for help needs to be objective and unencumbered by too much reference to mutual acquaintances and to your personal life as a pastor. For instance, a pastor was visited by a member of a nearby church. When he made a friendly reference to the pastor of that church, the woman became somewhat restless. The pastor, sensing her uneasiness, found it necessary to say: "But, of course, you know that when people come to me for a special kind of personal help I do not talk over their problems in any way with anyone else except at their request or with their permission. Also, let me ask that if you choose to talk with others about our conference, you will let me know." Promises of confidentiality work both ways, for if you choose not to talk of these matters and your pastoral counselee talks irresponsibly, you can be put into impossible ethical dilemmas.

The ministry of friendship and example may be the extent of your ministry to many people. It is the main necessity in your relationship with people of other denominations. In hospital visitation you find most valuable this "social approach" of a "hello visit" with Catholic and Jewish patients and with persons who are the responsibility of another Protestant minister. Likewise, the ministry of friendship to small children is exceptionally rewarding. Pastors give little children an example, a hero with whom to identify, and a friendship that lends security. Especially is this true in instances in which the home has been broken by death, separation, or the divorce of parents. Children of intact and happy homes need friends older than they are who are outside their family.

Whereas the objective, considerate management of a personal friendship is one of the least artificial and most effective means at the pastor's disposal of changing human character, naturally it has severe limitations. Many pastors complain that their people think of them as a hail-fellow-well-met, but that they seem to avoid situations in which a private, serious conversation about the deeper issues of life can be discussed. An example of this is the rural pastor who, upon arriving at the home of parishioners for a meal, finds there a large gathering of neighbors. The host and hostess feel the need for their neighbors' presence in "entertaining" the preacher. Whereas this may turn out to be an excellent opportunity for an informal kind of *group* guidance, it does not allow for a personal conference with an individual or for developing an intimate acquaintance with a family group.

Again, you may find yourself socially identified with your people in such a way that the amount of social distance necessary for them to reach out for your care and help will be lost. Familiarity need not breed contempt, but it does represent a loss of effectiveness in your leadership when you become just "another one of the gang" and your "separateness" as a person of God is completely obscured by this "togetherness" with the people of the community. As pastor you need enough detachment that when people do come to you they will feel that they have been somewhere when they get back.

This suggests the most outstanding limitation of the social level of your pastoral ministry: there are some things a person can tell only to a stranger. As one person said in conference with a pastor in a neighboring community: "I would not dare tell these things to my own pastor because he knows all the people I do. I have no doubt that he would never tell a soul. I have confidence in him, but I feel that I must talk to someone who is not so close to me." Certainly a pastor needs to be able to entertain strangers. The need for a stranger is a paradox with the need for a friend, distance and intimacy seeming to be alien to each other. Out of this paradox has grown the pastoral counseling centers that can provide distance, anonymity, and privacy that the togetherness of even the best church fellowship cannot provide.

But in spite of such limitation, your friendly pastoral access to people in the natural setting of their homes is your greatest opportunity for a careful observation of their personal needs and for a saltlike influence on their behavior.

Yet, with all these advantages of pastoral friendship, you as a pastor propose to be the friend of people who are actually enemies of one another. You are caught in the cross fires of hostile people. Inherent in your ordination is the fact that you are called to be a minister of reconciliation, with a multilateral partiality in family conflicts, vendettas between families in the church who feud with each other, and legal hassles of Christians who ignore the Biblical teachings in I Cor. 6:1–8 in which we are taught that "to have lawsuits at all with one another is defeat for you." Being a friend means often to take your stand apart from the measly motives that can beset people who have become consumed with enmity toward one another. They dedicate their lives to the idolatry of hating, plotting, and scheming against one another. Have the good sense to bear your witness and shake the dust of the situation off your feet. You have a higher calling and more valuable uses of your time.

THE LEVEL OF COMFORT

At your best, like Jesus, you are thought of as a person "of sorrows, and acquainted with grief." Under inevitable hardships, people turn to you for spiritual fortification, emotional support, and affectionate companionship. Here Christian shepherds go with people into the "valley of the shadow of death," stand beside them in the testing times of great tragedies such as economic failures, intolerable losses of self-respect, and terrors of such calamities as war, flood, pestilence, and economic depression. People of every walk traditionally give a minister this task in life, and expect the minister to fulfill a ministry of encouragement and comfort. "If you are not available when people are in trouble," said one lay person, "you need not be on hand any other time."

The different situations in which a ministry of comfort is needed are legion. *Bereaved persons* most often are in need of the supporting help of a minister. *Those who are facing death* lean heavily upon pastors and draw upon the sources of spiritual strength that the pastor offers and represents. Likewise, the pastor's approach to *persons with long-term chronic illnesses,* such as multiple sclerosis, the more serious kinds of arthritis, and the many afflic-

tions of old age, is usually one of companionate encouragement. A supportive ministry is also a necessity in the case
of *persons who are permanently handicapped,* such as
blind persons, persons who have lost a limb, or those who
have been paralyzed. Such losses are much like the loss of
a loved person by death, and the process of mourning over
the loss through which these persons go, in adjusting to
their plight, is much the same process as that through
which a bereaved person goes. Closely akin to bereavement is the plight of *parents of deformed or mentally
deficient children,* who continually need fortification of
spirit. In the same grouping of difficulties in which a supportive ministry of comfort is indicated are *those persons
who suffer from acute physical pain,* which often is so
intense that pain-killing drugs seem to be of little avail.
The pain itself is aggravated by the straining tension with
which the excited person fights to bear the suffering. The
first step in relief is relaxation, which quite often comes
through the efforts of a well-poised minister who does not
waver in the presence of trouble and is relatively serene
in the presence of fear. This is one reason why clinical
pastoral education should be considered an indispensable
part of every minister's education. The minister learns
under supervision and under "combat conditions" what it
is like to see people in acute pain, facing death, and losing
the persons who are important to them. The Association
for Clinical Pastoral Education, with central offices at 475
Riverside Drive, New York, N.Y. 10115, is an organization
that coordinates, certifies, and accredits training centers
all over the United States. By writing them you can find
the training center nearest you. The facilities are abundant, the supervision is experienced and disciplined. Let
me encourage you to make this a continuing part of your
education.

Furthermore, *mentally depressed persons,* whose reasons for being depressed lie unrecognized in the hinter-
lands of their awareness, need a supportive ministry of

comfort. Rational attempts at analyzing their troubles and giving them ready-made solutions quite often meet with failure, which in turn depresses such persons all the more. Most often they are in need of a physician as well as a minister, although they quite regularly go to the minister first. The possibility of suicide in such cases is rather high, and caution should be taken at every move. Recent methods of treatment make depression one of the most amenable disorders for successful recovery. The severe pain of depression *can* be healed.

Another group of persons who vitally need the ministry of comfort that you can afford are the *disappointed lovers* of your parish. A smile flits across most people's minds when such persons are mentioned, but you cannot afford to let humor be your only treatment for persons who have been seriously hurt in a love affair. Efforts at patching up such situations usually are less valuable than a ministry of comfort and supportive encouragement of the person who expresses such a grief to you.

More specifically, the "how" of your ministry of comfort consists of the oldest methods of personal influence that exist: *suggestion, catharsis,* and *reassurance.* These methods have been criticized by persons who have often seen them used to exploit rather than to bless human life. Nevertheless, even the worst use of an instrument does not justify the condemnation of the instrument itself, but only of the ends toward which it is used. But you, by reason of your consecration and ordination, "have renounced disgraceful, underhanded ways; you refuse to practice cunning or to tamper with God's word. You openly state the truth to people in their times of stress." Hence, you are endowed with a *weight of being.*

Therefore, you cannot underestimate the tremendous power of *suggestion,* which your presence itself carries even in the lives of those who actively despise the way of life in which you walk. Paul expressed it accurately when he said that "we are the aroma of Christ to God among those who are being saved and among those who are perishing. . . . Who is sufficient for these things?" (II Cor. 2:15–16). Your pastoral presence itself spiritually fortifies you as you come alongside people in time of stress. You sit where they sit as a reminder of the presence of God.

The knowledge of this should relieve you of the compulsive necessity of "saying something" on every occasion. If you have courage to wait and watch, you will see times when silence itself is a means of prayer during those "groanings which cannot be uttered." Especially within the fellowship of the household of the Christian faith, among those who share a common loyalty to a living Christ, "there is no speech nor language, without these their voice is heard" (Ps. 19:3, marginal reading). Job aptly railed at his comforters: "Ye are all physicians of no value. Oh that ye would altogether hold your peace! And it should be your wisdom" (Job 13:4–5). If you as a minister have not learned the disciplined and re-creative use of silence as a means of spiritual communication, you will draw similar reactions from those whom you seek to comfort with windy speeches and worn stereotyped "answers" to human suffering, and you are simply relieving your own anxiety by talking. You will be different because the sheer awe that doing things differently creates in you will make all other approaches seem hollow and shallow.

Not only is your presence a spiritual fortification to your people, but your capacity to bear with them in their griefs affords a *catharsis* of the spirit for them. Catharsis is something more here than confession: it is a sharing of difficulty in which the weight of pain, grief, and disappointment is actually lightened. As Bacon has said, the sharing of a trouble cuts it in half, but the sharing of a joy doubles its strength. If you observe your people's expressions of deep feelings in times of bereavement, you enter an unexcelled opportunity to cooperate with the Spirit of God in the growth of the soul through grief crises. You note that at the earlier stages the bereaved person quite often *cannot* talk about the loved one but that at a later stage wants to talk and by then friends are hesitant to let the person talk about the loss. Furthermore, recent studies of stress management repeatedly emphasize "debriefing" of overstressed people who have become fatigued, distorted in their perspective, and impaired in their judgment. In your daily work with lay leaders, supportive pastoral care in regularly debriefing them will bring harmony and serenity instead of frenetic misunderstandings and poor morale. This debriefing is a form of catharsis.

Such a catharsis restores the person's perspective and helps the person to lay hold of the positive forces. Likewise, it gives the person access to the pastor and the community resources, which the pastor represents. And in many instances your actual supportive ministry will depend more upon the way Christian fellowship groups can "prop up" a dependent church member or support a "wounded comrade" than upon your minute analyses of an unchangeable situation.

Much of your time, also, will be given over to reassuring people. *Reassurance* is a primary method of comfort, and is a necessary part of the pastoral ministry. A pastor says to a young college student who has an intolerable sense of inferiority because of the cultural backwardness of the family: "You are going to do an acceptable year of college work. I know you are, because your high school principal told me that you have good intelligence, and I have seen that you are willing to work." This is reassurance, and you as a pastor may find yourself saying it more than once. A reassuring letter, written in your own hand, may be read again and again. A pastor may say to a forty-one-year-old woman who has just recently given birth to a child and feels that she is not "a fit mother" and fears that the child may not be normal because of her late age for childbirth: "You have told me why you feel that you cannot go through with this. You have also told me that you would die if you had to give your baby up. You *can* carry through

if you really *want* to do so; I believe in you. I want to
encourage you in your struggle to be a responsible parent.
I am not alone in sustaining you; many people whom you
do not know yet stand ready to be your friend. You are not
alone." This is reassurance, and the woman may need to
talk with this pastor again and again and receive such
encouragement. The ministry of reassurance involves the
basic problem of low morale and the necessity for continued impartation of hope to the person. Sometimes the
person's hope hangs by the single thread of your concern
as a pastor yourself. If you can ward off the isolation by
building a community of concerned people around the
person, they and you together become a bridge over the
abyss of despair.

Naturally, the use of reassurance incurs many problems.
First of all, you should be careful that this encouragement
of people is in keeping with the facts of their own situations. Idle words said just to make them feel good are an
offense. Idle encouragement given as a palliative does
more harm than good. But a hardheaded optimism that
nevertheless faces the facts makes you one who imparts
hope and doggedly searches for fresh alternatives. Careless reassurances, on the other hand, can cause people to
feel that you are minimizing their troubles and do not
understand at all. Quite often this breaks the relationship
completely, and they search for help elsewhere.

Again, it is easy to become trite, impersonal, and vague
in the reassurances you give people. Your encouragement
in these instances is not based on attention to the personal
problem of the individual to whom you are talking, consideration of the way in which the person will hear what you
say, nor care for the essential well-being of the person and
those other persons to whom they are related. Therefore,
ministers are likely to say the trite things to everyone
regardless of the specific nature of the person's trouble.
For instance, a minister was talking to one of his most
substantial contributors during an illness that called for

hospitalization. At the age of forty-three this man was suffering from hypertension, arteriosclerosis, and a reactive depression. He was on the verge of a divorce from his wife for having carried on a clandestine love affair for ten years, and his business was facing failure. Not knowing these facts at all, his pastor visited him for about eight minutes, at the conclusion of which he said: "You are going through the deep waters. I have had all the troubles you are going through, and I can say to you from experience that if you will just put your trust in the Bible, you will come through."

Such an approach at best missed the mark of the man's life situation. This is not to say that the pastor's words were insincere; it is to say, however, that if they were "according to knowledge," the minister had a rather lurid history!

The resource of prayer is especially helpful in the ministry of comfort. The pastor brings the assurances of the power of God through prayer. Prayer therefore should be handled as prescriptively as any powerful medication would be handled. Several guidelines are of help in determining the use of prayer in any given situation:

Appropriateness of the atmosphere is one guide. To bring formal prayer into an atmosphere of frivolity or empty gossip often is to do violence to the nature of prayer.

Brevity is a guide to the use of formal prayer. This means that every word must count and that words should be chosen to fit the need of the person to whom the pastor is ministering. This rules out the trite, worn-out phrases that are used not only by liturgical ministers but also by persons who decry "form prayer." Spontaneity in prayer is to be desired, but this is not to say that the language of prayer is not a thing that can be learned. *The Book of Common Prayer,* especially in its most recent form, has been wrought out of specific situations of need. You will find it, regardless of your denominational affiliation, an enrichment of your prayers. The best-written prayers are found in the Bible. The language of the Bible is the language of prayer. Carry great sections of the Bible in your memory for use in your prayers. (Psalms 1; 15; 23; 37; 46; 51; 79:8–9; 90; 91; 103; 139; Isa. 40:28–31; Matt., ch. 6; John, ch. 14; Rom., ch. 8; I Cor., ch. 13; II Cor. 4:15–18; Eph. 3:14–21 are good examples of the "patience and comfort of the Scriptures.")

Prayer should not always be formal. You often find yourself ministering to persons in open wards in hospitals, in the crowded church corridors during the time between church school and the worship hour, and in the marketplace as you and they go about daily chores. You can pray with the person what has been called "an open-eye prayer." Instead of bowing the head and closing the eyes, you say to the person: "I want you to think of me as praying for you. When you do, remember that I will be praying that you will be strengthened with might to meet the challenge that every day gives you." Other words that are given to you in that hour will be tailored to the very pressures the person is facing. But the basic point to remember is that this kind of prayer is informal and ordinarily unobserved by other people. Similarly, prayers can be written into the text of a letter; outstanding examples of this are the letters of the apostle Paul. For example, as I write these words, I can pray for you—my reader—that you will catch my meaning even when my words are confusing to you. In doing so, I would also pray that you as my reader would be given the wisdom to push my meanings and words aside and to let the Holy Spirit be your teacher.

Relaxation is another principle of prayer. For this reason, prayer should never be "used" merely as an excuse to end a conference with a person. Often prayer will be the point at which a person moves from a social level of conversation to the deeper levels of concern. For example, a pastor was visiting a family in which the mother was seriously ill. After a brief conversation, the mother asked, as her custom was, that he read a passage of the Bible to her.

This he did and led a brief prayer for God's strength to be afforded the sick woman and for the love of her family to be a medicine in itself. After the prayer, the pastor did not hurry to say good-by. Rather, he paused in silence a long while. Then the mother told him of her awareness that she was dying. The pastor had broken through to depths of communion with her of which she had "protected" her husband and children by not discussing. She did not have to face death alone. A quiet pastor was her confidant. He could not have done this had he himself been tense, in a hurry, devoid of relaxation, and terrified by death.

Finally, *prayer means more to persons if they voluntarily ask for it themselves.* You can do much to enable people to be at ease in asking for such a ministry. In many cases it is taken for granted that you will pray—such as in cases of acute illness, impending death, or recent death. But these are not the rule. You can say, "There are many things a pastor can do for people, and I wonder if there is anything that I can do for you?" The tone of voice inflects meaning, and the person may ask, as one woman did, "Well, I had never thought of that; what *are* the things ministers do for people?" Then that pastor had an opportunity to interpret his ministry of prayer to her. It was made easy for her to say she would like him to pray.

Likewise, the use of the Scriptures for purposes of reassurance, comfort, and support is especially valuable. In Martin Luther's *Letters of Spiritual Counsel,* there are abundant examples of this. The use of the concise, easily remembered verses of the Scriptures, especially the winnowed wisdom of Psalms and Proverbs and the epigrams from the teachings of Jesus, provides an undergirding for the minds of people. Their effect increases with repetition and multiplies when they are memorized. For example, Jesus said: "Sufficient unto the day are the troubles thereof. Take no thought for tomorrow." This slows down the apprehensiveness of a person whose imagination is running away. You do well to leave a passage with a person for later reading by writing it in on one of a supply of cards you carry. You may with profit prepare a set of chosen Scriptures for people who have different types of difficulties, as a sort of "spiritual prescription." I have done this in my book *The Bible in Pastoral Care.* It should be emphasized that reassurance, support, and comfort are not the only purposes, or even the major purposes, of the use of the Scriptures. Interpretation, instruction, and historical wisdom take precedence over these purposes. However, our education as pastors so emphasizes the technical study of the Scriptures that their prescriptive use for people in all manner of difficulties is neglected. (Two books will be of specific help to you in exploring the use of the Scriptures in pastoral care: Donald Capps, *Biblical Approaches to Pastoral Counseling* (Westminster Press, 1981); and Wayne E. Oates, *The Bible in Pastoral Care* (reissue, Baker Book House, 1974).

THE LEVEL OF CONFESSION

A pastor visited one of his parishioners at her home inasmuch as she was the victim of an incurable cancer. She was thirty-nine years of age, the mother of two grown children by her first husband, from whom she was divorced. At this time she was married to a second husband, who had also been divorced previously. On his first visit the pastor was received cordially, and the woman told him how good the Lord had been to her and how she had been given divine assurance that she would be healed. Then she asked the pastor to pray for her. His ministry was that of listening and prayer. Twice a week he visited the woman. Each time she protested almost too much that everything was all right between her and God. Finally, the necessity for skilled nursing help prompted the family to move her to the hospital.

At the hospital the pastor visited her regularly, and was met with the same overstated assurances of God's care.

The pastor listened with a sympathetic concern but without challenging the woman's conflicting feelings. One day, however, the woman said with great force that she was sure she was a saved woman and that God was going to help her get well. Then the pastor ventured a remark: "Then *everything* is all right between you and God, is it?" In a startled fashion, the woman said: "Have you been talking to somebody? Do you know something that is not right between me and God?" The pastor said, "I know nothing about you except what you yourself have told me." Then the sick woman clutched at her pastor's hand and fearfully asked him to pray for her. He prayed that she might understand herself in the light of God's love and discover the peace of God that passes understanding. After a long silence he left.

Four days later he returned. The woman was very sick and close to death. When he entered the room, the woman sent all her relatives away in order that she might talk in private with her pastor. Then she said: "I have sins in my life that I must talk about before I die. I have confessed them to God many times and each time he has told me to confess them before people. You are God's minister and I must tell you." Then she proceeded to reveal a crushing load of guilts connected with a series of acts that involved her close relatives and friends over a period of twenty-three years. In great remorse she sought the assurance of God's forgiveness. Then the pastor brought to her the "patience and comfort of the Scriptures" that assured her of God's healing redemption in Christ.

This is an example of the confessional ministry which many veteran ministers can describe. This ministry was formally institutionalized by the Catholics on a compulsory basis. Luther taught that "confession should always be voluntary and freed of the pope's tyranny. . . . There has been no law quite as oppressive as that which forced everyone to make confession." Yet he also notes that some men "do whatever they please and take advantage of their

freedom, acting as if they will never need or desire to go
to confession anymore." But he says that the Lord's Prayer
contains a confession that should and must take place all
our lives." (Martin Luther, *The Large Catechism,* pp. 101–
102.) Today, the Catholic experience of confession is far
more voluntary than it is usually perceived to be by Protestants. In reaction, Protestants have neglected the importance of confessing their "faults one to another." This is
one of the first functions of the Christian community. The
restoration of those overtaken in faults is characteristic of
Christians who have not become so sophisticated that they
no longer feel the need for their own confession of sin. (See
Gal. 6:1–2.) As Martin Luther said, "A man who with fear
and trembling has made humble confession will receive
the grace of justification and forgiveness, even though he
may perhaps have done something from a hidden unbelief
of which he was not aware." (Pauck, ed., *Luther: Lectures
on Romans,* p. 105.)

Protestant ministers who are near to the heart of God
and sensitive to the feelings of their people still listen to
the confessions of their people. A mother cries in bitter
repentance for her mistakes in rearing her children. An
otherwise respectable bank teller confesses a series of
thefts for the first time to his pastor because he can no
longer bear the guilt alone, nor tolerate the fear of being
caught. A young man confesses the paternity of an unborn
child and seeks the aid of his pastor in protecting the
mother and child. A young white woman has suddenly
fallen in love with a black classmate in a large university
and knows that her southern parents will not understand.
A husband confesses his marital infidelity and seeks to find
its causes and remedy. A defense worker caught by tuber-
culosis confesses his money madness, which caused him to
work too many hours, too many days, and brought him to
his bed.

The common characteristic of all these confessions is
that they are social in nature, involving many other peo-

ple. But many confessions are more individualized, and the persons condemn themselves for the evil character of their private thought life. Or they may confess the practice of masturbation, as did one fourteen-year-old boy who felt that he was mentally affected by melancholia for having indulged in this practice. Of course, this was not so.

Several facts need to be considered in the practice of a confessional ministry. First, isolation is the main effect of a known transgression. The persons cannot face their community as they did before. They are "cut . . . off from the land of the living" and from the face of God. The confession is, therefore, more than a mere catharsis; it is also a socialization of an otherwise isolated experience. The person achieves a sense of togetherness with the people whose approval the person considers most worthwhile, as well as with the eternal God. As Washington Gladden has said, the load of shame and remorse can be removed if the pastor "can draw forth the rankling secret, and convince the troubled soul, *first by his own forgiveness,* that the Infinite Love is able to save to the uttermost all who trust in him." (Gladden, *The Christian Pastor and the Working Church,* p. 86; italics added.)

Again, you must be careful in your ministry of confession not to accept too quickly the stated problem or the confessed sin as the real one. This could be called the "A-ha reflex," in which a minister feels like saying, "Eureka!" when a person tells of some foul deed. Especially is this true of confessions of sexual sins. These gross offenses are often merely the symptoms of deeper and more persistent ones. For instance, a young unmarried woman may confess the fact that she is pregnant, whereas her heaviest burden of guilt hovers around a burning hatred of her father, who is chairman of the official board of the church. Her sexual act is an expression of her hatred of her father and a self-destructive way of bringing shame upon him.

Another hazard to avoid in the confessional ministry is that of taking the admission of a fault too lightly and reas-

suring the person to the point that the person is made to
feel guilty over having felt guilty. This is most common in
one's ministry to children and adolescents. An adolescent
may be having all manner of difficulty over some seemingly insignificant habit. The pastor may pass the whole
thing off lightly—even with humor—and miss the deep
feelings the person has about the behavior. This applies
not only to adolescents but also to adults. For instance, a
thirty-five-year-old woman, upon being asked by her pastor if she had been to church recently, said, "No, I do not
feel comfortable when I'm sitting in church." When
pressed unduly for a reason, she said with great embarrassment, "I constantly fear that someone will hear my insides
growl out loud." A touch of humor eased her tension. Then
the pastor said: "I know that is not completely funny to
you; I want you to know that I take it seriously. Would you
like to talk with me more about these fears sometime?
Maybe I can help you." This conversation led easily to
another, and the woman confessed to feeling great remorse over having had an abortion performed several
years before. Now she greatly desired children and could
not have them. There was a direct connection between
her fear of her "insides being noticed" in the church and
her guilt over this deed.

Probably the point at which individuals most need the
"disburdening" ministry of confession, as Calvin called it,
is when they first enter the Christian community as adults.
In some communions this will be when the young person
takes Communion for the first time. In others it will be
prior to Baptism and after a public profession of faith. But
you will carefully create a private conference situation in
which you can become acquainted with the person, learn
something of the person's spiritual history, and let the
person confide prayerfully in the atmosphere of trust that
develops.

Another point at which a confessional ministry is appropriate and often neglected is prior to marriage. Even

though a couple plan to become one flesh in God, they still exist as individuals before God in their histories of sin. Some of these sins are quite independent of their chosen partner and should be confessed to God and to no spouse. You can encourage these prayers of penitence, for if the person is left unassuaged by the forgiveness of God, it could tend to hobble the marriage relationship with fear and compulsion.

The ministry of confession is closely related to medical psychotherapy, but *there is a vital difference.* The woman to whom reference has just been made was referred to her pastor by a psychiatrist. He stated the difference this way: "Here was a woman suffering from a sense of sin about wrong deeds she had actually committed. She needed forgiveness from God, and there was very little need of my trying to turn theologian. I referred her to her pastor. Now the people whom a psychiatrist can help are those who are *deluded* and *think* they have committed crimes of which they are innocent, or who are hearing voices telling them that the room is electrically wired in such a way as to cause them to murder, etc."

The confessional ministry calls for different methods of approach according to the age of the person involved and the degree of "full-grownness" of the sins the person confesses. A child needs information and guidance in the presence of ignorance, temptation, and sin. An unwitting error cannot be treated in the same way a high-handed and premeditated crime is treated. Great care must be taken in distinguishing a temptation from a sin. Many people experience more guilt over the things they are tempted to do than they do over the sins they actually commit. Also, many people are afflicted with diseases that cause them to do things against their own good judgment, and they are powerless to control their actions. In such cases it is the minister's task to heal the volition and strengthen the person's sense of personal responsibility rather than to add to the loneliness and desperation by losing patience. Quite

214   *The Christian Pastor*

often such persons as epileptics, acute alcoholics, sex deviants, and psychopathic thieves and liars are in need of a physician as well as a minister. They are afflicted with diseases that express their symptoms in the moral behavior as well as in the psychosomatic disequilibrium of their personalities. When starting to deal with these persons, the minister needs the compassion that Christ had for the demoniac. Their communities have often ostracized them to the hinterland of isolation without the advantage of a funeral.

THE LEVEL OF TEACHING

As a personal counselor you find that some of your most effective teaching is done with individuals in a face-to-face ministry. Jesus most often appeared to his followers as a teacher. The matchless teachings that he left the world were often the outgrowth of his ministry to individuals who were drawn to him for help. As a Christian shepherd you function as an instructor of the conscious minds, the moral intentions, and the undisciplined desires of your people. On the teaching level of your personal ministry, therefore, you must know not only the content of Christian teaching and practice but also the process whereby these become a part of the spiritual tissue of the personalities of your people and the communal life of your fellowship of faith.

A person who comes to a Christian pastor for guidance in a personal difficulty usually expects that pastor to be an interpreter of the mind of Christ, "a teacher come from God." A distinct expertise is expected. You represent these realities to the person. Furthermore, you are supposed to be an authority on the teachings of the Bible and Christian history. People come to you with thorny personal problems at the base of questions as to what the Bible teaches about divorce, remarriage, adultery, the unpardonable sin, money matters, profanity, war, and a hundred other things. You are expected to know the historical context of Christian experience and to be able to use this knowledge in a way that edifies and does not tear down the person.

In addition, you are supposed to be an authority on the specific teachings and practices of your own church. A young engaged couple will come asking you to explain the difference between the teaching and practices of Catholics and Protestants, for instance, and your knowledge and attitude will have a determinative effect upon their decision. You are a clinical research person, too. If you do not know the precise facts, you can ask for time to research them. Many times you will have friends who are pastors of other denominations, priests in Catholic churches, and rabbis in synagogues. They are people whom you can call while the persons are in your office. If you define your role as a teacher, build a democratic relationship of give-and-take, and provide the couple with factual information, you can exercise genuine shepherdly care for such a couple regardless of the outcome of their decision. You as a minister also find yourself the interpreter of the social attitudes of your people all the way from such matters as personal amusements that are taboo to worldwide attitudes on race prejudice, draft registration, abortion, child custody, the need for legal counsel.

As a teacher you are caught between your stewardship of the absolute ideals of the teachings of Jesus on the one hand and the rigorism of special pressure groups in the church on the other hand. You bear a sensitive conscience in terms of your care for human persons who have failed to reach the ideals of Jesus Christ and the responsible instruction of the church in the Christian standards of human life. On such matters, an exploding body of knowledge is appearing in the literature under such topics as bioethics, medical ethics, and Christian social ethics. Even if you graduated from seminary only ten years ago, your information is out of date. Set aside some library time, consultation time, and seminar time for this kind of updating of your learning. It will enrich your teaching, preaching, and counseling.

On the teaching level of pastoral ministry, you as a Christian shepherd find a distinctive character of your work that sets you apart from professional counselors and necessitates a departure from their ideologies. This distinctive character, however, may bring you closer to the reality of people's problems, i.e., *you represent both the individual's and the group's interests, and you must combine individual and group counseling procedures.* The person-minded minister knows that many personal counseling opportunities come as the result of questions stimulated in group discussions. Conversely, you must confront the "reality principle" of your group connections and those of your counselees in all personal work with individuals.

But people come to you not only for guidance on specifically religious questions but also for information on the common ventures of everyday life. Parents who have not been able to have children want to know adoption procedures, problems in artificial insemination, and parent surrogating. Young people seek premarital instruction. High school graduates want to know about the college facilities available to them. Children of elderly parents want guidance concerning homes for aged people. Relatives of mentally ill persons want guidance concerning psychiatric help and legal procedures involved in institutionalization. Parents invariably want to talk over problems in child guidance with their pastor, seeking information about the simpler as well as the more complex problems in mental hygiene. The request for the recommendation of medical specialists in cases of physical illness is a very common appeal.

In all these instances and in countless others, you are expected to be a repository of information. As one young minister, after two years of pastoral work, said: "They came to me, but they did not ask me what I *thought*. They said, 'Pastor, do you *know* . . .?' " Therefore, take heed to know your Bible, your church, and your community resources. These are your equipment.

The methods of instructional guidance are varied, but in every instance these approaches must be distinguished from long lectures of moralistic exhortations filled with such phrases as: "Don't you know . . .?" "I think you ought . . ." "Maybe you don't realize it, but . . ." *Instructional guidance is the impartation of the facts necessary for an individual to make a voluntary choice with wisdom and informed consent. Recommending the use of good books is one of the most tactful methods* to be employed here. You should take care to separate heavier volumes that you would use for your own instruction from those briefer, more plainly written books you would use for guiding other people. Likewise, you should not recommend literature before you yourself have read it. Every pastor needs a loan shelf of books and pamphlets bought with extra gifts of money received from time to time. The pastor will lose a few books this way, but they will be valuable even so. Suggestions for such materials have been made throughout this volume. Most recently the Westminster Christian Care Books have been published for this purpose. They are highly specific in nature. Note the variety of their subject matter:

When Your Parents Divorce, by William V. Arnold
When the Mental Patient Comes Home, by George Bennett
Coping with Physical Disability, by Jan Cox-Gedmark
After Suicide, by John H. Hewett
The Two-Career Marriage, by G. Wade Rowatt, Jr., and Mary Jo Brock Rowatt
Coping with Difficult People, by Paul F. Schmidt
Pastor's Handbook, Vol. I, by Wayne E. Oates
Mid-Life Crises, by William E. Hulme
Understanding Aging Parents, by Andrew D. Lester and Judith L. Lester

For Grandparents: Wonders and Worries, by Myron C.
   Madden and Mary Ben Madden
Coping with Abuse in the Family, by Wesley R. Monfalcone
Parents of the Homosexual, by David K. Switzer and Shirley
   A. Switzer
Parents and Discipline, by Herbert Wagemaker, Jr.
Pastor's Handbook, Vol. II, by Wayne E. Oates

Supplying missing facts is another method of personal
instruction. You may be listening carefully to a mission
volunteer who is making educational plans, but you suddenly realize that this person is already beyond the age
limit for missionaries in the area in which the person wants
to serve. A member of the official board of the church may
want to make a certain change in the financial policy of
the church. You as the pastor supply the missing fact that
the charter of the church expressly forbids it. This type of
counseling is especially valuable to the religious counselor
on college campuses and to people who teach in institutions of learning. "The rules" become the grooves on
which much of their counseling progresses. Furthermore,
outlining various alternatives and exploring these as to
their possible implications, resources, and outcomes is another method of instructional counseling. This kind of pastoral care has the advantage of appealing to the responsible, healthy dimensions of the person. This in itself
amounts to treating the person with integrity, respect, and
dignity. This builds the kind of confidence necessary for
any more complex and profound problems the person
may wish to discuss.

Chapter VII

The Deeper Levels
of Pastoral Care

The previous chapter, "The Levels of Pastoral Care," dealt with the traditional, *expected,* ministries of the pastor. However, neotraditional expectations have been focused upon a pastor's responsibilty to be more technically competent than this. World War II, the Korean conflict, the continuing cold war, the Vietnam War, and the turbulent social changes of the '60s and '70s have imprinted upon millions of civilians the expectations that a pastor shall be far more than just a friend and a comforter. Less and less do they quietly expect the pastor to be a hail-fellow-well-met who "attends all the meetings." More and more they expect the pastor to be a person who will converse in depth with them about the main meanings and excruciating meaninglessness of their lives. Consequently, this chapter is devoted to two kinds of conversations that pastors tend to have with parishioners and nonparishioners alike, either in visits with them or in their visits with the pastor: *brief pastoral dialogues,* and *multiple-interview pastoral counseling.*

THE LEVEL OF BRIEF PASTORAL DIALOGUE

Pastoral care is essentially spiritual conversation. Three recent volumes on pastoral counseling, in different ways, emphasize spiritual conversation as the focus of pastoral care: Wayne E. Oates, *Pastoral Counseling* (1974); John B. Cobb, Jr., *Theology and Pastoral Care* (1977); and Howard Clinebell, *Basic Types of Pastoral Counseling,* rev. ed. (1981). Brief pastoral dialogue, styled along the line of the Socratic dialectic, is the most easily used technique for approaching the personal problems of an individual. This method is the commonsense approach to pastoral procedure that is most likely to do good and the least likely to do harm. It is also a preparatory approach to any longer-term counseling that needs to be done. The brief pastoral dialogue assumes that the person seeking help is of average intelligence, fairly stable emotionally, and capable of talking freely about the situation, with no unusual degree of mental blocking. Further, this dialogue assumes a strong degree of personal rapport between the individual and a pastor. It is usually appropriate with people to whom the pastor has been related over a period of time as pastor and teacher. Ordinarily there is a reasonably permanent bond of identification between the pastor and the person at hand. These are rather sweeping prerequisites for the use of such an approach. The psychologist or the psychiatrist may ask whether or not there *are* any such people living. But as pastors we deal with such people every day of our ministry, whereas these other experts do not see them professionally. We have the advantage of working with healthy as well as sick people.

The process of the brief pastoral dialogue is as follows: First, simply listen to the parishioner who comes to you in a time of decision and lays out a problem before you. Ask an occasional question in order to fill in missing facts. Here, in actuality, you yourself are a student, much as Socrates was a "student" with the youth of Athens, learning from the person at hand all the facts about the present situation confronting the person. You are "leading the person out" (in the Latin sense of the word "education").

Secondly, give a factual summary, a sort of recapitulation or "readback" of what the person has told you. You may initiate this by saying: "Now let me see whether or not I have really understood what you have told me." Then, upon finishing a concise statement of the situation at hand, you may say: "Do I understand you properly? Have we left anything out?" Quite often the person will say, "Yes, I failed to mention this . . ."; or, "No, I don't think you really understood what I meant . . ."; or, "I didn't mean to leave this impression, but . . ."

Thirdly, ask the person to help you outline the alternative paths of action, and with the help of the counselee explore the end results and methods of achieving results in each one of the alternative paths of action. Usually this may be initiated by asking the question, "Now what are the things you *can* do in the situation?" After these alternatives have been carefully enumerated, each one can be discussed freely in a give-and-take manner as to obstacles preventing their realization, ways and means of accomplishment, and unique advantages inherent in each choice. Often the condition of things calls for your adding another possibility for the consideration of the individual —a possibility that the person probably has not yet seen. Many times this "other possibility" may be a careful combination of the best advantages of the other alternatives. For instance, a young woman does not know whether to stay in school or to go to work in order that she and her fiancé can marry. Finally she decides to stay in school, lighten her class load, get a part-time job, and marry. Inasmuch as both of them have only one more year, she feels that they can "make it." Yet, you do best simply to say: "Had you thought of doing this?" Or, "Would a good working compromise be . . .?"

The fourth step is to appeal to the basic desire of the person. Often you may ask, "If all things were equal, now, which of these alternatives would you really want to follow —deep down inside?" Quite often an amused light comes to the person's eyes and the statement is made, "Well, I guess I did not want your advice so much as I wanted sympathy for what I have already decided to do." But on frequent occasions the answer may be: "I guess that is my big problem: I don't know what I want to do. I want to have my cake and eat it too, and I am not able to choose one thing and carry through with it." The more intense this feeling is, the more likely it is that the person is suffering from some type of anxiety state. At any rate, the "big problem" is out in the open. You are firmly established in the person's confidence, and now you may go into the deeper difficulties of the individual.

However, in the majority of the situations that confront a pastor, this brief pastoral dialogue produces a heightened degree of emotional reflectiveness, whets the sense of personal responsibility, reduces the chances of impulse decisions, and leaves the decision-making capacity of the person free and inviolate. It lends itself to one-interview situations more readily, and is adaptable to pressurized schedules. Be sure to take two precautions in ending such a brief pastoral dialogue. First, be careful not to break the relationship by giving fixed advice. It is better to develop working hypotheses or "experiments" and try things out to see if they will work. This is one of the main hazards of fixed advice: if the person cannot follow through with the recommendation, the person is hesitant to return to you. Of course, in some relatively rare instances, you may want this result. In the second place, you are able to make some arrangement for follow-up of the conference. Take great care not to forget about the persons who have conversed with you concerning the main issues of their life.

THE LEVEL OF PASTORAL COUNSELING AND PSYCHOTHERAPY

Not all personal encounters yield themselves to the rational approach suggested in the discussion of the brief pastoral dialogue. The Christian shepherd confronts many people who are suffering from deep inner conflicts over which they have no control. They stand in need of a minister who has psychological foundations and knowledge of psychotherapeutic skills as well as the healing power of God. Such persons have come to the point where *they do not want to do what they want to do.* Their decision-making powers are deadlocked in a filibuster of *one* of their many selves in the congress of their soul. Unhappy people, they come to the pastor complaining that they cannot control their thoughts and actions. In the thought of Paul, they do not understand their own actions, for they do not the things they want, but do the very things they hate (Rom. 7:15).

The large majority of such persons are not "insane." They do not suffer from gross delusions of grandeur and persecution. They may live their lives in quiet desperation, but are not definably depressed to the point of suicide or homicide. They do not stand in need of institutionalization and protective care. Accordingly, they are not candidates for a psychiatrist ordinarily. Usually they are not wealthy enough to afford a psychoanalyst who specializes in their kind of troubles. Rather, when they come to a pastor, they are usually people of limited means who are acutely unhappy and blocked out of the abundant life. Nevertheless, they may be conscientious church members and active in the affairs of the community. Their religion, unhappily, seems to be conformed to the pattern of their unhappy way of life rather than a transforming power that renews their mind. They do not have the joy of their salvation. Yet they hopefully look to their faith in God as a promise of redemption from their inner bondage to the legalism they have mistaken for Christian faith.

In order to deal effectively with the basic religious needs that these conflict-weary persons manifest, you must become acquainted with the "heart's native language" of feelings as well as with the rational precepts of theological formulations. As Nathaniel Hawthorne says:

If he show no intrusive egotism . . . ; if he have the power, which must be born with him, to bring his mind into such affinity with his patient's that this last shall unawares have spoken what he imagines himself only to have thought; if such revelations be received without tumult, and acknowledged not so often by an uttered sympathy as by silence, an inarticulate breath, and here and there a word, to indicate that all is understood; if to these qualifications of a confidant be joined the advantages afforded by his recognized character as a physician—then, at some inevitable moment will the soul of the sufferer be dissolved, and flow forth in a dark but transparent stream, bringing all its mysteries into the daylight. (Hawthorne, *The Scarlet Letter*, Signet Classics, p. 123)

Such a "feeling for the feelings" of people, a careful clinical study of people's troubles, and an equally careful reexamination of the New Testament reveal a Christian explanation of the difficulties of people: Idolatry in the sphere of values is the basic religious component in the malformations encountered in these particular neurotic processes. The person suffers, as Søren Kierkegaard said, from "inwardness with a jammed lock." They are in bondage "to the elemental spirits of the universe . . . , in bondage to beings that by nature are no gods" (Gal. 4:3, 8).

Primarily such a person is possessed by the demand of one part of the self that the rest of the self bow down in its worship. As Plato said, this type of sin is "the rising up of a part of the soul over the whole." Such individuals are not persons, but many selves. They condemn themselves roundly on every hand, giving the key to their plight when they say: "I could never forgive myself . . ." Thus it is seen clearly that they are inordinate worshipers of fictitious goals in life, borrowed standards for life, fantasies of what they think themselves ideally to be. The viciousness of this idolatry lies in its self-destructiveness, its prating itself as humility, self-denial, self-rejection, and religious devotion. Their desire to become a person in their own right overshoots the mark and they aspire to become their own god.

The only answer to this plight is that the eyes of the inner understanding be opened to irresponsibility and a childish sense of omnipotence. The inner life must be opened to the ethically severe love of God. This convinces these persons that the root of their sins is in self-enchantment, that God is consistent and can be depended upon to work within them as they make and carry out decisions, and that God is "a rewarder of them that diligently seek him." Such a picture is seen in the life of the man whom Jesus asked, before he healed him, "Wilt thou be made whole?" And the surest thing that you can do for such conflict-weary persons who come to you is to put them on their own before God, to give them all the loving confidence and intelligent affection that you have time and opportunity to give. But do so on a clear covenant and disciplined basis.

But a theological orientation to the problems of such trouble-ridden people is inadequate unless it takes into account what is observably known about the processes of recovery from such states. The busy pastor needs a clear conception of *how* to go about "putting persons on their own before God and giving them all the intelligent affection that time and opportunity make possible." Every responsible pastor knows that the neurotic personalities in the church not only are unhappy themselves but cause unhappiness to others all out of proportion to their own number. We as ministers ourselves are at least as important as any other one factor in causing church splits and church failures. Therefore, the minister may be forced by circumstances to ask, "What am I going to do for and about the neurotic processes in my church and in myself?"

The core of neurotic processes is anxiety and fear. Long-standing inabilities to trust people fuel impairments in the capacity to trust, commit, and bond oneself to others. This universalizes itself in the struggle of the Spirit to perceive and relate to God as a loving friend rather than an ever-present opponent or enemy. The love of God is a perfect one. Yours and mine are impeded by fear. "Perfect love casts out fear. For fear has to do with punishment, and he who fears is not perfected in love" (I John 4:18).

The field of counseling and psychotherapy three decades ago was thinly populated. Resources for this kind of care were few and far between. However, as of this writing, the field is becoming heavily populated. One criticism in the field leveled at pastoral counselors and psychotherapists is that we as ministers are too authoritarian and moralistic to accomplish effective results. A controlled study of this was made.

From 1956 to 1961, Seward Hiltner and Lowell G. Colston clinically contrasted the two different contexts of counseling—that of the clinical psychologist and that of the pastor. They published their findings in the book *The Context of Pastoral Counseling.* They used the term "context" for "what differentiates the pastor's counseling from that of other counselors." They concluded that "the attempt to understand and to articulate to ourselves the feelings people have about the whole context in which pastoral counseling takes place is not a nuisance but a vital instrument in the giving of help." (Hiltner and Colston, *The Context of Pastoral Counseling,* p. 220.) One important result of the study was that counselees felt *less* judgmentalism and authoritarianism in a church counseling service than in a psychological clinic.

The subtle conditioning factors discussed are integral parts of the context of counseling. The religious history and the characteristic modes of selfhood developed over the years of a person's life exercise a reciprocal effect on counselor and counselee. For example, pastors, psychiatrists, social workers, and psychologists seem to have equally difficult times in activating those individuals who are aggressively dependent and who insist that the counselor shall take total responsibility for their care.

For this reason and because of my own hypothesis that in the design of selfhood a particular counselee and a particular counselor reciprocally shape the responsible covenant they form and the techniques that eventuate, my position, simply stated here, is: (1) The structure of the context in which a person seeks the pastor's help—informal or formal—may be or become confused, and must be continually defined, redefined, and clarified. (2) The methodology of the pastor is shaped by the patterns of self-confrontation that emerge in the relationship and that, in turn, must be sensitively appreciated, identified, and understood. (3) The religious history of the person is important to the person seeking a pastor's counseling, and the person should be given every opportunity to discuss it in detail, as is indicated in the previous chapter. (4) The preponderant majority of pastoral counseling situations involve marriage conflict, which moves through a definable process of deterioration. This process shapes the procedures of the pastor and cannot be ignored. Therefore, you as a pastor can most productively use continuing education opportunities in studying marriage and family therapy.

My hypotheses have been considerably influenced by my own specific counseling experience studies, but also by the additional help of the work of Harry Stack Sullivan in his discussion of "Developmental Syndromes" in his *Conceptions of Modern Psychiatry* and his discussion of the "Detailed Enquiry" in his book *The Psychiatric Interview* (pp. 94–182). These hypotheses are sufficiently clear from extensive clinical application to be good foundations for effective pastoral counseling when generously laced with common sense. However, each one is open to continuing refinement by more sophisticated and detailed research design. New generations of pastoral counselors can no longer rely upon anecdotal and "hunch" approaches to methodology. But it is sustaining to find one's previous "hunches" validated from clinical studies. More recent studies for your consideration are András Angyal, *Neurosis and Treatment: A Holistic Theory*, ed. by E. Haufmann and R. M. Jones, and Irvin D. Yalom, *Existential Psycho-therapy.*

However, without *supervised* application and research the pastor cannot appreciate or understand safely such literature as has been discussed and recommended here. In actuality, the only effective means of testing the hypotheses described in these books is that of engaging in intensive clinical work under adequate supervision and in a setting where you can have a group of other professionals with whom to study in a fellowship of learning. You can get this training in theological curricula in many schools today. If you are already in a pastoral situation and cannot easily gain access to a training center during a summer, you can try to get a leave of absence or commute to the nearest center of training. In such a center of training you become a part of the healing team. Physicians, social workers, psychiatrists, nurses, and ministers are all helpfully related to the same persons in need. Furthermore, you are given close personal supervision in your individual work with people by trained theological supervisors. Here "the living human documents of flesh and blood" become the textbooks for you. The gospel comes alive to you in the face-to-face ministry to people.

Some persons ask, "How far should a pastor go in 'deeper-level counseling' ?" The answer is threefold: You should go as far as your training has equipped you to accept responsibility for the outcome of your treatment. You should go as far as the uncontrolled environment in which you work will permit you to accept responsibility for the person's life. And, finally, you should go as far as the limitations of your time and social role will permit you to give yourself to the needs of the individual.

The counseling work of a minister is a dynamic and growing relationship. You do well to think of yourself as counseling in the creative processes of spiritual birth and maturation, and to think of the person before you as needing new life and spiritual maturity. *This creative process moves naturally through five phases.* The phases may take place quickly in one interview, but more often the relationship may extend over several or even a large number of conferences. This allows time for growth and reflection, during which the person has the opportunity in between interviews to deal with problems alone and in fellowship with the Holy Spirit.

The Preparatory Phase of Counseling

The more inexperienced pastor usually asks the question, "How is it that people come to their pastor for counseling help?" The veteran minister asks, "How can I get people who ask for help started off in an effective relationship for the best results in my counseling with them?" Others may ask, "How can I stimulate the need for counseling help in a person who does not yet feel either the need for help or that I am the person to give it?" All these questions indicate a *preparatory phase* in most counseling relationships. In this phase you as pastor do several things. You first discover who needs help and establish an initial contact with that person. If the person comes to you in an informal situation, you seek to construct a more formal one in which time, privacy, and quietness can be achieved. If the person must be sought out by visitation or by cultivation of friendship, you seek to stimulate the sense of need for help and to shift the initiative in the relationship in such a way that the person "stretches forth a hand" for help.

1. *Discovering persons in need and establishing an initial contact.* The pastor is one of the very few persons in modern society who is still expected to visit people. In some communities even this expectation is losing its strength. But ordinarily, you as pastor have a right to visit in the homes of your community. This is one of your best means of discovering persons in need and of establishing an initial contact with them. Purposeful and patient home

visitation reveals to the observant pastor, especially when visits are made in times of crises, many of the quieter and more desperate needs of individuals and families. It establishes a rapport that will be necessary to any future counseling. It gives a distinctly personal touch to your interest in people. Learn to use the pastoral visit in a disciplined, professional way. It offers you opportunities to see the individual in the context of the family and to sense the feelings of other members of the family toward that person. Home visitation presents you with a *systems analysis* of the way of life of the person which only many hours of individual counseling would ultimately reveal.

Likewise, as has already been indicated in the discussion of preaching and teaching, your public ministry affords you "after meeting" conversations with persons who have private matters they wish to discuss. This is the pastoral counselor's "outlet to the sea" of human suffering. Careful, perceptive, and humanly tender preaching and teaching are avenues of exchange of feeling between a pastor and the individual who needs personal counseling.

Furthermore, a patient educating of the leadership of the church to guide persons in actual need to you as pastor rewards you with an abundance of initial contacts with such persons. This is best illustrated by a negative example. A middle-aged woman who had been married only about six years became deeply depressed and took her life by self-poisoning. One of her neighbors called the pastor immediately and asked that he make his services available to the husband of the woman in making plans for and conducting the funeral. In the telephone conversation, she said, "I have known for some time that she was thinking of doing such a thing, but I never believed she would!" If the woman had been trained to do so, she could have notified the pastor long *before* the tragedy. As it was, all she knew to do was to call him for the funeral!

Probably the most Christlike method of establishing initial contacts with persons in need is that of the pastoral "marketplace ministry." As you read the Gospels, you find only one example of a formal interview in the ministry of Jesus, the conversation with Nicodemus. The rest of his conversations were beside wells, in people's homes, along the roadside, and in or near places of worship. In the casual, informal contacts of everyday living with people—in the grocery store, at the service station, at the bank, at the garage, at social gatherings of all kinds—you as a contemporary pastor also hear the "uplifted voices" of human need. A young pastor tells of this experience: He read in his morning paper that a man and a woman, both members of his church, were seeking a divorce. That morning he stopped, as his custom was, to get some gasoline at the man's service station. He stood reading his paper inside the man's place of business. The proprietor was posting his books, while the attendant filled the gas tank. Everything was tensely quiet until the owner looked up and snarled at the pastor: "Well, go on and say it. I know what you are going to say anyhow!" The pastor countered by saying: "I am not sure whether or not you feel that I am your friend. I don't want to say anything unless you know that my friendship belongs to you and that I care what happens to you."

The man was taken aback by this approach. Then he broke into a warm, anguished outpouring of his difficulties with his wife that had culminated in divorce proceedings. The pastor did not try to deal with it at that moment, but said: "I will be responsible with your confidence in me. Do you think you and I could get together tonight, after your station closes, and talk this over?" An appointment was made, and the more formal kind of counseling relationship had been established.

2. *Making counseling appointments.* This latter step suggests one of the important essentials of the preparatory phase of counseling work: you learn to be very effective in the use of an appointment system. Unless it is otherwise unavoidable, you do not attempt to deal with intimately

personal problems of individuals in public places where
other people can surmise and draw their own conclusions.
You make appointments either to visit in the person's
home or else to meet in your study. Such a simplified
procedure will do much toward making your time more
valuable to others and to yourself. This is much wiser than
setting arbitrary office hours for people to come to see you
if they need help on their personal problems. It is more
personal, less of an affront to the autonomy of the people
of the community, and therefore less likely to create un-
necessary hostility. Furthermore, your identity as a
preacher, teacher, and overseer of the flock will not be
obscured by arbitrarily set office hours which "strike the
pose" of a formal counseling ministry which some people
may resent. But more important than this, such a plan
does much toward "tailoring" your relationship to the individual in such a way that you can counsel without too
many personal obstructions and uncontrollable interruptions.

3. *Stimulating the initiative of the person who needs
help.* A difficult task in the preparatory phases of counseling is that of switching the initiative from yourself as pastor to the person whom you are seeking to help. This is
more easily illustrated than it is defined. For instance, a
young woman called her pastor, asking for an appointment *for her husband* to come and talk with him about
some marital problems in which they were involved. The
pastor, in the preparatory phases of the counseling relationship, said: "I will be glad to talk with *him* as to a time
that is convenient for both of us. Will you have him call me
about it?" The purpose of the pastor was to shift the initiative in the search for help away from the wife and onto the
husband. Yet, in some instances, it might be clear that the
husband's work prevented his own calling and you would
feel that there was no manipulation of the husband by the
wife.

Sometimes you will recognize an acute need in a person

in your community, but are aware that the person is hostile and resistant to any offer of help. You want to lessen the hostility and to uncover in the person a desire for your guidance. This is one of the most difficult relationships with which you deal. For example, a pastor learned that one of the members of the church had made a vow that he would never return to church after seeing his father, the senior elder of the church, with "another woman sitting in my dead mother's place," as the man himself stated.

The pastor visited the home of the man regularly, inasmuch as the man was physically ill a good portion of the time. Little mention was ever made of the fact that he did not come to church. No reference was made to the fact that the pastor knew of the conflict between him and his father, nor to the fact of his father's remarriage. The pastor "waited him out" until the man himself felt secure enough in his affections to tell him about the conflict without being asked. At this point, the man sought the pastor's guidance and became durably related to the pastor as a caring person. This relationship lasted—at differing levels of intensity—over a period of sixteen years.

Another situation in pastoral care and personal counseling that calls for a switch of initiative is that of major moral offenses among persons in the congregation. These usually first come to your attention in rumors from different persons within the community. Whispers of embezzlement, shady business dealings, sexual promiscuity, sexual perversions, and any item of the catalog that each community compiles come to the ears of the minister. Next, the person's place of authority and leadership in the church is questioned. A rift in the unity of the congregation is in the making. In smaller congregations, the whole unsavory situation can come to a crisis in a clash of personalities in the open meetings of the church. Your own leadership may become so involved that you may want to resign or be asked to resign.

Such a situation may best be handled in the rumor stage by a pastor who has a firm hand in dealing with people. The following case record shows how one pastor handled the situation:

PASTOR:
Wilhelm, I called and asked you to come by to see me for a reason. Before I tell you what I have on my mind, I want to say that my confidence in you as a person runs pretty deep and my affection for you is true and sure. Otherwise, I would not have been concerned about you. Then, too, I want to assure you that no one else knows that you are here and that all you say to me will be handled responsibly and with your full knowledge ahead of time.

You may justly tell me, when I say what I have on my mind, that I am sticking my nose into your business and have no right to do so. You will be right except in the fact that I would want you to do for me what I am trying to do for you, because I feel that you are my friend.

Now to come to the point, before you lose your patience in curiosity, let me say that I am not concerned about the truth or error of the reports that have come to me. They could be false and still do you harm. If they are false, I think you are entitled to know that these things are being said. If they are true, I think you are entitled to a sympathetic friend with whom you can talk safely about your side of the story. There are, as you well know, two sides to all such things.

The word has come to me that you have been sexually molesting some of the young boys and girls in our church. The exact situations are these: ——; ——; ——; ——. I will not tell you who told me all this, because I do not want to do all of you harm. But you can imagine for yourself, and if this is not true, you can be secure in knowing that they do not know that I am talking to you either.

What do you think about all this?

WILHELM:
Well, for a good while I have wanted to talk with you about this, but I never knew quite how to go about it. I have been doing some of those things. Not all of them, though. I came here a stranger and thought I had found a really Christian

crowd that didn't do those things. I got into it, though, and found that they were not so different from myself. . . .

The conclusion of the whole history is too lengthy to report in full, but this part of the record indicates that confidence was established. The preparatory phases of such counseling can move from an authoritarian to a permissive relationship between the counselor and the counselee. However, catching in time an explosive interpersonal condition like this is not always this easy. In later stages of deterioration the situation may spread so far and so deep in the life of the church and the community that you would be forced to distribute responsibility to members of the official board and to the members of other helping professions—medicine, the law, and businesses. Making a referral to an outside uninvolved professional may be the thing to do. You may have many difficulties in dealing with such a problem in the next phases that are to be discussed, but, at least if you are as fortunate as the pastor who was mentioned in the preceding record, you have stabilized your relationship in such a way that the initiative is with the counselee more than it is with you.

The Phase of Relaxation and Development of Trust

At the outset of this discussion of the process of counseling, the problem of the place and time of the counseling ministry needs to be considered. The initiative factor has already been discussed in connection with "making the contact." You cannot afford to be careless about the place at which you meet the person. Whether the counselee is a man or a woman, in either instance you communicate your identity as a caring pastor by the place where you suggest that you meet. It is highly preferable that the person come either to your study or to your home at a time when other persons are also in the church building or at your home. This can usually be done and still allow discreet and unobserved privacy for the conversation. If this cannot be done, another time should be arranged when it will be possible. Responsible attention given to finding a place of discreet privacy, but with someone nearby, forestalls your being alone in a building with the person in the event that an emergency arises or in the event that your presence with the person would be for any reason misinterpreted either by the person with whom you are counseling or by other persons. For example, one pastor was alone in his study early one morning talking with a businessman about a personal problem, and the businessman had a heart attack. The pastor had great difficulty in handling this emergency alone.

Furthermore, you need tactfully to interpret the time situation to a person at the outset of a conversation. Thus, both you and the person will be more relaxed in the time you do have together. This avoids some of the stress and divided attention that may otherwise come at the end of the conversation. Usually an interview should be about an hour in length. It may be shortened to forty-five minutes or even to a half hour when the relationship has matured and strengthened. It may be lengthened a bit on the first interview or in the event that circumstances of distance in travel or length of time between the interviews necessitate this. Rarely should an interview continue over an hour and a half without a break. The pastoral counseling relationship does not really develop fully in hurried conditions. The amount of time the pastor, teacher, or administrator can give to one person usually begins to be strained when the more intensive phases of the relationship extend beyond a dozen interviews. However, effective pastoral counseling often comes in "rounds" of three to five interviews at a time, with months and even years elapsing between groupings of interviews.

Most persons who are suffering from emotional handicaps are discouraged, tense, suspicious, and self-conscious. In the earliest phases of your relationship to such persons, you put them at ease and disarm them of their personal mistrust of you. Likewise, you establish some meeting point of feeling with them and define clearly your own relationship to them. The success or failure of a counseling situation is often determined within the first half hour of the discussion. A "relationship of a trusted motive" must be established and the suspicions of the person relieved before progress can be made. Erik Erikson speaks of the element of trust as the foundational factor in human integrity and development. He says that in "adults the impairment of basic trust is expressed in a basic mistrust." He also perceives that the positive function of religion is to restore a sense of trust. "Whoever says he has religion must derive a faith from it which is transmitted to infants in the form of basic trust." (Erikson, *Identity and the Life Cycle,* pp. 56, 64–65.)

The pastor in this phase of any relationship, therefore, will be sensitive to three trust-building and trust-interfering factors in the experience of the person who is being counseled:

1. *The relief of nervous tension.* The person is often frightened at talking with you and especially about personal concerns. Breathlessness may indicate either fear of the interview situation or haste in arriving for the appointment in time. Drawn features may indicate sleeplessness, loss of appetite. Clenched fists, sweaty palms, and twisted handkerchiefs may point toward a burden of unrelieved anxiety. Rigid perching on the edge of a chair, furtive movements of the body—all these and many other signs are the tattered edges of a tense spirit showing themselves. Be alert and sensitive to the degree of tension in a counselee at all times. By the composure within yourself, the unhurriedness of your manner, and the steady certainty of your tone of voice you can communicate confidence and peacefulness to the person. Often purposely avoid talking about significant and painful matters until the person feels more at ease and under less tension. The

person must be relatively free from the mental blocking that arises from emotional tension before being able to discuss difficulties profitably. This process of relaxation, by whatever legitimate means you most aptly can use, is the first prerequisite of good counseling. The small talk, superficial conversation about places and relations, a brief prayer for peace and clarity of vision, and direct suggestions such as: "Sit in this chair. I think you will be able to relax more"; "Why not pause a little while and catch your breath? You've been running"; "Lean back in your chair and take it easy"—all these point toward an easing of tension.

2. *The acceptance of personal antagonism.* The occasion that brings many people with deep-seated emotional disturbances to a minister quite often is one of anger and resentment. A person may come to you under pressure from someone else and resent both that other person and you for being put in such a position. But occasionally the point that stimulated the person's anger may be something you yourself have done that the person did not like.

Anger is regularly denied. The word itself is taboo to many people within and outside the church. They are more likely to use the words, "I am hurt," or "frustrated," or "it's not fair." Deep wells of antagonism prevent these persons from having a relaxed relationship with you. The most common fear is that you will condemn them if you know them as they really are. They fear that you will betray them in some unknown way. But even more subtle are those antagonisms which cause persons to misinterpret and distort your words, to ascribe to you meanings that you did not reflect to them, and even to deny the truth of their own words that might be repeated back to them verbatim.

You also have the task of disarming your counselee of any antagonism toward former ministers that may be spilling over into the person's feelings toward you, the present pastor. The resentments that the person holds toward other people in the church also inhibit a friendly relationship.

By careful definition of your own relationship with and an undivided attention toward the person, you can tactfully disarm the person of much of this resistance. Sometimes this may take a whole interview; with others a "meeting point of feeling" is never established. But no smoothness of ministry can be achieved until the thermostats of the person's heart have been opened by the warmth of friendship and sustained by the strength of a basic trust. This does not mean you are doing no good for these persons. Later, in some instances they will return and thank you for not either giving in to their anger or responding in kind.

3. *Mutual acceptance of personal responsibility.* One hazard in the establishment of rapport is that the person will shirk personal responsibility for the difficulties and shift to a complete dependence upon the pastor for a solution. Whereas some people refuse to trust a minister at all, a great many take the relationship of mutual trust as a parasitic opportunity "to pass the buck" of their troubles to the pastor. When you fail to measure up to their expectations, then you begin to get resistance from them. The genius of effective counseling is to leave the responsibility for the solution of the problem with the person who has the problem, without causing the person to feel abandoned. You provide a permissive and warmly personal atmosphere in which a counselee can objectively work through the problem to a satisfactory solution. Religiously stated, it is the careful observance of the principle of the autonomy of the individual personality before God. The counselor exercises a confident trust in the lawful working of the Holy Spirit both to will and to do for the good pleasure of God in the life of the person. Furthermore, perceive persons as they perceive themselves! Get their

internal frame of reference. Exert the religious discipline
of self-emptying which in itself is "good news" to your
stress-ridden counselees.

From your point of view as a pastor, you take preventive
measures in order that you may not become so encum-
bered with the difficulties of one person that you cannot
minister to the many other people who come to you. It
aids you in your own personal relaxation to get over the
compulsive necessity of doing something about every
problem that is brought to you and to accept the realism
of Paul's maxim, "Each man will have to bear his own
load" (Gal. 6:5). The sense in which you are fulfilling the
law of Christ by bearing the other person's load with that
person lies in your provision of a faithful presence of togetherness with the person. Thus the person is neither
alone nor wrapped up in the self; the person is sharing the
reality of the Christian community.

These three problems—the degree of tension, the degree of personal antagonism, and the degree of personal
responsibility—are the issues at stake in establishing rapport with the person who comes to you with a more profound personality problem. At all stages of counseling, the
degree of rapport may be strengthened or weakened in
such a way as to help or hinder any further progress. No
smoothness of ministry can be achieved at all, however,
until the person has accepted you through the warmth of
friendship and the power of genuine trust.

The Phase of Listening and Exploration

Blending into the phase of relaxation and the development of trust is the period of "talking it out." Your counselee has a story to tell, a mosaic of present events and past
connotations. The person feels that life is slipping away
and some real decisions need to be made. A tangled
schemata of events needs to be unraveled. You listen to
this intently, you create at all times an atmosphere of

safety in which long-harbored events may come to light. The person socializes, often for the first time, the thoughts and feelings that have hovered in the hinterland of the consciousness, creating anxieties that could not be explained but could only be felt and responded to with blind compulsion.

1. *The ministry of listening.* The pastor at this phase of the counseling situation depends almost entirely upon the ministry of listening. Much needs to be said at this point on the use of this powerful tool of pastoral work.

The easiest way to help people is to understand them. As Lin Yutang has said, "To understand is to forgive." The easiest way to understand people is to listen to them, to hear them out. Listening creatively is an art in itself. It calls into action those other nonverbal forms of communication which are dramatically more powerful than the use of words: eye expression, bodily responses of muscle and movement to meaning, and the effect of total silence. As Reik has said, "It is important that we recognize what speech conceals and what silence reveals." (Theodor Reik, *Listening with the Third Ear,* p. 126.) Listening essentially means three things.

a. It means *actually hearing what the person says,* hearing with an "evenly hovering attention." You are most susceptible to letting your attention wander from the person to whom you are listening to any one of the thousand other things that you have to think about. Preoccupation with other things is like damp rot in your counseling ministry. Shuffling papers on the desk, searching out a letter from your pocket, furtively glancing at your watch—all these are subtle ways of indicating that you are giving halfhearted attention to what is being said. Likewise, we quite often miss the mark in understanding people because we do not pay attention to seemingly insignificant details concerning their attitudes and feelings.

But it would be a mistake to assume, as Reik says again, that "all observation is purely conscious. Not until we have learned to appreciate the significance of unconscious observation, reacting to the faintest impressions with the sensitiveness of a sheet of tinfoil, shall we recognize the difficulty of transforming imponderabilia into ponderabilia." (Ibid., p. 142.) In this sense, listening is a sort of "free-floating attention," which "makes note of everything equally."

b. Listening means *letting the person do the talking.* Suppress the temptation to make comments and observations to the person with whom you are counseling. Don't give your own understanding of the difficulties *as soon as you yourself have seen them.* Careful restraint and attentive listening instead often reveal that the person has already thought of these things. Almost a miracle occurs to hear a person say that which it seems impossible for the person even to see, much less articulate. The counselee whom you genuinely trust to work faithfully at problems will often utter the very words *you would have* uttered, without any prompting from you.

In the sense of *letting* counselees do the talking, listening is a passive process. Here your passive listening lays hold of the "active power of silence," which "makes small talk transparent, and has a force that pulls them forward, driving them into deeper layers of their experience than they had intended." Also, it calls upon your initiative as the pastor.

Of course, the use of silence, in the sense of letting the person do the talking, depends upon the degree of trust that is present between the pastor and the person at hand. Subtle miracles can and do occur as you do this. Douglas Steere describes the process in an exquisitely written section in his book *On Listening to Another:*

> Have you ever sat with a friend when in the course of an easy and pleasant conversation the talk took a new turn and you both listened avidly to the other and to something that was emerging in your visit? You found yourselves saying

things that astonished you and finally you stopped talking and there was an immense naturalness about the long silent pause that followed. In that silent interval you were possessed by what you had discovered together. If this has happened to you, you know that when you come up out of such an experience, there is a memory of rapture and a feeling in the heart of having touched holy ground. (Steere, *On Listening to Another,* p. 1)

The silence of a physician of the spirit slowly changes its significance to the person with whom you are working. I was interviewing a thirty-year-old man who had always been passively dependent upon his pastors, college professors, and parents for the motivation of his behavior. The interviews consisted of many long and painful silences in between jerky, halting outbursts of insight into this infantile dependence upon others. On the fourth interview, the man said, "I have decided that I have been coming to talk with you just to get on the good side of you, just as I did with my pastor and my professors in college."

Then I said, "Have you been that eager to have my approval?" Then a long, stringent silence ensued, at the beginning of which I felt a sense of impatience at the fact that the man would not talk any further. Then I remembered that silence could uncover what speech would hide, remained silent, and felt the impulse to pray silently in the man's behalf. During the meditative silence, the man arose from his seat and walked out of the room.

Two weeks later, the man sought another conference and told me this: "During that exceedingly talkative [laughing at his own humor] interview we had the last time we were together, I made up my mind that, in order to clear my own thinking, I would just have to break my dependence on you. I felt that the only way to do this was to come in and engage you in conversation and get up and walk out and leave you. But when I came, you just sat silent. *At first I felt that your silence was an unfriendly silence, but suddenly it changed and I felt it was a friendly silence. I had the feeling that if I did leave your office, you would understand."*

Therefore, the use of a passive listening is predicated upon the "friendliness of the silence" of the pastor. This can best be approximated by facial assurances of understanding, and by creating the illusion of talking by using such interjections as "Uh-huh," "Yes," "I think I see," "Did he?" Or it can be accomplished by repeating the trailing ends of sentences, such as, "You say you went from home to work that morning." This is a continual flow of encouragement from you to the person with whom you are counseling, stimulating the person's confidence to talk and making it easier for the person. If, however, you are preoccupied with trying to formulate what you yourself are going to say as soon as you find an opening, you may find the opening sooner than you think. It is much more effective to follow the lead of the most emotion-laden response of the counselee and encourage the person by reflecting these feelings back to the person to explore them more thoroughly.

c. Listening, in the third place, means *actually getting the person to talk.* In this sense, listening is an active experience on your part. Here you take some positive initiative. At this point the pastoral counselor is no longer hobbled by earlier demands for "nondirectiveness." Nevertheless, you maintain person-centeredness rather than problem-centeredness, positive regard and respect for the counselee, and a steady practice of getting the person's own internal frame of reference, values, and anxieties. In the first instance, you can take the initiative in the listening by following the lead of the person and picking up the specific trailing end of the sentence that is spoken with the most feeling and strength of tone. This amounts to asking the person to talk a little bit more about the particular subject being discussed, without using those words at all.

Again, active listening calls into action your right to ask questions. This is directive listening. What the scalpel is to the surgeon, the question is to the pastoral counselor. Therefore, the question is used with antiseptic motives, clean hands, and a pure heart devoid of vanity and deceptiveness. The important thing for you to remember is that you not run ahead of the sense of trust that you have with the person. You do not ask a question that the person has not given you the spiritual privilege to ask. Then, for the sake of time and because of the informal nature of much pastoral counseling, you can, with safety for all concerned, encourage the person to talk by asking well-placed questions. Here you may fill out a gap of information, you may reflect a feeling, or you may even suggest an association by the way you ask a question.

These are the three significant meanings of the listening ministry—hearing what the person says, letting the person do the talking, and actively encouraging the person to talk. They should be borne in mind as you enter upon the phase of counseling that has been called "listening and exploration." However, certain precautions as to the use of a passive or an active listening approach need to be made. Such a method may cause the pastor to spend time that should be used more valuably by a person with greater skill who could give more concentrated attention to the person. An example of this would be the case of those persons who are so acutely depressed that they become more agitated and depressed as they talk more and more to their own confusion. In fact, they may be so depressed as to be mute. An attempt on the part of the minister to explore their difficulties through a listening approach might even make things worse. Total dependence upon listening as a pastoral procedure, to the exclusion of basic knowledge and skillful evaluation of the different patterns of emotional reaction in people's lives, is ineffectual at best and dangerous at worst. For example, this approach is limited in dealing with passive-aggressive persons. In my book *Pastoral Counseling* these patterns of self-structure are dealt with in detail.

2. *The achievement of insight.* Your frank objective in this second phase of the ministry of counseling is that the person with whom you are dealing will achieve insight into the difficulties the person has *and* develop control over them. This is done by indirection rather than by frontal assaults on the besetting difficulties of the individual. It comes to pass through the process of listening and exploration somewhat after this manner:

Repressed memories return in the present feelings of the person. Do not think of these memories as being *past* experiences. They live actively in the present existence of the individual, who unconsciously considers them as present realities rather than as things that are in the past. For example, if a person had a sadistic, cruel parent as a child, the chances are that the parent is *still* treating the person that way. Or, the present dream life of the person reenacts the old events. As one hospital patient said upon having dreamed of her childhood, "All those people who have long been dead are now alive again in my mind." These are memories, yes, but they were buried alive, and, like Hamlet's father's uneasy spirit, find their way back into the daily affairs of the person's life. The ministry of attentive, careful, and considerate listening provides the atmosphere in which these memories and present feelings may return for the person's own reconsideration and for assimilation into the person's reasonable way of life.

You will also be alert to the *expression of ambivalent feelings* on the part of the person, or opposing feelings about the same point of concern. For example, in one context an attitude of almost worshipping the father may be expressed, and in another connection the person may mention having discovered recently that the father is dismally wrong about many things. In the presence of the contradictions, you may be prone to say, "But I thought you said you almost worshiped him!" This would give the person a trapped feeling. *Simply to reflect these feelings back to the person in a mirror fashion lets the person see the contrast, not hear it.* Whereas people see through a glass darkly, and know only in part, this is one way of moving them toward a conviction of insight that *may* eventuate in constructive actions.

This acceptance, clarification, and balancing of contradictory needs in the lives of people is vital concerning their feelings toward God. The tensions in the person between the need for aggression and the need for passivity, the need for independence and the need for dependence, the need for individuality and the need for social approval, the need for rebellion and the need for authority, constantly call for a frank conversation about God's relationship to the person. Encouraging this balance in the lives of people is a frankly accepted objective of a good pastor. In reality, these ambivalences are conflicts in the value structures coming to fresh focus in their perceptions. This struggle is an ethical struggle of the self for consistency of values. (See Prescott Lecky, *Self-Consistency,* ed. by John F. A. Taylor.)

The *need for self-rejection and the need for self-acceptance* constantly tend to stalemate each other. These opposing needs usually appear in the context of the question that arises as to whether the persons at hand should express or deny themselves in the search for personal satisfaction. They may have in mind aggressive impulses and feel very guilty over losing their temper but feel that they cannot accept themselves as a weakling! Or they may realize freedom in Christ to enjoy the sexual life but do not know what to do with this freedom. Of course, such instances are illustrations of ambivalent feelings toward the self. They reflect a fear of one's own emotions and a confusion as to one's purposes in life.

Naturally, the problems of self-acceptance are basically of a religious nature. (Robert H. Bonthius, *Christian Paths to Self-Acceptance.*) They suggest that the achievement of insight in the process of personal counseling may be superficial or profound, destructive or creative, temporary or permanent, depending upon the level of truly religious feeling it reaches. *The Christian pastor frankly accepts the fact that ethical values make a difference in the mental health of a person.* Discriminating judgment of such values reveals about four qualitatively different levels of insight.

a. On the *ascetic level of insight,* individuals refuse to accept the idea of even having negative feelings of aggression, passionate feelings of a sexual nature, power drives of domination, acquisitive desires for possession, and self-destructive drives because of meaninglessness. These persons live on the basis of complete repression and inner blindness to their humanity. In a word, they feel not only that they are without sin but that they are not tempted.

b. On the *fatalistic level of intellectual insight,* individuals are "sicklied o'er with the pale cast of thought," accept intellectually that they have certain problems but find more satisfaction in analyzing themselves than in attempting any changes in their way of life. Quite often they will use the opportunity for an interview as a mirror before which they can preen their symptoms. It is as though they had a filmlike image of themselves before them. Their descriptions of their difficulties become means of satisfaction rather than an unhappiness to them. Again, such persons may subtly defy the counselor to solve their problems and, when the house is swept clean, they may return a few days later with "seven other" problems to take the place of the first one.

Or these persons may take the fatalistic attitude of a stoic and become one whose "head is bloody, but unbowed," engage in heroics of their determination, and resign themselves to their fate. Stoicism is often mistaken for Christian faith by such persons.

c. On the *sociopathic level of Machiavellian insight,* these persons see their antisocial and asocial tendencies and rejoice in the new freedom of their insight. They take their knowledge as an occasion to the flesh. They take a delinquent turn, and the people around them pay the price for this newfound "understanding" of themselves. Their insight is that of creativity gone berserk. They take advantage of society to get their own wishes, although they may use the appearance of socially acceptable standards to get their own way. This "acting out" of impulses may create havoc in the life of a church, a school, or a society as a whole.

d. On the *level of the Christian stewardship of insight,* which is the profoundest level of insight, these persons will to give up immediate pleasures for more lasting and eternal satisfactions. Impulses are used as "instruments of righteousness" unto life rather than as instruments of sin unto death. They interpret their own good in terms of social feeling for other people. They use newfound freedom as a means to liberate and understand other people. They alleviate their suffering even as theirs has been alleviated for them. This sounds the depths of Christian experience and lays hold of the need of the individual for community with other people who share in the fellowship of agreed-upon values, also. Here individuals have achieved insight not only into the nature of their own imperfections and lack of omnipotence. They also have entered into an acceptance of the imperfections and fallibilities of those about them. Temporal reality takes its proper relation to the Eternal.

The gift of such insight moves from "deep . . . unto deep" in the reality of the counseling situation. You as pastor need to be very careful not to accept the first statement of a problem as the real one. For instance, a young university student came for his first interview saying that he had begun to doubt "that God exists." Then in the third interview he said, "I have no doubt that God exists and that he is good, but I am beginning to see that my real trouble is that I am afraid my father and mother will not approve my marrying until I finish school." In the fourth interview he said, "I guess my main problem is that my mother has never wanted me to marry." In a later interview he stated, "I am going ahead with my plans to be married this summer, and I think I can help mother to take it."

The problem in this instance changed its form in the student's mind as the level of his understanding deepened. Like Job, he did not begin to lay hold of the resources of strength until he sought help for those who were at one and the same time the closest to him and his greatest vexation.

Much has been said here about the revelatory experience of insight. The qualitatively different kinds of insight I have described reflect the fact that insight for its own sake may be a waste of time and energy. It is not enough to beg the question by saying that the person simply needs more insight.

Let me go one step further and say that insight is not always necessary for a real change of heart. Change often occurs in people from their becoming exhausted with ineffective ways of being. Change may occur when a traumatic event gives them a glimpse of death and a glaring light of deliverance. Change may come when they see their firstborn child. Change often comes when people meet, hear, and choose to follow a gifted leader. Change often takes place when individuals discover that they are no longer powerless, helpless, and in the clutch of fate.

Yalom rightly says that insight is of value only when it prompts a person to "take some stand toward change." (Yalom, *Existential Psychotherapy*, p. 339.) In my own words, insight must jell into convictions that involve a change of direction in life, and specific behaviors must result that coincide with the convictions. The counselee, as Emerson says, "learns to speak his latent convictions, to believe in his own thoughts, and to believe that what is true for him is true for all people." Yalom calls these "leverage-producing insights." Examples are: "Only I can change the world I have created." "There is no danger in change." "To get what I really want I must change." "I have the power to change." (Ibid., pp. 340–341.) This all sounds good except for the overtones of self-sufficiency.

Other therapists today insist that insight comes *after* the behavior has changed. Emotional response comes after a self-imposed discipline such as breaking an addiction such as obesity, being released from a phobia, or being set free of a dangerous habit such as fire-setting, exhibitionism, or child molestation. These therapists ask for an act of surrender to the person's own helplessness, participation in a group of fellow sufferers, and learning new adaptive rather than maladaptive habits. You can learn much about this from persons like William Glasser, M.D., in his book *Stations of the Mind: New Directions for Reality Therapy*, and Halmuth H. Schaefer and Patrick L. Martin, in their book *Behavioral Therapy*.

The Phase of Reconstruction and Guidance

You are concerned not only with helping persons with their inner conflicts. Their reconstruction of purposes requires your interest in and guidance in a new way of life. God works in reorganizing personality in essentially a redemptive way. God helps a person to back the new commitments in a way of growth and consecration. Therefore, you, in this fourth phase of your counseling ministry, are present when the person begins to turn a plan of action into a new freedom and a new walk of life in God. Consequently, your approach may change considerably in order that the person may be encouraged to sustain the new selfhood.

Usually you are most meaningful when you appeal to the sense of adventure and experimentation of the person with whom you are dealing at the time. Several opportunities present themselves at this stage of the relationship.

1. *The interpretation of the life situation.* You may want to give a brief interpretation of the basic causes of the trouble, or make a series of concrete suggestions. It is best

that these avoid wordiness, be to the point, in simple language, and easily understood. *Usually, as in all phases of
personal counseling, it is better to use the same words that
the person uses and to lay hold of any figures of speech or
ways of expression that the counselee has presented.* I am
reminded of a member of one of my rural churches who
once asked me "what to do when the plow hits a stump
and a fellow swears before he can stop to save his life."
Being in the midst of the preparation of a sermon on
temptation, I went into a long, detailed, catacomblike explanation of how to stop swearing. The man listened with
interest and attention, and when I had finished he said,
"Yes, but, pastor, by the time I remember all that, I've
done gone and cussed!" A few words would have been
much easier to remember.

Several tested ways of interpretation are valuable: You
may interpret by the kind of questions you ask, the order
in which you ask them, and the tone of voice in which you
speak. The interview that Jesus held at the well with the
woman of Samaria is a case in point here. He interpreted
her problem by asking her to go get her husband. Again,
you may interpret by giving a short summary of the relationship and the different turns the conversation has
taken. Another method that Jesus used constantly was that
of an appeal to the experience of other people, the use of
a parable, or the use of a proverb. Sometimes the parables
the persons themselves use are invaluable. One person
said that his life was like a wagon full of barrels which was
used to haul water from the river to the church baptistry:
by the time the wagon got to the church, all the water that
had been in the back barrel was in the front and vice versa.
He averred that his family discord had so affected his
work, and vice versa, that he could not tell which was
which! This is a valuable "homemade parable" for use in
interpretation.

But the best way that you can interpret the life situation
of a person is to encourage the person to express frankly

and objectively the personal responses of affection and antipathy that the person feels toward you as counselor. This was called "relationship" counseling, devised many years ago by Jessie Taft and Otto Rank. An illustration is the young woman who, for several years, had moved from one denomination to another as she became attached to a different pastor. In bringing her difficulty to the pastor at this particular time, she finally came to the conclusion that she would unite with his church. He registered no surprise or undue elation. In the next interview the pastor was able to interpret tactfully what the changing of denominations had meant to her and to disentangle her church affiliation from too much dependence upon the minister. The pastor's interpretation of the relationship was the basis for counseling her.

2. *The brief pastoral dialogue.* You as the pastor may be asked by the person to whom you are ministering to confer about a specific plan of action with reference to marriage, parental responsibilities, educational plans, or vocational readjustments. Here you may resort to the use of the brief pastoral dialogue that was suggested earlier in this chapter.

3. *The introduction to Christian friends.* At the same time, you may take on the functions of a teacher-evangelist, seeking to relate the person to the church, to fellowship groups, and to other sources of spiritual undergirding. Also, you may feel that some particular member of your church or community, such as a physician, an attorney, a business person and employer, or maybe one of the dependable members of the church, could be a meaningful friend to this person. Therefore, you may introduce the person to one or more of these friends for specialized help.

4. *The selection of appropriate literature and Scripture passages.* At this stage of the counseling process, you may deem it advisable also to refer the person to certain literature that will be specifically applicable to reconstructing the person's outlook on life. You may find that the person

knows next to nothing about the Bible, and that you have the opportunity to cause the New and Old Testaments to come alive to the person in the light of the person's life situation. By and large, the persons who come to a pastor are religious illiterates and stand in need of this sort of help. You should be very careful not to hand the whole Bible to them and make some generalized and vague remark as to its healing power. You should carefully (ahead of time if possible) select the sections that give the clearest guidance to the persons in terms of their educational background.

Whatever interpretation, instruction, or introduction to other people is given to the person, it should indicate a plain path of action. The person will need reassurance, spiritual support, and vital encouragement. The encouraging power of your own confidence in the person cannot be overestimated. You are wise to use down-to-earth common sense in suggesting goals as you evolve plans along with the person. These goals need to be in keeping with the abilities of the person to achieve them. All these procedures are appropriate only after you and the parishioner together have a relaxed sense of certainty that you have arrived at the real issues of the person's life situation. If you have any doubt at all that the person has not come to the core of the problem with you, or if you are confused in your own mind as to what the situation actually is, you should begin to angle for another interview. Reflection, maturation, and the opportunity for more conversation are the only things that can clarify the matter.

The Phase of Follow-up and Experimentation

Much effective counseling has gone to waste because of a failure on the part of pastors to follow up the progress of the persons with whom they have dealt. This is notoriously true of the counseling done by pastors in evangelistic meetings, religious retreats, college religious emphasis weeks, etc. In this final phase of personal counseling, several issues are at stake:

1. *Overdependence.* The breaking of the continuity of regular interviews creates an emotional crisis in the life of the person in and of itself. The chances are that the person has become too dependent upon the counselor, and the interviews have become something of a sedative to soothe anxieties. The person may interpret the breaking of a series of formal interviews as a personal rejection. At this point you are made to feel more keenly the powerful charges of affection that have been transferred to you by the person. One person said to his pastor, "What will I do when you are too far away for me to find you?" The pastor interpreted the relationship in this manner: "You seem to wish that I were capable of being everywhere and probably are assuming that I am all-powerful also, as far as you are concerned. This is your attempt to deify me, but only God can be God in your life. It is God who is all-present and all-powerful, and you can talk with him any time. We call this prayer, and I should like for you to try to develop that practice in your life." In your ministry of "follow-up," you can do nothing more effective than "tutor" in the art of prayer the people with whom you counsel. This can be done on a group basis as well as on an individual basis.

Another difficulty of an overdependent relationship between a pastor and a parishioner at the point of follow-up is that the parishioner will continue to bring each minor decision to you as the pastor for your opinion or in an attempt to sustain the former continuity. This is especially true of pastors or student counselors in a college setting. Adolescents draw a great deal of personal strength from being near a person with whom they can identify and like whom they would seek to become. They have an abundance of "free-floating" anxiety that they allay in this way when they are away from home and from those people who have naturally filled voids in their lives.

2. *Fear and hostility.* The failure to provide room for

false starts and mistakes and relapses to old patterns of behavior by holding over the person's head a perfectionistic, "sure cure" goal to be achieved may cause the person to avoid you in the event such things should happen. Persons feel that, if one slip is made, facing you who had such high hopes for them would be too much. Later they may say that they have "let the pastor down." In a real sense they have let you displace God on this score also.

Another way of falling into the same error is by dominating the decisions of persons in such a way that the only means by which they can become persons in their own right is to rebel completely against the whole relationship with you. In the context of a pastoral community, such rebellions can take vicious turns and do more damage than can be undone in a long while. Yet a measure of real hostility—frankly and warmly accepted—may be a healthy sign of growth, even necessary for the continued autonomy of the individual. Your calling as a pastor is to be a faithful servant, not to be liked or disliked!

3. *Gossip.* The gossip hazard also conditions the form that a "follow-up" ministry may take. Parishioners may become very uneasy as they get more removed from a face-to-face relationship with you. Then they will become apprehensive lest you be irresponsible in references about them as counselees to others. Out of sheer discomfort, they may move their church membership elsewhere. Or, in the pressure of a momentary crisis, they may seek out irresponsible persons in the community and give an emotionally distorted version of some snatch of their conversation with you. Jesus, in his pastoral ministry, was continually plagued by the results of such gossip. Little wonder that he charged people to go and tell no one of their interviews! A part of the covenant of communication involves the counselees' responsible commitment to confer with the pastor if and when they plan to discuss their pastoral conversations with others.

4. *Positive follow-up.* But more positively, the pastor

may follow up private conferences with people by visits in their homes. You have this privilege and will often be invited into the homes of newfound friends. You may be asked to perform the wedding ceremony of the young man or woman whom you counseled prior to the marriage. These same persons will occasionally invite you to conduct a dedication service in their new home, or when a baby is born to them. A young minister may ask you to preach an ordination sermon, or a young business person may want you to speak at a civic club. Although you have numerous outside contacts such as these, the majority of persons with whom you counsel will be members of your church. You will see them in church services, have them in discussion groups, and preach to them Sunday after Sunday. These contacts can enrich or impoverish your counseling ministry, depending upon your appreciation of the dynamics of group life and your sensitivity to people's feelings toward one another.

Quite often you will counsel with people whom you will not see again because they are not so closely knit with your own community. They may be people from another city who have been sent to you by someone you have helped before and who has moved away. They may be the relatives of a member of your church and are hospitalized in the city where you minister. Or they may come to you from having read something you wrote, from having heard you over the radio or on television, or from having seen you in a religious assembly. As one "person-minded" minister wrote: "I sometimes wonder how it is the word gets around about one, if he is competent to help others when they need him. But I am learning daily how much it does get around. I count it a privilege to counsel with those who come, although I am constantly amazed at my total inadequacy—but by leaning hard on the counsel of the Holy Spirit, the friend and I work out in our thinking helpful avenues through many and varied problems."

This defines the feeling of a minister who is concerned

with the inner peace of people: you feel competent and full of confidence in your ministry, yet you sense our inadequacy as you confront the magnitude of human suffering. When you discover your own perennial source of dependence in the Holy Spirit and a sense of community with the person in need, helpful avenues are found.

Never become overconfident of your own skill in the use of any technique of pastoral care. If you do, you soon begin to depreciate and think irreverently of the personalities of those with whom you deal. You begin to "play on their souls," which causes them to turn on you. Shakespeare describes such careless irreverence in Hamlet's dialogue with Rosencrantz and Guildenstern, who had been sent to lure Hamlet's secret from him. Hamlet begs Guildenstern tauntingly to play upon a flute that he offers him. But Guildenstern says: "I have not the skill. . . . These cannot I command to any utterance of harmony." Then, with much vehemence, Hamlet replies:

> Why, look you now, how unworthy a thing you make of me!
> You would play upon me, you would seem to know my
> stops, you would pluck out the heart of my mystery, you
> would sound me from my lowest note to the top of my
> compass; and there is much music, excellent voice, in this
> little organ, yet cannot you make it speak. 'Sblood, do you
> think that I am easier to be play'd on than a pipe? Call me
> what instrument you will, though you can fret me, you
> cannot play upon me. (*Hamlet,* Act III, Scene 2)

EXTENDED PASTORAL PSYCHOTHERAPY

The discussions of counseling thus far in this book have been aimed entirely at the working situation of the pastor who leads a congregation in worship and the celebration of the Lord's Supper. At different points I have described and affirmed the specialized forms of pastoral counseling done in pastoral counseling centers which may or may not be related to a local church, an association of churches, a diocese, etc. Increasingly, such centers are being by economic necessity forced to solicit funds for themselves as nonprofit corporations and to complete their budgetary demands by charging fees for service to counselees. In turn, counselees ask if the services of a pastoral counselor are "covered" by private insurance carriers and/or Medicare. These are called "third-party payments." Certification agencies, such as the American Association of Pastoral Counselors and the American Association for Marriage and Family Therapy, have committees and lobbying groups in Washington, D.C., to see to it that such payments are duly qualified and permitted. How the time-consuming work of the specialist pastoral psychotherapist is to be financed is as yet an inadequately answered question.

You readily see that the persons and processes to and for which a pastoral counselor ministers are quite apart from direct answerability to the face-to-face community of Christians, although not from the reign and rule of the sovereignty of God. The inroads of secularism are ever present. Yet the critical problem is the lack of theological seriousness on the part of the churches in providing for their people's psychotherapeutic needs. The inroads of secularism are on the ground the churches leave unattended, i.e., the unconsidered quiet desperation of their people. This ecclesiastical irresponsibility is the stuff that catalyzes secularism.

Yet, whether the churches come alive to their responsibilities or not, the specialized function of Christian pastors for intensive pastoral psychotherapy is growing and will continue to grow. Enterprising and gifted men and women called of the Lord for this work will find ways and means of doing this ministry. After many years pass and severe sacrifices of a few intrepid spirits have been made, the movement has weight, becomes popular, and many will want to climb on the bandwagon. In the meantime, if you are one of those intrepid spirits and want a guidebook for traversing the terrain over which you have to travel to become established as a disciplined and consecrated pastoral counselor whose whole discipline is in this ministry, then read the book *The Organization and Administration of Pastoral Counseling Centers,* ed. by John C. Carr, John E. Hinkle, and David M. Moss III.

The most sensitive areas in the specialized practice of pastoral counseling, it seems to me, are: (1) The pastoral and theological confusion that arises out of the allure of third-party payments for the service. The person who pays the piper calls the tune. Answerability to one's ordination is primary in my value system, and the dilution or confusion of this is inherent in dependence upon third-party payments. (2) The problems of sustaining a unique theological core and content in shaping the methodologies of counseling used are inherent in the specialized function of counseling. (3) The problem of elitism exists that would make a "guild" of pastoral psychotherapists who discount the pastoral counseling done by general parish pastors. Recently some references have appeared in the literature which frankly say that the pastor of a church *cannot,* by the nature of the social context in which the pastor works, be a counselor. (See Richard L. Krebs, "Why Pastors Should Not Be Counselors," *The Journal of Pastoral Care,* Dec. 1980, pp. 229–233.) What the authors of those references mean is that a pastor cannot be a psychoanalytically oriented psychotherapist. Yet, if you are a generalist pastor of a church, do not let this elitist stand discourage you. You have other ways of accomplishing some of the same goals a psychoanalytically oriented pastoral psychotherapist uses. The generalist pastor may effectively accomplish similar goals—some as good, some better, and some not as good—with individuals through new disciplines of systems orchestration.

Nothing we can do can ignore, safely permit us to lower our consciousness of, or make purely implicit the centrality of God's claim upon us as his ministers of reconciliation. Elitism in pastoral counseling confuses both the good theology and the good psychotherapy of the generalist pastor.

Chapter VIII

The Pastor as a Minister
of Introduction

As the years have added new perspective to the kinds of relationships described in the foregoing pages, three major impressions stand out in my mind as both indigenous to and primary in the values of the Christian pastor. First, you as a pastor not only *represent* God as he is revealed in Jesus Christ through the Holy Spirit; you actually *introduce* people to the God and Father of our Lord Jesus Christ. You do this through your teaching and pastoral care, both as preacher and shepherd. Thus, you are an evangelist in the best sense of the word, i.e., you are personally acquainted with the Lord Jesus Christ. You want your friends to "come and see him" who brought all that you ever did to focus with a whole new meaning, calling, and destiny. Secondly, you as a pastor, therefore, are at work meeting new people and establishing lasting and creative relationships with them. Human relationships, once formed, cannot be broken; they can only be changed into more creative ones or deteriorate into indifference or destructiveness. Tragically enough, you and I as pastors struggle with the theological complexity of what has been called "the death of a relationship," as in the case of some divorces. Yet these "deaths," spoken of metaphorically, are like actual biological deaths—their influence, history, and effects of the person continue. In all such rifts and chasms in human relationships, you as a Christian pastor

are like John Bunyan's Mr. Faithful. You establish covenants with people and keep them. You are sensitive to and
scientifically informed about the processes that human
relationships undergo in time. You are steadfast, immovable, and abundant in your devotion.

Thirdly, as a Christian pastor you become durably
related to persons, and you introduce them to each other
and to persons who can enable them to help themselves
by providing them with the rich resources that friendship,
professional skills, and winnowed wisdom can afford them.
Thus you multiply your own service to parishioners and
other counselees and at the same time create a bond of
service between them to each other in your church, and
between them and other professional persons within and
outside the church. You yourself orchestrate, inspire, and
lead.

As Daniel Aleshire says in *Ministry in America,* one of
the first five most commonly agreed upon expectations of
you as a minister is that you are "sharing ministry and
developing a community that nourishes and sustains that
ministry." "Building . . . a strong sense of community
within a congregation" calls for the ability to "handle administrative responsibilities with understanding, effi-
ciency, and careful planning." (Aleshire, "Eleven Major
Areas of Ministry," in *Ministry in America,* pp. 34–35.)
Earlier, Niebuhr spoke of being as a "pastoral director,"
and "building and edifying the church." (H. Richard Niebuhr, *The Purpose of the Church and Its Ministry,* pp.
79–94.)

As a pastor caring for the well-being of individuals, and
for individuals and families, this is your "ministry of introduction," a ministry that is an alchemy in human relationships. It takes the unsightly, seemingly valueless, and even
detrimental stuff of human suffering and turns it into a
community of significant and committed persons for people in distress. As one handicapped person, made so in an
unfortunate accident, put it: "I met five lifetime friends

through this awful thing that happened. It doesn't change what happened, but it has gone a long way toward making what happened worth a lot to me."

In the first edition of this book, I called this ministry of introduction the ministry of referral. However, use of the word "referral" itself creates some bad side effects in the minds of many people. Especially, the mind of the inexperienced theological student and the mind of the new pastor tend to take "referral" as a symbol of helplessness on their own part. The minister and the student often take the easy way out and make quick, irresponsible referrals. This grows out of a feeling of inadequacy, the harassed feeling of being hurried and busy that hovers over all that ministers do, and preoccupation with other things the minister enjoys better. To "refer" the person both assuages the conscience and leaves the minister feeling that the person has been helped. What is really being said nonverbally is that the minister does not want to be bothered. Similarly, one detrimental side effect of making a specialty of pastoral counseling is that the general parish minister may ditch the whole responsibility to hear, consider, and spiritually direct individuals, couples, and families.

Another bad side effect of the idea of "referral" is that you are likely to feel that once this is successfully done, there is nothing left for you to do. Especially is this true of psychiatric referrals and referrals to marriage counseling services. Consequently, you do not continue to give emotional support, reinforce the person's trust in the other counselors, and be a spiritual confidant, a fellow sufferer in the ministry of prayer with and for the person. The *distinctly* confessional needs, spiritual direction, and church involvements of these persons are yours to accomplish. That which you can uniquely be and do becomes much more apparent when the psychotherapeutic work is being done by other professional people. "Referral" often leaves the minister, the patient, and the other professional person feeling that "there is nothing now left for the minister to do." But being a friend, a "continuity sustainer," before, during, and after such professional services have begun, taken place, and ended is the unique identity of a minister who is durably related to people.

Another side effect of the idea of referral is that it carries with it the connotation of sickness, pathology, and acute emergency for many who hear it. It does not include the sheer joy that comes from introducing one friend to another, or relating a new convert to a small group of persons with similar interests, or getting people with great religious doubts and questions together with people who will relish the quest of a group of spiritual seekers, or introducing people with shared interests or stations in life—such as two musicians or two widows, or two working women who each need a roommate with whom to share an apartment.

In order to offset these bad effects of the idea of "referral," I have chosen to call attention here to "the ministry of introduction" of the Christian pastor. We can turn to the New Testament for an example of what is meant by "the ministry of introduction."

Possibly the most outstanding example of a "minister of introduction" was Barnabas, "the son of encouragement," told about in the book of The Acts. He it was who introduced the apostle Paul to the Christian community. His efforts failed when he introduced Paul to the church at Jerusalem. But apparently he kept a durable relationship of even warmth and acceptance with the apostle Paul. It was several years later before he succeeded in introducing Paul to the church at Antioch. We might surmise, also, that he introduced John Mark to Paul, and, although they had their differences, all three of them maintained a continuing relationship to one another.

Likewise, the letters of Paul are replete with greetings to friends, introductions, and intercessions. The whole letter to Philemon is devoted to the pastoral care of a new convert who also happened to be a slave. He reintroduced

Onesimus, the slave, to his owner, Philemon, in his new relationship as his, Paul's, son in Christ "whom he had begotten in his bonds." He could just not have thought to do that. He could have neglected the continuity of care of a new Christian. This is the main defect in modern evangelism—the sustaining ministry of introduction and reintroduction is missing.

If you do your pastoral work in a widely varied context of persons who are devoted to helping others and who are trained in ways of doing so, your daily work is that of getting acquainted with these persons who can serve those whom you serve. When you go to a new community, a systematic church survey of the community as a whole will get you in touch with many persons, groups, and institutions. Your lay leaders can do much to introduce you first to the members of your own church, then to the leaders of the community who may not be in the church of which you are pastor, and then to persons who are especially in need of the ministry of the church and you, its new pastor. A living organism of "known persons becoming known to each other" is thus built through pastoral attention, considerateness, and care. Your own isolation is thus overcome in your concern for others. You need not feel yourself to be the *only* servant of the Lord in your land.

You as a Christian pastor cannot work alone and in a vacuum. You do not minister to your flock without soon finding that you are not the only person in the community who is concerned with the welfare of your parishioners. Nor are you alone in the depth of your devotion to people, in the clarity of your sense of mission in the world, and in the favor of those to whom you minister. Within the context of the Christian community in even a small city may be found *many* ministers who have "gifts that differ" accordingly from those of the pastor of the congregation, such as employers, landowners, teachers, attorneys, physicians, psychiatrists, social workers, clinical psychologists, and—most important of all—parents. In the rural community, the consolidated school staff, the athletic coach, the county agent, the home demonstration agent, the general medical practitioners, and parents offer similar ministries in a less complex and more intimate manner.

Often the fascinating vocations of these people pull them away from the church rather than bind them more closely to it. They rarely have more than an elementary education in the galaxy of wisdom, literature, heritage, tradition, and roots of the religious spheres of existence. Their public school and secularized university educations have by law deleted such from their learning. As a result, the mechanistic education of many highly trained specialists sometimes has driven a wedge between their present way of life and the original sense of mission with which they started, and which often was stimulated by the church. Many times, careless neglect and harshness on the part of the pastors of these valuable persons have further alienated them from a vital Christian activity. You, on the other hand, are likely to devalue your own rich education in the humanities, the arts, philosophy, and religion. Hence you put yourself down. Stop it! Move toward these people with confidence, an open and inquiring spirit about their special work and their history, good or bad, with previous religious leaders and groups. They may have not been made to feel the hospitality of the Christian faith. Nor do they think that their skills and resources are indispensable necessities for the total witness of the church to the community. No one has convinced them. They have often in ignorance thought of the church as the one-person activity of the pastor rather than as the cooperative teamwork of all the members in a ministry to the total personality of individuals according as each person has need. It comes to them as good news to see small groups in churches become warm and loving support groups for their patients or clients.

Therefore, your responsibility as a pastor, upon having come to a new community, is, first, to visit the aged patriarchs and matriarchs of your community. Do not hurry as you do so. Let them tell you *their* memories of the church and the community. They are repositories of the family-tree knowledge, the tragic-event records, the customary ways of doing funerals, weddings, and handling church fights! You need them as badly as they need you. Of course, you will inquire into their own living situation and make clear note of their needs. Secondly, make friends with your fellow shepherds, i.e., the other pastors of the community regardless of denomination; thirdly, with the family-practice physicians, surgeons, internists, pediatricians, gynecologists, and psychiatrists in the community; fourthly, with the social workers, heads of institutions, and public school teachers; and fifthly, with the parent-teacher organizations and the child-care agencies. And, of course, you should consider the parent of any child as your greatest ally or your potentially most effective opponent in the spread of the gospel. More so than all the others put together, you are at the zenith of your function when you come to know each little child as your personal friend. All these persons are members of a koinonia of healing helpfulness to people. As a general rule, they, like the minister, are passionately devoted to what they are doing. Almost any pastor with initiative and common sense can gain their respect by showing an intelligent, informed, and careful devotion to the same people to whom these persons also minister daily. As you become acquainted with these ministering people yourself, you in turn become a "minister of introduction" to the persons who need their care. You "bridge the gaps" between the nonprofessionals and the professionals and represent their inseparability from each other. At the same time you communicate a realistic and creative witness of your church and its ministry to the people of all walks of life who care what happens to their neighbors.

You soon learn the drastic limitations of your abilities to help people, even though you are no more limited than any other trained workers who are also circumscribed in their own particular ways. Then you discover that it is not so important that you yourself help your parishioners as it is that you see to it that their own personal energies be so strengthened that they can help themselves. When you discover how to lay hold of the resources of all those about you (especially the resources of "those who are of the household of faith"), you will be less likely to become discouraged and "weary in well-doing." You will find your most loyal friends among those comrades in helping to bear the loads of people whose burden is not light and whose yoke is not easy.

You are responsible, in the presence of a wealth of community abundances for helping people, for more than you yourself are capable of doing for people regardless of how well trained you are. You are also obligated to see that they get the help of people who are equipped to help them with their specialized difficulties. It is just as important that you see that a person gets help as it is for you to give that help yourself.

For instance, a pastor in a small county seat received a letter from a soldier in Vietnam. The soldier was distressed over the economic welfare of his wife and children, who lived about ten miles out in the country from the town in which the pastor lived and worked. The soldier had tried other avenues of learning about the needs of his wife, who would not write him about the health and economic status of the family. The pastor was much too weighed down in his own community at the time to give personal attention to the man's request. He knew, too, that he might not be able to give the assistance needed, even if he should visit the home. Instead of going himself, therefore, he asked a social worker in the county welfare department (who was a devoted member of his church) to investigate the matter. She did, and, having discovered the needs of the family to be acute, brought the welfare resources of the community to their rescue. Then the pastor could contact the soldier in Vietnam through the chaplains he knew at a nearby military base. They called the man's commanding officer in the advance firebase in Vietnam and advised him of the health and welfare of his family, informing him that the economic problem was solved.

In order that you may take your place with confidence on such a complex network of care, you need specific guidance on the ministry of introduction. You need to know something of the indications as to *when* you should introduce a person to another professional worker. You need to know some of the methods and the hazards involved in making such introductions. You need to know the resources of your own community well enough, and, it is hoped, you will stay in a community long enough to establish a working understanding with other members of the comradeship of service to others.

RECOGNITION OF THE NEED
FOR THE MINISTRY OF INTRODUCTION

You need to ask yourself in every situation of pastoral care and personal counseling: "Is this parishioner in need of help in addition to the specific ministry that I, by the nature of my ordination, the substance of my education, and the weight of my influence, am equipped to offer?" The question may be answered both generally and specifically.

General Indications of the Need for Additional Help

1. *Lack of available time.* You generally try to introduce a parishioner to others when you know that more time and attention will be required than you have to offer. For instance, you may have the necessary training to carry through with intensely complex counseling over a period of weeks and months. Nevertheless, your load at that moment may be so heavy that you cannot give adequate

attention to the person. Or, you may be planning to be out of the community, or may be so involved in other responsibilities that you cannot possibly find the time to do what needs to be done. Then you will need other disciplined persons whose time will be available. This may mean that you will ask the individual to see an associate, another pastor, a marriage and family counselor, a family physician, a psychiatrist, or a social worker, as the conditions warrant. The person to whom the individual is sent will be determined entirely by the kind of problem in need of solution and the kind of persons available for the assistance needed. No specific rule can be devised. This is a clinical decision made on inspection, clarification, and commitment.

2. *Social and emotional involvement.* Another general consideration in regard to the ministry of introduction is whether you may be too socially and emotionally involved with an individual to supply the kind of help needed in a given situation. You do not have the leverage needed. One instance can be cited. A student pastor in a part-time pastorate in the suburbs of a large city sought to counsel with two married couples in his church. All four persons were active members of his church, having places of important leadership. They were contemplating trading spouses in a double divorce and remarriage arrangement. Before they did so, they brought their confusion to the student pastor, who sought to deal with the problem directly, without help. The whole church became involved, and the problem culminated in the student pastor's resignation from the church. As you see from this example, you as pastor have the oversight and care of the well-being of your whole church. Yet you have the responsibility for the care of an individual, a family, or a pair of families, as in this instance. You do not shirk either responsibility. However, you create enough privacy from the rest of the church to give the pair of families their best chance to localize the problems and deal with them without spreading them

throughout the whole church. Your "overseeing" function enables you to "see to it that" they get this care. If the student pastor mentioned above had known that the trouble was too involved for him to handle alone, he could have introduced the couples to the marriage and family counseling agency in the nearby city. There they would have received expert help. Neither he nor the church would have been hurt so deeply. At the same time, the service of the marriage and family counseling agency would likely have opened up an ongoing relationship between their personnel and the people of the church.

3. *Lack of specialized training.* In the third place, the pastor generally seeks additional help for parishioners whose problems require specialized treatment that the pastor has not been trained to give. For example, if a young unmarried member of your church says to you in confidence that she is pregnant, you cannot tell whether this is so or not. Only an obstetrician-gynecologist or other physician can do this. Therefore, a rabbinical rule can be laid down: "Get a physician to see her." She may simply be filled with guilt and fear. However, even the most highly trained pastors can be identified by their ability to know the limitations of their equipment for dealing with special difficulties.

Specific Indications of the Need for Additional Help

1. *Illness.* Parishioners who are physically sick, or who *think* they are physically sick, need the help of a good physician. You should be thoroughly informed as to the medical help available both in your community and in the larger region in which you live. Especial attention should be given to the availability of specialized diagnostic and therapeutic services in medical centers. The cost of such treatment, the various services of clinics, and the distances of the clinic from the person who needs it are practical problems to be confronted. Usually, if a parishioner is al-

ready under the care of a physician, by all means confer
with that physician, as is appropriate in counseling with
the person about the person's spiritual difficulties. If the
person does not have a physician at the time, you are at
liberty to suggest the names of physicians whom you yourself know and with whom you have a working understanding.

Today, we do not neatly separate mental and physical
illnesses. Many mental illnesses are epiphenomena of
physical disorders, substance abuse, etc. Classic psychotic
and depressive illnesses have clinically demonstrable
physical correlates in severe vegetative disorders and dys-
functions of the neurotransmitters of the neurological and
biochemical interrelationship. As has already been suggested, these persons quite often come to the attention of
a minister *before* they go to a physician. If a person is
threatening suicide, or is dangerous to the personal safety
of other people, or is not amenable to reason but is
deluded and irrational, or if the person shows any of the
less obvious signs of mental illness, the family and you
should collaborate about getting adequate psychiatric care
for this person. If you are acquainted with the family of the
person, you may seek tactfully to instruct the closest of kin
as to the seriousness of the situation. In doing so, you share
the responsibility wisely. The extent of your ministry will
be directly dependent upon the cooperation of the family,
the availability of psychiatric help, and the ability of the
family to tolerate the patient.

However, if you are a pastor in a community where
there are no psychiatric facilities and where medical services are scarce, you face the heavy responsibility of doing
for the patient what you can. You do it "with fear and
trembling," taking care to do no harm. Your situation in
the event that a psychiatrist *is* available is much like your
situation in relationship to a surgical patient: *Before* and
during the illness, your best help is offered in establishing
the confidence of the patient and the family in the physi-

cian's trustworthiness. Your ministry *after* the illness is primarily that of helping the person to find a place of security after recovery.

2. *The problem pregnancy.* Since the days of earliest Hebrew-Christian history, problem pregnancies have been the concern of the spiritual directors of people. You as a pastor will be concerned, as our forebears have been. Today, the issues are much more complex because of the explosion of knowledge and technology in preconception, prenatal, perinatal, and postnatal medicine. Genetic counseling is indicated for persons with family histories of malformed and/or mentally retarded persons. Sonar, amniocentesis, and other predictive tests present parents with the choice of a medical interruption of the pregnancy. Fierce propaganda battles rage over this issue, many of them financed and waged by different religious groups. When a young woman becomes pregnant out of wedlock, the alternatives of keeping the child and raising it as a single parent, of carrying the child to full term and letting the baby be adopted by an unknown family through a social agency, of having a medical interruption of the pregnancy, of marrying the father of the child, or of having an abortion *and* marrying the father of the child present a confusing ethical array of possibilities. Within marriage itself, a woman may become pregnant and one or both partners do not want the child although there is no evidence to suggest an abnormal birth.

As if these were not complex enough, the sterile couple bring their spiritual plight and frustration to you the pastor. They are the brunt of many cruel jokes from friends and relatives, subtle pressures from unrequited wishes of their parents for grandchildren, etc. The alternative of adoption is very dim for them because the sources of newborn adoptive babies have been severely reduced by the casualness with which the populace takes abortion. Many older children need adoption, but few people want to adopt older children. The alternative of artificial insemination of the mother by the sperm of either the father or an unknown donor presents hope for parenthood. The degree of conscience-ease or discomfort may be presented to you as a pastor. Now, the obverse side of this surrogate, anonymous, sharing of the power of parenthood is the most recent ethical dilemma. In a chauvinistic society, little question was raised when the sperm of a man was shared with a mother-to-be by artificial insemination. However, when a woman decides to share a child with a sterile couple, a furor is raised! This problem is as old as the Abraham, Sarah, and Hagar triangulation of parenthood (Genesis 16). However, it seems that the conflict-stress lies between the adults involved and not between God and the children.

These issues are such as to involve you as a working associate in the therapeutic process. I know of no better place in the caring process than this for you to realize that you are *expected* to be the ethicist, the spiritual mentor, and the technically educated person in moral theology. An excellent source for your disciplined study in these issues is the book *A Matter of Life and Death: Christian Perspectives,* edited by Harry N. Hollis, Jr.

3. *The problem of substance-abusing persons.* Another concrete example of the need for multiple sources of help are the substance-abusing persons and their families, with whom every pastor deals. As Dean Willard Sperry pointed out long ago in speaking of alcoholism: "Hitherto ministers have regarded drunkenness as a moral scandal and a vice. They looked to the mourners' bench at a revival meeting as the safest and surest cure. It is only fair to say that this remedy has worked in many classic instances. But today ministers are beginning to realize that there is a point beyond which drunkenness becomes a bodily disease, and the moral resolutions of penitence may well need the fortification of sober medical treatment." (Willard L. Sperry, *The Ethical Basis of Medical Practice,* p. 23.) Today we would have to add substances like marijuana, cocaine, and

heroin. Tobacco, coffee, food, and work also are abused. Addiction is no respecter of social class. Both men and women are victims, and it seems that it is either on the increase among women or we are finding out about it more readily.

Personal discipline is one of the main claims of the religious way of life. Seventh-day Adventists have been leaders in devising programs for enabling people to break these shackling habits. The methods of Alcoholics Anonymous have been applied to problems like overeating in Overeaters' Anonymous and Take Off Pounds Sensibly. Set yourself to become expert in dealing with this array of troubles and introduce these persons to the people who take them as seriously as you do. For example, the reliability of the methods of the Alcoholics Anonymous groups has been demonstrated, and you are wise to depend upon the help of these men and women in dealing with acute alcoholism.

4. *Economic disability.* The poverty-stricken person, in need of economic assistance, is another for whom the pastor usually relies upon the expert casework assistance of welfare agencies. Much harm has been done to people who were given economic assistance by well-meaning persons who did not know how to get the facts and foundation for wisely doing so. You and your church should be participants in the general welfare program of the community, both in terms of giving support and in terms of relying upon the guidance of these agencies in the care of destitute persons. The personnel of these agencies are trained to meet the needs of hungry, naked, and shelterless people. If they are not available to do so according to wisdom and tenderness, you will usually be held in enough confidence among the people of the community to be heard when you suggest the need for more adequate workers. The church, of course, will have ways and means of meeting the emergency economic needs of its own members. If a dependable family in the community should

lose their house and other belongings by fire, the fellowship of the church should be strong enough to keep the family from too much hardship. If a long-term chronic need appears in some family (such as a mother being left a widow with several small children and no relatives to whom to turn), you may confer with the community service organizations and make a plan whereby a consistent and intelligent program of help can be offered cooperatively. You do well to seek the advice of the welfare agencies as to *how* to help families or individuals without taking away their self-respect and causing them to lose personal initiative. The long-range strategy must be to enable people to be self-supporting and to avoid addiction to welfare.

5. *Other areas of need.* Many other specific situations can be named in which you need the help of people to whom you may introduce parishioners who come to you for guidance. Young people seeking work may be referred to employers, young persons seeking premarital counseling will be introduced to physicians, and those seeking guidance about the adoption of children will be helped through both physicians and social agencies. Parishioners making educational plans will be referred to college and university authorities; veterans with specific difficulties will be guided to government agencies that have been established for such purposes. The United Way, Community Chest, or other centralized community service agency usually publishes a directory of services in its area. As soon as you come to a new pastorate, visit these agencies and ask if you may purchase a copy. It usually costs a small fee. Thus you begin having personal contact with these agencies. It is a rare thing for them to have a minister come to see them!

THE PROCESS AND THE METHODS
OF THE MINISTRY OF INTRODUCTION

The process of the ministry of introduction and the methods used in carrying through with that process determine to a large extent the amount of good the person gains by the referral.

Recognizing Limitations

Your own inspection, recognition, and definition of a person's problem is primary. You recognize not only the nature of the parishioner's difficulty but also your own obligation to diffuse and distribute the responsibility when you become overextended. Naturally, you can overdo this. You can feel so inadequate in the presence of even the most trivial problem that you run for cover when you see the first sign of suffering. Or you may simply not want to be bothered at all and pass the buck to someone else. But ordinarily pastors are overconscientious instead. We mistakenly feel that we should have the resources within ourselves and from our knowledge of the Bible and religion to solve any and every problem that arises. In such an instance, when you recognize your need for help you have made a real step in understanding yourself.

Interpreting the Person's Problem

The second step in calling in the help of other professional people is to interpret the person's own difficulty to the person. A young man comes to his pastor and describes many physical symptoms such as headache, loss of appetite, and sleeplessness. He says, however, that these are all caused by his fears that he is going to "do something" at night to hurt his wife, and by his fear that he is losing his mind. He breaks down, cries profusely, and falls all over the chair, writhing with anxiety. After calming the young

man, the pastor gets a little more of the story, discovering
that the man is hearing strange voices "out of nowhere."
Obviously the man needs help, but the pastor recognizes
the immediate need for medical care as well as pastoral
care. Therefore, in a persuasive and suggestive manner,
the pastor says to him: "You have had many stresses pile
up during the rapid events of a very short time. You have
not been married long; you are facing new responsibilities;
you have had several misunderstandings with those who
are very close to you; you are afraid of what you think; you
are upset, nervous, and have not slept or eaten properly.
I think you realize that you are not in any frame of mind
to think through your problems clearly or to make any
important decisions at this time, until you have rested
your body, relaxed your thinking, and steadied your self-
confidence. You are exhausted and need medical care. Let
me help you get just that." This is a commonsense interpretation of the man's trouble, aimed at suggesting to him
the idea that he does not just *think* he is sick, but that he
really *is* sick and needs help in addition to that which the
pastor can offer.

Confessing Limitations

The third step in a ministry of introduction is your confession of your limitations and explanation of your need for
the help of the professional person to whom you hope to
send the individual. Great care should be exercised here.
Do *not* say: "There is nothing I can do to help you." You
literally pronounce doom upon the person, for you represent God to the person. Preface your confession of limitations with a confident assurance of the things you *can* do.
In the case cited above, the pastor went on to say to the
man: "Of course, your health is the most pressing stress at
this present moment. I can be your faithful friend and talk
with you about your relationship to God. I can pray with

you and keep you reminded of God's love and sustaining power. I will stand by you. Your health needs the attention of a physician. I know that you cannot be your best spiritual self as long as you are ill in your total being. You need to go to a physician, who can give you treatments that will relax you and restore your perspective, who can talk with you about your ideas and feelings after you have rested for a while. A good psychiatrist can help you with your troubles." Also, ask for the privilege of talking with the person's most intimate and trusted family member. If the person needs psychiatric help, the family's cooperation will be especially necessary.

Introducing the Other Professional Person

The fourth step in the ministry of introduction is that in which you put the parishioner in touch with the other professional person. This is usually done by telephone, but occasionally it is done personally. Sometimes, if the situation is not one that involves emergency action, a letter will do. In the case mentioned above, the name, address, and telephone number of the psychiatrist were given to the patient and his wife. It is a helpful and meaningful ministry for you on occasion to go with the person in need to the office of the physician, the social worker, etc. This man was admitted to a hospital the next day and received treatment. At this stage, the most important need is that you "transfer" whatever confidence the parishioner may have in you as a pastor to the other professional person. You will find it necessary to reassure both the patient and the family after this order: "I have known this physician for some time. I know from observation that this physician is trustworthy and deserves your complete confidence. Be sure to depend upon the physician's guidance without too much fear. You will find great reverence for your religious faith

280 *The Christian Pastor*

in this physician's care." Simple honesty requires that you do your best to know persons about whom you can sincerely say such things.

Showing Concern While Not Interfering

The fifth phase of such a ministry includes cooperative concern and a minimum of interference on your part. These persons must not feel that you are "trying to get rid of them." In the case under discussion, this was avoided by directly reassuring the patient, by following his progress by telephoning his wife, and by visiting him during his hospitalization. The process of reassurance could have been aided by letters, as well.

In referring a patient to a physician, you do the physician a great service by writing a letter in which you give a brief summary of the facts that you know about the patient's situation. This summary should include a word about how this parishioner came to your attention, a concise description of the number and nature of conversations you have had with the patient, a description of the person's problem *in the same words the person used,* insofar as is possible, and a statement of the facts that you may know about the life history of the parishioner. The summary may be followed by another paragraph in which you give your own interpretation in *nontechnical language* of the life situation of the person. Lengthy letters are not indicated in most cases.

The case of a psychiatric cooperation has been cited here because it is the most difficult type of situation with which a pastor has to deal, and because requests come more often as to how to introduce a person to a psychiatrist. Tender persuasion and strong suggestion are necessary in most cases of this kind. However, some of the most important ministries of introduction come under much happier circumstances. A pastor introduces a strange couple to other couples in the church as friends. You write a letter of introduction for a college freshman to one of your own former professors. You introduce a jobless young person to a prospective employer whom you know. You introduce a skeptic or an avowed atheist to a professor of philosophy. You *may* even introduce a young man and a young woman! They may even become husband and wife. Who knows! But more than this, you as an evangelist are always at work introducing people to Jesus Christ.

Following Up

The final phase of the ministry of introduction is the follow-up. This corresponds to the phase of follow-up and experimentation characteristic of all good counseling.

A procedure of this kind, skillfully executed, leaves your hands free for a definitely religious ministry in the life of people. You can rely upon the resources of your community to help you in such a way that you can do a distinctive task without being a "jack-of-all-trades and master of none," dabbling in this, that, and the other and not "sticking to your own last"—the reconciliation of persons with God. Nevertheless, this does not relieve you of the responsibility of knowing enough about the work of the other members of the community effort to help people to be able to function smoothly in relation to them.

The question may be properly raised at this point: What should be done in case a person does not want to cooperate with efforts to call in outside assistance? An instance of this is the sixty-five-year-old woman who constantly sought the help of the church with her financial difficulties. She had no family except a sick brother, had no work, wandered about the city begging, would call the wealthier members of the church by telephone and ask them for help. If they did not do what she wanted them to do, she would threaten to kill herself, call them profane names, and become incensed with anger. She was the first seeker for help who came to the attention of every new pastor.

One of the pastors, when she came to him, listened carefully to her story and asked her to come back to see him the next day. In the meantime, he called the city relief agencies and discovered that she had a sixteen-year record with three of them. She had an epileptic brother and was considered by the agencies to have "epileptoid personality traits" herself. They suggested that the pastor ask her to return to see them, and that the church itself contribute what it could to the total program of medical and financial relief that the agency would plan for her.

When the woman returned the next day, the pastor, after having conferred with the social service committee of the church (which had long since lost patience with her), asked the woman to return to the social agency. He said to her: "The church plans to help you if you will cooperate with us in the program we have outlined for you. I have talked with the family service organization and asked them to study your whole financial problem. I have told them that we will do for you what they suggest. We will pay our funds directly to them, and they will add whatever else you need." The woman became irate and refused to cooperate. It finally became necessary for her to be institutionalized in a state hospital. However, the pastor had no hand in this. Two of the lay leaders of the church took the case of the elderly widow to two physicians and arrangements for her commitment were completed. The state hospital, which formerly would have had little but custodial help to offer her, now has an extensive geriatric rehabilitation program. It has two chaplains for the pastoral care of the patients. The members of the Woman's Missionary Union visit with the woman regularly.

But there is a limit beyond which a pastor cannot go in trying to help people. You do them harm when you try to overrule their objection to being helped. Remembering this will help you to be objective at the same time that you will do all that can be done to meet people's needs. You give your time and energy to people who are willing to make at least minimal use of it.

Anton T. Boisen is fond of saying that the pastor deals with three groups of people. First, there are those who are capable of taking care of themselves, and will get along nicely regardless of the care the pastor gives them. These people need encouragement and appreciation. Secondly, there are those who will become progressively worse, regardless of the care and attention the pastor can offer them, and will not profit by anything the pastor does for them because they do not want to be helped. These people need patience and resistance to being manipulated and exploited. Thirdly, there are those who stand at the crossroads, and the outcome of their lives will be *largely determined* by the pastor's patient efforts in ministry to them. These people need intensive attention at crucial moments of teachability. Of course, these are loose but very valuable generalizations. You as pastor are under obligation to devote your time, energy, and equipment where they will do the most good. The parable of the sower and the seed and the parable of the wheat and the tares can be appreciated best by the veteran pastors who see the magnitude of human suffering and the finitude of their own abilities in the light of the eternal wisdom of God. Never forget that you are not alone as a pastor; God has people of his own who care for your parishioners, too! Together with them you are a part of the royal priesthood of believers.

Bibliography

Ahlstrom, Sydney E. *A Religious History of the American People.* Yale University Press, 1972.

Aleshire, Daniel O. "Eleven Major Areas of Ministry." In *Ministry in America,* ed. by David S. Schuller, Merton P. Strommen, and Milo L. Brekke. Harper & Row, 1980.

Allport, Gordon W. *The Individual and His Religion.* Macmillan Co., 1950.

Angyal, András. *Neurosis and Treatment: A Holistic Theory.* Ed. by E. Haufmann and R. M. Jones. John Wiley & Sons, 1965.

Arnold, William V. *When Your Parents Divorce.* Christian Care Book. Westminster Press, 1980.

Augustine, Saint. *The Christian Combat.* Tr. by Robert P. Russell. In *The Fathers of the Church: Writings of Saint Augustine,* Vol. 4. Robert P. Russell. Cima Publishing Co., 1947.

———. *Faith, Hope, and Charity.* Tr. by Bernard Peebles. In *The Fathers of the Church: Writings of Saint Augustine,* Vol. 4. Cima Publishing Co., 1947.

Bailey, D. S. *The Mystery of Love and Marriage.* Harper & Brothers, 1952.

———. *Sexual Relation in Christian Thought.* Harper & Brothers, 1959.

Baldessarini, Ross J. *Chemotherapy in Psychiatry.* Harvard University Press, 1977.

Barclay, William. Article on "Metanoia." In *The Theological Dictionary of the New Testament,* Vol. 4. Ed. by Gerhard Kittel. Wm. B. Eerdmans Publishing Co., 1967.

———. *Turning to God: A Study of Conversion in the Book of Acts and Today.* Westminster Press, 1964.

Barnette, H. H. *Exploring Medical Education.* Mercer Univer
sity Press, 1982.

Barth, Karl. *Church Dogmatics,* Vol. III, Pt. 2. Tr. by H. Knight
and others. Edinburgh: T. & T. Clark, 1960.

Baxter, Richard. *Gildas Salvianus: The Reformed Pastor,* 1656.
2d ed., rev. Ed. by John T. Wilkinson. London: Epworth Press,
1950.

Bennett, George. *When the Mental Patient Comes Home.* Christian Care Book. Westminster Press, 1980.

Blizzard, Samuel. "The Minister's Dilemma," *The Christian Century,* April 25, 1956.

Boisen, Anton T. *The Exploration of the Inner World.* 1936.
University of Pennsylvania Press, 1971.

Bonthius, Robert H. *Christian Paths to Self-Acceptance.* King's
Crown Press, 1948.

Bowlby, John. *Loss: Sadness and Depression.* Attachment and
Loss, Vol. III. Basic Books, 1980.

Brister, C. W. *Pastoral Care in the Church.* Harper & Row, 1964.

Bunyan, John. *The Pilgrim's Progress.* Ed. by Hugh Martin. Macmillan Co., 1948.

Calvin, John. *Commentaries on the Catholic Epistles.* Tr. and ed.
by John Owen. Wm. B. Eerdmans Publishing Co., 1948.

————. *Commentaries on the Epistles to Timothy, Titus, and
Philemon.* Tr. by William Pringle. Wm. B. Eerdmans Publishing Co., 1948.

Capp, Donald. *Biblical Approaches to Pastoral Counseling.*
Westminster Press, 1981.

Carr, John C.; Hinkle, John E.; and Moss, David M., III (eds.). *The
Organization and Administration of Pastoral Counseling
Centers.* Abingdon Press, 1981.

Chamberlain, William Douglas. *The Meaning of Repentance.*
Westminster Press, 1943.

Chrysostom, Saint John. *The Priesthood: A Translation of Peri
Hierosynes.* Tr. by W. A. Jurgens. Macmillan Co., 1955.

Clebsch, William A., and Jaekle, Charles R. *Pastoral Care in
Historical Perspective.* Prentice-Hall, 1964.

Clinebell, Howard J., Jr. *Basic Types of Pastoral Counseling.*
Rev. ed. Abingdon Press, 1966.

————. *Contemporary Growth Therapies.* Abingdon Press, 1981.

————. *Growth Counseling: Hope-Centered Methods of Actualizing Human Wholeness.* Abingdon Press, 1979.

————. *The People Dynamic.* Harper & Row, 1972.

Cobb, John B., Jr. *Theology and Pastoral Care.* Fortress Press,
1977.

Cox, James W., (ed.). *The Twentieth-Century Pulpit.* Abingdon Press, 1978.

Cox-Gedmark, Jan. *Coping with Physical Disability.* Christian Care Book. Westminster Press, 1980.

Dittes, James E. *When the People Say No: Conflict and the Call to Ministry.* Harper & Row, 1979.

Dobbins, Gaines S. *The Church at Worship.* Broadman Press, 1963.

Draper, Edgar, M.D., et al. "On the Diagnostic Value of Religious Ideation," *Archives of General Psychiatry,* Vol. 13 (Sept. 1965), pp. 202–207.

Erikson, Erik. *Identity and the Life Cycle.* International Universities Press, 1959.

——. *New Perspectives for Research on Juvenile Delinquency.* Ed. by Helen L. Witmer and Ruth Kotinsky. Washington, D.C.: Children's Bureau, U.S. Department of Health, Education, and Welfare, 1955.

Freud, Sigmund. "Observations on Transference—Love" (Further Recommendations on the Technique of Psycho-Analysis III) (1915 [1914]), *The Standard Edition of the Complete Psychological Works of Sigmund Freud,* Vol. XII (1911–1913). (Papers on Technique, 1911–1915 [1914]). Tr. and ed. by James Strachey. London: Hogarth Press and Institute of Psycho-Analysis, 1958.

Gennep, Arnold van. *The Rites of Passage.* Tr. by Monika B. Vizedom and Gabrielle L. Caffee. University of Chicago Press, 1961

Gerkin, Charles V. *Crisis Experience in Modern Life: Theory and Theology in Pastoral Care.* Abingdon Press, 1979.

Gladden, Washington. *The Christian Pastor and the Working Church.* Charles Scribner's Sons, 1898.

Glasser, William, M.D. *Stations of the Mind: New Directions for Reality Therapy.* Harper & Row, 1981.

Glock, Charles Y., and Roos, Philip. "Parishioners' Views of How Ministers Spend Their Time," *Review of Religious Research,* Spring 1961, pp. 170–175.

Group for the Advancement of Psychiatry. *Assessment of Sexual Function: A Guide to Interviewing.* Jason Aronson, 1974.

Havighurst, Robert J. *Human Development and Education.* Longmans, Green & Co., 1953.

Hawthorne, Nathaniel. *The Scarlet Letter.* New American Library, Signet Classics.

Hewett, John H. *After Suicide.* Christian Care Book. Westminster Press, 1980.

Hiltner, Seward. *Ferment in the Ministry: A Constructive Approach to What the Minister Does.* Abingdon Press, 1969.

Hiltner, Seward, and Colston, Lowell G. *The Context of Pastoral Counseling.* Abingdon Press, 1961.

Hollis, Harry N., Jr. (ed.). *A Matter of Life and Death: Christian Perspectives.* Broadman Press, 1977.

Hovland, C. Warren. "*Anfechtung* in Luther's Biblical Exegesis." In *Reformation Studies* (Essays in Honor of Roland H. Bainton). Ed. by Franklin H. Littell. John Knox Press, 1962.

Hulme, William E. *Mid-Life Crises.* Christian Care Book. Westminster Press, 1980.

Hutschnecker, Arnold A. "Personality Factors in Dying Patients." In *The Meaning of Death.* Ed. by Herman Feifel. McGraw-Hill Book Co., 1959.

Justice, William G., Jr. *Guilt and Forgiveness.* Baker Book House, 1980.

Kemp, Charles F. (ed.). *Life-Situation Preaching.* Bethany Press, 1956.

———(ed.). *Pastoral Preaching.* Bethany Press, 1963.

Krebs, Richard L., "Why Pastors Should Not Be Counselors," *The Journal of Pastoral Care,* Vol. XXXIV, No. 4 (Dec. 1980), pp. 229–233.

Law, William. *A Serious Call to a Devout and Holy Life.* Ed. by John W. Meister and others. Westminster Press, 1955.

Leas, Speed, and Kittlaus, Paul. *The Pastoral Counselor in Social Action.* Fortress Press, 1981.

Lecky, Prescott. *Self-Consistency.* Ed. by John F. A. Taylor. Island Press, 1945.

Leech, Kenneth. *Soul Friend: The Practice of Christian Spirituality.* Harper & Row, 1980.

Lester, Andrew D., and Lester, Judith L. *Understanding Aging Parents.* Christian Care Book. Westminster Press, 1980.

Luther, Martin. *The Large Catechism.* Tr. by Robert H. Fischer. Muhlenberg Press, 1959.

———. *Letters of Spiritual Counsel.* Ed. and tr. by Theodore Tappert. The Library of Christian Classics, Vol. XVIII. Westminster Press, 1955.

———. *Luther: Lectures on Romans.* Tr. and ed. by Wilhelm Pauck. The Library of Christian Classics, Vol. XV. Westminster Press, 1961.

Lutz, Theodore. *The Person.* Rev. ed. Basic Books, 1976.

McNeill, John Thomas. *A History of the Cure of Souls.* Harper & Row, 1951.

McSwain, Larry L., and Treadwell, William C., Jr. *Conflict Ministry in the Church.* Broadman Press, 1981.

Madden, Myron. *The Power to Bless.* Broadman Press, 1979.

Madden, Myron, and Madden, Mary Ben. *For Grandparents: Wonders and Worries.* Christian Care Book. Westminster Press, 1980.

Marty, Martin E. *Friendship.* Argus Communications, 1980.

Masters, William, et al. *The Pleasure Bond.* Bantam Books, 1976.

Mayer, Herbert T. *Pastoral Care: Its Roots and Renewal.* John Knox Press, 1978.

Menninger, Karl. *Theory of Psychoanalytic Technique.* Basic Books, 1958.

Monfalcone, Wesley R. *Coping with Abuse in the Family.* Christian Care Book. Westminster Press, 1980.

Moustakas, Clark. *Loneliness.* Prentice-Hall, 1961.

Niebuhr, H. Richard. *The Purpose of the Church and Its Ministry.* Harper & Brothers, 1956.

Niebuhr, H. Richard; Williams, Daniel Day; and Gustafson, James M. *The Advancement of Theological Education.* Harper & Brothers 1957.

Oates, Wayne E. *The Bible in Pastoral Care.* Baker Book House (Reissue), 1972.

―――. *Christ and Selfhood.* Association Press, 1961.

―――. *Pastoral Counseling.* Westminster Press, 1974.

―――. *Pastor's Handbook,* Vol. I. Christian Care Book. Westminster Press, 1980.

―――. *Pastor's Handbook,* Vol. II. Christian Care Book. Westminster Press, 1980.

―――. *The Psychology of Religion.* 1973. Word Books, 1981.

―――. *The Religious Care of the Psychiatric Patient.* Westminster Press, 1978.

―――. *The Revelation of God in Human Suffering.* Westminster Press, 1959.

―――. *Your Particular Grief.* Westminster Press, 1981.

Oates, Wayne E., and Rowatt, Wade. *Before You Marry Them.* Broadman Press, 1975.

O'Connor, Elizabeth. *The Call to Commitment.* 1963. Harper & Row, 1976.

Oglesby, William B., Jr. *Biblical Themes in Pastoral Care.* Abingdon Press, 1980.

Otto, Rudolf. *The Idea of the Holy.* Tr. by John W. Harvey. Oxford University Press, 1958.

Prenter, Regin. *Spiritus Creator.* Tr. by John M. Jensen. Muhlenberg Press, 1953.

Price, Reynolds. *Love and Work*. Atheneum Publishers, 1975.

Pruyser, Paul W. *A Dynamic Psychology of Religion*. Harper & Row, 1968.

———. *The Minister as Diagnostician*. Westminster Press, 1976.

Radin, Paul. *Primitive Religion*. Viking Press, 1937.

Rank, Otto. *Will Therapy; and, Truth and Reality*. Tr. by Jessie Taft. Alfred A. Knopf, 1945.

Reik, Theodor. *Listening with the Third Ear*. Grove Press, 1956.

Roberts, David E. *Psychotherapy and a Christian View of Man*. Charles Scribner's Sons, 1950.

Rowatt, G. Wade, Jr., and Rowatt, Mary Jo Brock. *The Two-Career Marriage*. Christian Care Book. Westminster Press, 1980.

Sager, Clifford, and Kaplan, Helen (eds.). *Progress in Group and Family Therapy*. Brunner/Mazel, 1972.

Salzman, Leon. "The Psychology of Religious Ideological Conversion," *Psychiatry*, Vol. XVI, No. 2 (May 1953).

Satir, Virginia M. *Conjoint Family Therapy*. Rev. ed. Science and Behavior Books, 1967.

Schaefer, Halmuth H., and Martin, Patrick L. *Behavioral Therapy*. McGraw-Hill Book Co., 1969.

Schmidt, Paul F. *Coping with Difficult People*. Christian Care Book. Westminster Press, 1980.

Schuller, David S. "Identifying the Criteria for Ministry." In *Ministry in America*, ed. by David S. Schuller, Merton P. Strommen, and Milo L. Brekke. Harper & Row, 1980.

Schuyler, Dean. *The Depressive Spectrum*. Jason Aronson, 1974.

Sherrill, Lewis J. *The Gift of Power*. Macmillan Co., 1955.

———. *The Struggle of the Soul*. Macmillan Co., 1951.

Snygg, Donald, and Combs, Arthur. *Individual Behavior*. Harper & Brothers, 1949.

Sparks, Jack (ed.). *The Apostolic Fathers: New Translations of Early Christian Writings* (The Didache). Thomas Nelson, 1978.

Sperry, Willard L. *The Ethical Basis of Medical Practice*. Paul B. Hoeber Book. Harper & Brothers, 1950.

Spurgeon, Charles H. *An All Round Ministry*. London; Carlisle, Pa.: Banner of Truth Trust, 1972.

Stagg, Evelyn and Frank. *Woman in the World of Jesus*. Westminster Press, 1978.

Steere, Douglas V. *On Being Present Where You Are*. Pendle Hill Pamphlet 151. Pendle Hill Publications, 1967.

———. *On Listening to Another*. Harper & Brothers, 1955.

Stewart, Charles W. *The Minister as Family Counselor.* Abingdon Press, 1979.

Stinnette, Charles. *Anxiety and Faith.* Seabury Press, 1955.

Sullivan, Harry Stack. "Detailed Enquiry." In his *The Psychiatric Interview.* W. W. Norton & Co., 1962.

———. "Developmental Syndromes." In his *Conceptions of Modern Psychiatry.* William Alanson White Institute of Psychiatry, 1948.

Switzer, David K., and Switzer, Shirley A. *Parents of the Homosexual.* Christian Care Book. Westminster Press, 1980.

Thurneysen, Eduard. *A Theology of Pastoral Care.* John Knox Press, 1962.

Tiebout, Harry M. "Conversion as a Psychological Phenomenon," in *The Treatment of the Alcoholic, Pastoral Psychology,* Vol. 2, No. 13 (1951), pp. 28–34.

Tournier, Paul. *A Place for You.* Tr. by Edwin Hudson. Harper & Row, 1968.

Usdin, Gene (ed.). *Schizophrenia: Biological and Psychological Perspectives.* Brunner/Mazel, 1975.

Wagemaker, Herbert, Jr. *Parents and Discipline.* Christian Care Book. Westminster Press, 1980.

Wainwright, Geoffrey. *Doxology: The Praise of God in Worship, Doctrine, and Life—A Systematic Theology.* Oxford University Press, 1980.

Wesley, John. *John Wesley* (writings), ed. by Albert C. Outler. Library of Protestant Thought. Oxford University Press, 1964.

Wilde, Oscar. *The Picture of Dorian Gray.* World Publishing Co., 1946.

Williams, Daniel Day. *The Minister and the Care of Souls.* Harper & Row, 1961.

Wimberly, Edward P. *Pastoral Care in the Black Church.* Abingdon Press, 1979.

Wise, Carroll A. *Pastoral Psychotherapy.* Jason Aronson, 1980.

Yalom, Irvin D. *Existential Psychotherapy.* Basic Books, 1980.

Index

Alcohol abuse, 28, 36, 40–42, 48, 111–112, 119, 188–189, 274–275
Aleshire, Daniel, 17, 23, 63–64, 262
Allport, Gordon, 34
Ambivalence, 247–248
Anger, 112–113, 238–239
Appointments, counseling, 231–232
Arnold, Matthew, 113
Assessment, pastoral, 167–189
Augustine, 10, 32, 37, 42

Bacon, Francis, 202
Baptism, 31, 34, 160, 212
Barth, Karl, 21
Baxter, Richard, 11, 37–38
Behavioral sciences, 188–189
Bereavement, 17–18, 22, 57–60, 73, 86, 202–203
Bernanos, Georges, 155
Bible, use of, 206, 217, 254
Birth, 17–18, 22, 27–33, 63, 250
Blizzard, Samuel, 119, 129–132, 135, 137
Boisen, Anton T., 57, 161, 283
Bonhoeffer, Dietrich, 183

Bunyan, John, 42, 94, 262
Bushnell, Horace, 143

Calvin, John, 97–98, 112, 212
Catharsis, 202–204, 211
Change, 250–251
Children, 22, 29–33, 52, 79–80, 107–110, 139, 197, 203, 210–211, 216, 267
Christian Care Books, 217–218
Chrysostom, John, 117–118
Clarification, 175–180
Colston, Lowell G., 92, 226
Comfort, 58, 86, 116, 148, 199–208
Commitment, personal, 93–94, 159–160, 162–163, 170–173, 175–176, 186
Communication, 48, 77, 81–82, 202
Concern, 280–281
Confession, 60–61, 87, 120, 208–214, 263
Confidentiality, 81–82, 196–197, 235
Conflicts, emotional, 52–53
Conscience, 71, 73–74
Convalescence, 55–57

Conversion, religious, 27–28, 34–39, 42, 186
Cosby, Gordon, 162
Crisis ministry, 17–64

Death, 17–18, 25, 27–28, 33, 37–38, 41, 48, 53–54, 57–64, 150, 197, 199–200, 207–208, 250
Depression, 41, 200–202, 230
Developmental perspective, 22–28
Diagnosis, pastoral, 50, 173–187
Dialogue, brief pastoral, 219–222, 253
Discipline, 114, 123, 159–163, 169
Divorce, 28, 33, 41, 47–48, 52, 63, 104–106, 139, 197, 214, 261
Dobbins, Gaines S., 151
Draper, Edgar, 181–183, 187
Drug abuse. *See* Alcohol abuse, Substance abuse

Economics, 30, 31, 44–45, 51, 62, 91, 99–100, 104–105, 109, 112, 199, 259–260, 268–269, 275–276, 281–282
Edwards, Jonathan, 144
Emerson, Ralph Waldo, 250
Empathy, 78–79, 168–170
Erikson, Erik, 23–24, 28, 44, 237
Ethics, 18, 24, 32–33, 47–48, 81, 91, 98, 104–106, 114, 124, 139, 143, 170, 182, 184, 215, 225, 247, 274

Faith, 22, 36–38, 68–69, 73, 77–80, 87, 115, 124, 128–129, 148, 158, 160, 162, 185, 187, 214

Faith, the Christian, 18, 42, 65, 91–94, 187, 202
Faithfulness, 24–25
Fear, 53–54, 62, 78, 80–81, 88, 187, 209–210, 225–226, 255–256
Fellowship, 19, 22, 31, 44, 56, 59, 75, 81, 119–120, 124, 126, 138–141, 155, 157–162, 203
Follow-up, 222, 254–258
Forgiveness, 22, 81, 87, 143, 146, 209, 213
Fosdick, Harry Emerson, 144
Fox, George, 42
Freud, Sigmund, 170
Friendship, 20, 26, 44, 149, 194–199, 253

Gennep, Arnold van, 18–19, 28
Gladden, Washington, 12, 196, 211
Glock, Charles Y., 132–135
Goethe, J. W. von, 118
Gossip, 100–101, 205, 256
Greed, 78, 112, 123–124
Grief, 29, 38, 41, 57–60, 118, 143, 199, 202–203
Guilt, 58, 70, 87, 93, 140, 150, 152, 187, 209, 211–212, 247
Gustafson, James M., 115–116

Handicaps, 32, 51, 114, 200, 236–237, 262–263
Havighurst, Robert J., 24, 28
Hawthorne, Nathaniel, 72, 223–224
Hiltner, Seward, 92, 130, 150, 226
Holy Spirit, 9, 18, 63, 65–66, 68, 71, 77, 80, 83–89, 106, 126, 141, 163, 169, 172, 187, 239, 257–258, 261

Hope, 27, 54, 204
Hostility, 255–256
Husserl, Edmund, 169

Identity, 20, 23, 35, 41, 50–55, 78–83, 85, 93, 128–163, 174, 179–180, 182, 255
Idolatry, 59, 72–75, 199, 224
Illness, physical or mental, 18, 27–28, 33, 35, 37–38, 42, 46, 48–58, 63, 110–117, 158, 199–201, 204–205, 207, 214, 216, 222–223, 271–273, 278–279
Initial contact, 229–231
Initiative, 178–179, 232–235
Inner world, 50–55, 225
Insight, 60, 74–75, 148, 246–251
Inspection, 175–180
Integrity, 128–163
Interpretation, 251–253, 277–278
Introduction, ministry of, 261–283
Involvement, emotional, 270–271
Isolation, 19, 44, 50, 138, 154–155, 160, 175, 204, 211

Jesus, 12, 21, 36, 62, 69, 75–76, 77, 81, 83, 95, 98, 99, 100, 110–111, 189, 225, 231, 252, 256

Kemp, Charles F., 143, 148–149
Kierkegaard, Søren, 125, 224

Law, William, 38
Levels of pastoral care, 190–260
Lewis, Sinclair, 93
Life-support system, 174–175

Limitations, 277–279
Lin Yutang, 241
Literature, use of, 27, 253–254
Loneliness, 19, 48–49, 95, 138, 143, 155, 186–187
Luther, Martin, 11, 29, 37, 58–59, 67, 183, 207, 209–210

Marriage, 17–18, 27–28, 43–48, 51–52, 102–107, 160
Marty, Martin E., 196
Maugham, W. Somerset, 72
May, Rollo, 78
Menninger, Karl, 169
Morality, 46, 71, 73, 102–107, 111, 115, 150, 153, 214, 233

Nervous tension, 154, 237–238, 241. *See also* Stress
Niebuhr, H. Richard, 66–68, 115–116, 128, 136, 262

O'Connor, Elizabeth, 163
Overdependence, 255

Pain, 48, 52–53, 118, 152, 200
Parenthood, 22, 29–33, 41, 51–52, 73, 79–80, 104, 107–110, 139, 160, 203–204, 216, 273–274
Pastor
  characteristics desired in, 17, 67–68, 128
  and Holy Spirit, 83–89
  mental health of, 110–118
  as minister of introduction, 261–283
  personal qualifications of, 96–127
  as reminder of Jesus Christ, 75–83

as representative of God, 62, 69–75, 108

as representative of a specific church, 44, 62, 89–91

as shepherd of the non-Christian, 91–95

symbolic power of, 65–95

Pastoral care and counseling, 24–25, 35, 39, 42–46, 66, 77, 98, 123, 130, 132–134, 138–150, 190–260

Pastoral care, levels of, 182, 190–260

friendship, 20, 26, 44, 149, 194–199, 253

comfort, 58, 86, 116, 148, 199–208

confession, 60–61, 87, 120, 208–214, 263

teaching, 24–25, 87, 110, 130–133, 135–150, 159, 214–218

dialogue, brief, 219–222, 251

counseling and psychotherapy, 53, 88–89, 222–258

Pastoral counseling, phases of

preparatory, 229–235

relaxation and development of trust, 235–240

listening and exploration, 53, 88–89, 240–251

reconstruction and guidance, 251–254

follow-up and experimentation, 254–258, 281–283

Paul, 36–37, 42, 65, 75, 81, 87, 98–99, 104–105, 118, 125, 173, 180, 201–202, 223, 264–265

Place of meeting, 178–179, 235–236

Plato, 224

Power, desire for, 112, 124

Prayer, 28, 31, 83, 88–89, 121, 123, 130, 151–153, 205–207, 209

Preaching, 128–138, 141–150

Pregnancy, 31–33, 45–46, 211, 271, 273–274

Prenter, Regin, 86

Professional training, 11, 46, 145, 200, 228

Pruyser, Paul, 184–187

Radin, Paul, 18, 19

Rank, Otto, 72

Rauschenbusch, Walter, 125

Reassurance, 148, 201, 203–204, 208

Reconciliation, 70, 80–81, 85, 198–199

Referral, 235, 263–264. *See also* Introduction, ministry of

Reik, Theodor, 53, 241–242

Religious subcultures, 188–189

Repentance, 168–170

Repression, 113, 246, 248

Responsibility, acceptance of, 70, 239–240

Retirement, 42

Rites of passage, 18–20, 28, 44, 55

Roberts, David E., 75, 186

Roos, Philip, 132–135

Salinger, J. D., 93

Salzman, Leon, 35–36

Sandburg, Carl, 93

Schuller, David S., 17, 23, 67–68, 103, 128

Self-acceptance, 247

Self-concept, 52

Self-control, 113–114

Self-rejection, 224, 247

Index

Shakespeare, William, 258

Shepherd, the pastor as, 9, 17, 21, 65, 69, 75, 78, 81, 91–95, 100, 108, 122–124, 129, 136, 150, 152, 156, 214, 216, 222, 261

Sherrill, Lewis J., 28, 159, 185

Sin, 22, 48, 60, 76–77, 86–87, 100, 105, 126, 179, 209, 211, 213, 224–225, 248–249

Social involvement, 270–271

Sperry, Willard L., 274

Spiritual factors, 18–19, 21, 24–25, 31, 34–35, 43, 54, 63, 87, 93, 102, 106, 109, 114, 116–122, 124, 126, 139, 147, 155–163, 173, 187, 194, 202, 208, 212, 263, 272–273

Spurgeon, Charles H., 116

Stability, emotional, 110–118, 140

Steere, Douglas V., 88–89, 242–243

Stinnette, Charles, 73

Stress, 17, 49, 64, 126, 184, 202, 240, 278

Substance abuse, 272, 274–275

Suffering, 37–38, 49, 86, 199–201, 224

Suggestion, power of, 201–202

Suicide, 201, 230, 272

Sullivan, Harry Stack, 227

Systems approach, 136, 230, 260

Teaching, 24–25, 86–87, 110, 130–133, 135–150, 159, 214–219

Temptation, 183

Tension, emotional, 49, 140, 150, 152

Theological perspective, 18–22, 66–67, 82, 106, 186–187, 259–260, 261

Theological students, 114–117, 160

Thomas a Kempis, 152

Thurneysen, Eduard, 77

Tiebout, Harry M., 36

Time, use of, 91, 131–135, 145–146, 177–178, 236, 269–270

Transference, 169–171

Trueblood, Elton, 160

Trust, 78–79, 158, 225, 235–240

Understanding, pastoral, 54, 86, 167–189

Visitation, 20–21, 25–26, 31, 49–50, 56, 59, 69–70, 94, 132–134, 140, 161, 197, 208–209, 229–231, 233, 257, 266–267, 280

Vocational crises, 19–20, 27–28, 39–43, 73, 121–122, 186–187, 221

War, 63, 86, 195–196, 199, 214, 219

Warmth, 79, 92, 170–173

Wesley, John, 38

Whitman, Walt, 79–80

Wilde, Oscar, 72

Williams, Daniel Day, 20–21, 69, 76, 115–116

Wilson, Woodrow, 195

Wisdom, pastoral, 27–64, 98–99, 193

Women in ministry, 97–100, 102–107, 113–116, 179–180, 184

Working mothers, wives, 40–42, 104

Worship, 49, 79, 129–130, 150–155, 160–161

Yalom, Irvin D., 250